Chelsea Porcelain

Chelsea Porcelain

ELIZABETH ADAMS

THE BRITISH MUSEUM PRESS

To the Memory of
my Grandmother
FLORENCE BEATRICE LAVER
1865–1949
in whose house, many years ago,
my interest in porcelain
was first awakened

First published in 1987 by
Barrie & Jenkins Ltd

This edition published in 2001 by
The British Museum Press
A division of The British Museum Company Ltd
46 Bloomsbury Street, London WC1B 3QQ

ISBN 0 7141 2806 6

A catalogue record for this book is available from the British Library

Designed by Andrew Shoolbred
Typeset by Wyvern 21 Ltd

Printed in Singapore
Under the supervision of
M.R.M. Graphics Ltd Winslow Bucks

Half-title page: Cup and saucer with decoration of theatrical figures.
Height of cup 6.3 cm (2½ in), diameter of saucer 13.9 cm (5½ in).
Mark: a Gold Anchor on bottom of both cup and saucer. *c.*1760–65.
The British Museum
Title page: Group of Tyrolean dancers, based on a Meissen model of *c.*1740.
Height 18.2 cm (7⅕ in). Mark: a Red Anchor on base by foot of male
dancer. *c.*1755. The British Museum
Frontispiece: Portrait group of Nicholas Sprimont, his wife Ann (right)
and sister-in-law Suzanne Protin (left). Oil on canvas, unsigned and
unattributed, *c.*1758–62. Private collection, USA

Contents

Acknowledgements

I should like to record once more my gratitude to the late Reginald Haggar, R.I., who was a continual source of encouragement, constructive criticism and enthusiasm from the conception to the completion of the first edition of *Chelsea Porcelain*.

For this new edition, I have to thank particularly Dr and Mrs Paul Riley, without whose most generous support it would not have been possible to proceed. Their help and advice have been essential.

A photograph of an elaborate Gold Anchor porcelain clock case in the Royal collections is included by gracious permission of Her Majesty the Queen.

I owe thanks to a number of other people for their help and support in the publication of this new edition of *Chelsea Porcelain*. In alphabetical order they are: Don Adie, Gilbert Bradley; Aileen Dawson, Curator in the Department of Medieval and Modern Europe at The British Museum, whose help has been a main part of the foundation of the project; Mrs Anne George of Albert Amor Ltd; Mrs Patricia A. Halfpenny, now Curator of Collections at the Henry Francis Du Pont Museum, Winterthur, Delaware, USA: Mr and Mrs Colin Hanley; Margaret MacFarlane, now retired from the Hampshire County Museum Service; Jessie McNab of the Metropolitan Museum, New York, John V.G. Mallet, formerly Keeper of Ceramics at the Victoria and Albert Museum, for his provision of most helpful articles; Errol Manners for enabling me to reproduce the Sprimont portrait scene as the Frontispiece; Robyn Robb, who supplied several splendid photographs; John Sandon of Phillips Auctioneers; Simon Spero; and Hilary Young of the Victoria and Albert Museum. I also thank my excellent editor, Coralie Hepburn.

Finally, I thank Mrs Eileen Sankey, who took care of the domestic chores while I wrote, and Mrs Elizabeth Aydon, who again produced the typescripts and also the disks required.

Chelsea Porcelain Marks

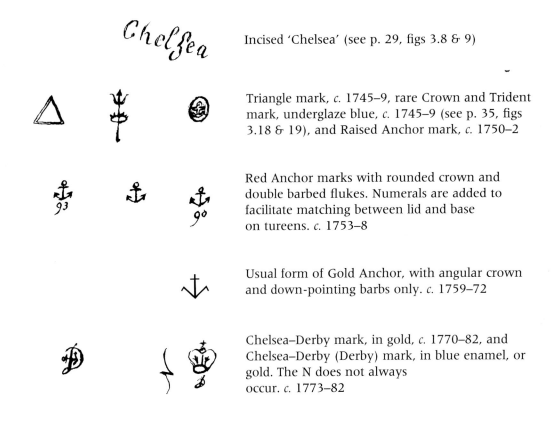

Incised 'Chelsea' (see p. 29, figs 3.8 & 9)

Triangle mark, *c.* 1745–9, rare Crown and Trident mark, underglaze blue, *c.* 1745–9 (see p. 35, figs 3.18 & 19), and Raised Anchor mark, *c.* 1750–2

Red Anchor marks with rounded crown and double barbed flukes. Numerals are added to facilitate matching between lid and base on tureens. *c.* 1753–8

Usual form of Gold Anchor, with angular crown and down-pointing barbs only. *c.* 1759–72

Chelsea–Derby mark, in gold, *c.* 1770–82, and Chelsea–Derby (Derby) mark, in blue enamel, or gold. The N does not always occur. *c.* 1773–82

CHAPTER 1

Chelsea in the Eighteenth Century

The village of Chelsea in the old county of Middlesex was well advanced in the process of becoming a suburb of the adjacent metropolis of London by the middle years of the eighteenth century. It was an ancient settlement on an attractive stretch of the north bank of the River Thames, immediately opposite Battersea on the Surrey shore, no more than two miles from Westminster, and since Tudor times a favourite place of residence for people of rank and culture [fig. 1.2].

The place name 'Chelsea' is derived from the Anglo-Saxon *Cealchythe* or 'Chalk Wharf' – the landing-place for chalk. Alfred Beaver, whose book *Memorials of Old Chelsea* was published in 1892, said that 'such a haven, or dock, did exist at Chelsea from time immemorial', and also that the remains of a causeway leading to a ford and constructed of 'chalk stones' was then still in existence. In addition, he pointed out that the most ancient part of Chelsea Old Church was built of chalk.

By the end of the seventeenth century the still rural village of Chelsea was famous for its market gardens, some of which had been founded by Huguenots, people of Protestant faith fleeing from religious persecution in France. Fine private gardens were already a feature of the area, but the most famous of Chelsea gardens is certainly the Physick Garden. This was founded on land leased from Sir Hans Sloane in 1673 by the Apothecaries' Company, for the cultivation of useful medicinal herbs and trees. It is still in existence today, though no longer under the care of the Apothecaries, the first public botanic garden to be established in this country.

The air at Chelsea had always been considered particularly healthy. For this reason in the eighteenth century Chelsea was a favourite place for private boarding schools and for the residence of invalids. Tobias Smollett the novelist settled in part of the Monmouth House complex in Lawrence Street in 1750, hoping that by so doing he would help his beloved consumptive daughter, though unhappily it proved in vain.

Chelsea village was concentrated round its riverside church, and *c.* 1700 had a population of about 1000 people. On west, north, and east it was surrounded by

Fig. 1.1 Plate with decoration in 'Hans Sloane' style. Diameter 23.7 cm (9¼ in). Mark: a Red Anchor. *c.* 1755. The British Museum

farmlands, meadows, nursery gardens and the Common. The Common, lying north-east of the village, was divided from it by the King's Road, a private road made by Charles II and running diagonally from north-east to south-west, linking Westminster with Fulham.

Charles II had provided 'the chief feature of the place' at Chelsea when he founded the Royal Chelsea Hospital for retired soldiers between 1682 and 1690, the architect of the great building being Sir Christopher Wren. But there were other palatial buildings near the river at Chelsea, among them Shrewsbury House, the Palace of the Bishops of Winchester, and Ranelagh House, to mention only a few. Ranelagh House with its beautiful grounds, its water-gardens and rotunda was opened to the public in 1742 and was one of the most famous of eighteenth-century pleasure grounds. The people of society who flocked to the balls, promenades and masquerades held there were without doubt some of those whom Nicholas Sprimont especially intended to tempt as purchasers of the luxury porcelain which his factory produced at Chelsea.

To a modern way of thinking it seems strange and even anti-social to found a pottery or porcelain factory with its attendant industrial fumes, noise and traffic in the middle of a residential area. In the eighteenth century such ideas carried no weight; the considerations were primarily those of commercial convenience. Suitable property could be easily bought or rented, transport for raw materials and finished goods was available by water, there was housing in the village for workers, and

Fig. 1.2 A view of Chelsea. Robert Sayer's print after the painting by J. Maurer made in 1744. Guildhall Library, Corporation of London

the place was accessible to and frequently visited by prospective purchasers from London.

Nicholas Sprimont had not only fixed on the right location for his porcelain factory by setting it up in Chelsea, but by doing so in the early 1740s he had also chosen the right time. It coincided with a growing enthusiasm and desire in England for wares and ornamental pieces made of the strange and beautiful substance which had about it the mystery of the Orient. Chinese porcelain, imported into Europe in growing quantities throughout the seventeenth century, and by the turn of the eighteenth augmented by the porcelains of Japan, inspired the acquisitiveness and then the emulation of Augustus the Strong, Elector of Saxony and King of Poland. In 1710 he founded the great factory at Meissen, chiefly to indulge his own passion for porcelain. He had coerced the cooperation of Johann Böttger, a chemist who thought himself an alchemist, and Böttger was helped in his quest by the Graf von Tschirnhausen. Von Tschirnhausen succeeded in discovering in Europe the necessary kaolin, the 'bones' of hard-paste porcelain, a clay which combines with petuntse, or 'china stone' (both are varieties of decayed granite), to form a true oriental-type hard-paste body, and it was in production at Meissen by 1710.

The secrets of the fortress-factory at Meissen, though rigorously kept, could not altogether be prevented from escaping. They spread with migrant workmen, and porcelain factories in emulation of Meissen were founded at Vienna in 1719 and Venice in 1720. Like Meissen itself, the European factories relied on funds provided by some noble or influential private backer, but none succeeded immediately in making porcelain exactly like the oriental. Guesswork was necessarily used in the formulation of porcelain recipes, and the earlier French factories of St Cloud and Chantilly produced extremely beautiful artificial (soft-paste) porcelains.

Augustus the Strong already possessed a fine and extensive collection of oriental porcelain at the time when he founded the manufacture at Meissen, and copies of oriental decoration often occur on Meissen porcelain. It was partly by way of Meissen that oriental designs found their way on to English porcelain, but large quantities of Chinese porcelain had been imported into England long before the end of the seventeenth century, and its importation continued throughout the next hundred years. The Chinese style in form and decoration had therefore a very great influence on the nascent English porcelain factories in the eighteenth century. At Bow the works were founded expressly to imitate and undercut the enormous imports of cheap blue and white oriental porcelain ware.

The earliest collection of oriental porcelain in England was that made by Queen Mary II, wife of William of Orange, and its remnants can still be seen at Hampton Court and Windsor Castle. They include blue and white porcelain, and also examples of the white variety from Dehua, usually known as *blanc-de-chine*. Throughout the eighteenth century oriental porcelains were the most highly prized by English collectors, but as the English factories arose, their products began to be collected as well: for instance, the collection of James West (1704?–72), President of the Royal Society and MP for St Albans, which was sold in 1773, contained not only an amount of Meissen porcelain, but items of Chelsea as well. Horace Walpole's famous collection of curiosities, which included a considerable amount of china, was housed at Strawberry Hill, his 'little plaything' house near the Thames at Twickenham (itself bought from Mrs Chenevix, the toywoman and china dealer of Charing Cross). The collection contained pieces of Chelsea porcelain, and Walpole described it as 'made out of the spoils of many renowned cabinets; as Dr Mead's, Lady Elizabeth Germain's, Lord Oxford's, the Duchess of Portland's, and of almost forty more of celebrity.'[1] Porcelain was the rage, and collectors of porcelain were numerous.

From the beginning, Nicholas Sprimont intended his porcelain for the rich, fashionable and aristocratic. Mrs Papendiek, Assistant Keeper of the Wardrobe to Queen Charlotte, wrote in 1783, more than ten years after Sprimont's death, of the setting up of her first home years earlier.

> Our tea and coffee set were of Common India china [i.e., Nankin porcelain], our dinner service of earthenware, to which, for our rank, there was nothing superior, Chelsea porcelain and fine India china being only for the wealthy. Pewter and Delft ware could also be had, but were inferior.[2]

In the late seventeenth century, after the revocation of the Edict of Nantes[3] by Louis XIV, over 200,000 Huguenots left France in order to escape the subsequent savage religious persecution. The majority, perhaps as many as 700,000, remained behind, but abjured their faith. Those that left France settled mainly in European Protestant countries, in particular in Holland, Britain and Germany. The exodus continued, though on a lesser scale, during the earlier years of the eighteenth century.

This dispersion of French people had a tremendous impact on the arts and manufactures of the countries to which they went. They took with them the style and customs of France, but with their religion they also carried a belief in upright dealing and hard work, reinforced by the necessity to support themselves decently in their new dwelling places. In England they left a mark in almost every commercial field besides banking, the law, medicine, and the applied and fine arts, palpable even today.

In London, which was a particular magnet to them, Huguenot settlers in England after 1685 found themselves at first with the choice of worshipping either in the traditional French non-conformist manner at the French church in Threadneedle Street, or with a French translation of the Anglican liturgy at the chapel of the Savoy. This second use had been established by Charles II in 1663 as the condition on which he would allow to continue a congregation founded in Westminster in the 1640s by Jean d'Espagne.

New congregations which followed one or other of these forms were founded to meet the needs of the refugees. By 1700 there were about twenty-eight Huguenot churches in the area now comprising Greater London, but they were particularly concentrated in Spitalfields, Westminster and Soho. The City also had a few Huguenot churches, and they were established as well at Greenwich, Wandsworth and Chelsea.

There is a noticeable thread linking the Chelsea Porcelain manufacture to the Huguenots, but as Hilary Young states, there is no positive evidence to confirm the tradition that Nicholas Sprimont was a Protestant refugee.[4] He was baptized and brought up in a settled, extended and well-found family, including goldsmiths and jewellers, in Liège, a city where there was little or no persecution of Protestants. Though his contemporaries thought of him as a Frenchman, it is, as John Mallet says,[5] 'worth recalling that this designer and entrepreneur, like several of the other foreigners who led the rococo movement in England, came from the periphery of the French speaking world'. Liège, now in Belgium, was in a Prince-Bishopric 'then linked to the Germanic world of the Holy Roman Empire'. In London he certainly had friends among the Huguenot congregation, and his earliest partner in the Chelsea porcelain undertaking was Charles Gouyn, a French jeweller who was known to be a Huguenot. The porcelain factory was founded *c.* 1744 and carried on in a house and premises in Church Lane East, Chelsea, of which the tenant, Anthony Supply, was a medical man, and likewise a Huguenot.

In a paper read to the English Ceramic Circle in October 1994,[6] which was based on the convolutions of the notorious Elizabeth Canning scandal of 1753–4 and its direct and indirect connections with the world of ceramics, Bevis Hillier gave details of the career of Mr Anthony Supply which he had discovered in a book, published in 1905, *Memories of Madras*, by Sir Charles Lawson. Hillier describes the book as 'a loosely framed history' of Fort St George, the great centre of trade established as long ago as 1643 by the original English East India Company. In a chapter of Lawson's book entitled 'Governor Harrison', which concerns Edward Harrison, Captain of the *Kent*, East Indiaman, who was appointed Governor of Fort St George in 1710, Hillier discovered a passage which, as he says, 'carries us straight back into the early history of English porcelain':

> [In 1711] the Directors stated that they had allowed "President Harrison to bring with him to Madras Mr Anthony Supply, and if you judge it for our Service wee consent that he be entertained one of the Surgeons when a vacancy happens."

Hillier goes on to explain that a directory of medical men[7] who served the East India Company shows that Anthony Supply had been appointed a surgeon's mate at

Masulipatam, a port north of Madras, in 1702. In 1703 and 1704 Supply's salary was £30 per annum. In 1705 he was appointed as successor to the surgeon at Fort St David (Cuddalore) who was described as 'a wild young fellow'.

'We having had complaints from the Deputy Govr. and Council of Fort St David of the insolent and saucy behaviour there of their Surgeon Charles Atkins, Agreed that Mr Suplee who was the . . . Surgeon at Metchlepatam (Masulipatam) be Entertained for his roome, and that he goes thither at the first opportunity.'[8]

In March 1709 Supply resigned because of ill health, in spite of having at Cuddalore had the convenience of a palanquin rather than simply a horse in order to attend his many patients, especially in times of 'great raines and excessive heats'. He went home to Britain on board the *Kent*, as surgeon, but as we know returned to Madras with Governor Harrison in 1711. He resigned finally in January 1716, once more through ill health, and returned to England on the *Mary*, his departure from India coinciding almost exactly with the birth of Nicholas Sprimont, with whom he was to be connected as landlord over a quarter of a century later, as we learn from the fire insurance policy issued by the Hand-in-Hand Company to 'Anthony Supply Surgeon' on 12 September 1744.[9]

The actual owner of the property at this date was John Offley of Wichnor, Staffordshire, a village about 6½ miles north-east of Lichfield. He held estates in Chelsea through his mother Margaret Lawrence, the last of that family whose name is commemorated in Lawrence Street. Margaret Offley is buried in Chelsea Old Church. During the 1740s and early 1750s John Offley sold off a good deal of his Chelsea estate, including all the ground pertaining to the porcelain factory. Bevis Hillier's paper also supplies many interesting details of the Offley family.

Anthony Supply was therefore probably in his sixties when he rented the property in Church Lane East to Nicholas Sprimont. His name appears in the list of Middlesex Oath Roll Naturalisations made under Queen Anne between 1702 and 1712, entered as 'Entony Suply' on 10 January 1710/11,[10] and he would then perhaps have been in his thirties.

When Nicholas Sprimont wrote his anonymous *Case of the Undertaker of the Chelsea Manufacture of Porcelain Ware*[11] *c.* 1752, an appeal to the government to prohibit the import of Meissen porcelain in order to assist the nascent Chelsea industry, he mentioned in it that 'casual acquaintance' with a 'chymist' had first roused his interest in porcelain manufacture. For many years a body of opinion assumed that the chemist was Thomas Briand, who exhibited examples of a soft-paste porcelain before the Royal Society in February 1742/3. Briand was described in the minutes of the Society's meeting as 'a Stranger that was present'. This almost certainly means that he was a foreigner. Dr Johnson's definition of 'Stranger' given in the first edition of his *Dictionary* (1755) is 'A Foreigner; one of another country'. If Briand was a Huguenot, and he was long assumed to be so, the description by the Royal Society clerk is exact. However, since the publication of a paper by Arnold Mountford in 1969,[12] it has been plain that Thomas Briand was probably not involved in porcelain-making in London, much though he may have wished it, but certainly in Staffordshire, where by 5 February 1746 he was 'of Lane Delph' and in partnership with Joseph Farmer. On 26 February the following year he was buried. Briand's knowledge of porcelain manufacture appears to have been both limited and faulty. Before he went up to Staffordshire, between 1743 and 1746, he had fallen foul of John Weatherby and John Crowther, the London wholesale pottery dealers, who were already interested in the science of porcelain manufacture and very shortly to be in partnership with Edward Heylyn and Thomas Frye at the factory of New Canton at Stratford Bow. A letter from them to John Wedgwood of Burslem dated 24 September 1748 survives, and in it they wrote as follows:[13]

> If you remember we told you in few words that we had nothing good to say of the deceased Briand (nor of his wife) that we had been greatly deceived by them, that they had from time to time made great promise to us of what they could do; & Mr Briand shew us several patterns of good China which he protested was of his making & yt he would convince us he could make the like but upon trial all his promises ended in words he never performed any one thing he proposed & it's our Opinion they knew nothing of what he pretended to know & we firmly believe the design of the deceased was only to make an advantage to himself of those he was concerned with …

This does not sound as if Briand was the sort of person who could have been working alongside Sprimont. To me it seems possible that the medical man Anthony Supply was perhaps the 'chymist' who first interested Sprimont in porcelain manufacture; his work for the East India Company must have at least acquainted him with oriental porcelain.

In pursuit of this thought I wrote to the Royal College of Surgeons of England. M.E.H. Cornelius, the Librarian, replied most helpfully, saying that in the eighteenth century the term 'surgeon' was often used to refer to a general practitioner, who would have learned his art by apprenticeship to another surgeon, and probably had no formal education or qualifications. It was perfectly possible for a surgeon to have an interest in chemistry or pharmacy, since as a general practitioner he would almost certainly have compounded his own drugs. He could well have been referred to as a chemist 'if he carried out chemical experiments, and was perhaps locally better known for these than for his medical practice'. In the light of these remarks, it is perhaps not beyond the bounds of possibility that the infant manufacture of Chelsea porcelain, that of the Triangle period *c.* 1744–9, was undertaken in 'Mr Supply's House'.

Nicholas Sprimont
Silversmith and Porcelain Maker

Nicholas Sprimont [see frontispiece] was probably not only a Huguenot, but by birth also a Walloon. His parents, Pierre Sprimont and Gertrude Goffin, lived in the Struvai quarter of Liège, where their son was baptised at the church of Notre Dame aux Fonts on 23 January 1716. Pierre Sprimont was a noted goldsmith in Liège, as were his brother Nicolas-Joseph Sprimont and the elder of Nicolas-Joseph's two sons, Jean-Joseph Sprimont.[1] Nicholas Sprimont is believed to have been apprenticed to his uncle Nicolas-Joseph (who was also his godfather) at 16 Rue du Pont. For whatever reason, perhaps feeling family pressure and competition too close at home, not long after he was out of his apprenticeship Nicholas Sprimont must have decided to seek his fortune in England, and he emigrated to London, never to return to live on the Continent. His brother Jean-Pierre Sprimont remained in Liège and became a jeweller.

Nicholas Sprimont registered his mark as a silversmith in London in the records of the Worshipful Company of Goldsmiths on 25 January 1742/3, when he was just twenty-seven years of age. It consisted of the cursive letters NS beneath a star:

Sprimont's address was given as Compton Street, St Anne's Soho. Two months earlier, on 13 November, he had been married at Holy Trinity, Knightsbridge, to Ann Protin of Kensington, a girl who was of Huguenot descent; and in the same year he took on an apprentice silversmith, James Lamistre, with a premium of 35 guineas.[2] [See figs 2.1–2.2 for some of Sprimont's silver designs.]

Pieces of silverware are in existence which carry Nicholas Sprimont's mark with dates ranging from 1743 to 1747. H. Bellamy Gardner, writing of 'Silvershape in Porcelain'[3] in 1939, said that he could indicate only fifteen items made by Sprimont and known then to be in existence. He included two large salts, each in the form of

Fig. 2.1 Design for a tureen and cover; pen and ink and ink wash. Signed 'N:s Sprimont in & Del'. Inscribed on the verso: 'My full intention'. 26 x 43.2 cm (10³⁄₁₆ x 17 in). The Victoria and Albert Museum, London

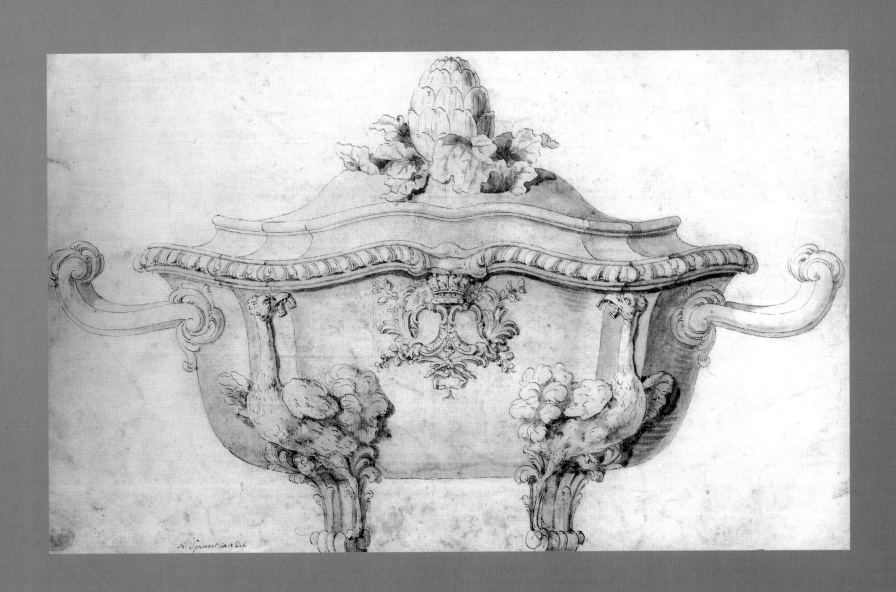

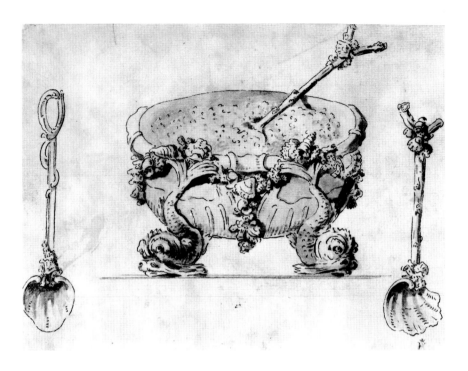

Fig. 2.2 Design for a salt cellar and two spoons. Attributed to Nicholas Sprimont. Pen and ink, ink wash and pencil, 14 x 9 cm (5½ x 7⁷⁄₁₆ in). The Victoria and Albert Museum, London

a crab holding a whelk shell, dated 1742/3 and in the Royal Collection at Windsor Castle, and a companion pair formed as a shell each with a crayfish beside it, at Buckingham Palace. Porcelain salt cellars of this form were made at Chelsea from *c.* 1745 to *c.* 1753 [see fig. 3.2], and appeared in the sale catalogues as late as 1756. They were apparently sold in pairs, and though generally in the white, sometimes had enamelled decoration. The design was probably suggested by a print in a series published in France in 1734 based on vegetables and game, after originals by J.A. Meissonnier.

Bellamy Gardner also lists four '11 inch oval deep Dessert Dishes with chased shells inside' and dated for 1743/4. They weigh 83 oz 10 dwt and are in the collection at Windsor Castle. In addition, there are four large sauceboats in the Royal Collection of which two were exhibited in the Rococo Exhibition at the Victoria and Albert Museum in 1984. They carry hallmarks for 1743/4 and are silver gilt. The Royal Inventory describes them as 'Of plain shell-shape, with seated figures of Venus on two, and Adonis on the other two. They are supported on two large dolphins, rocks and shells. Weight 229 oz 5 dwt. London date letters for 1743/4 and 1744/5.'

The 1984 exhibition catalogue entry suggests that the dolphins are smaller versions of those in a marine centrepiece marked by and accredited at the time of the exhibition to Paul Crespin, though this is now disputed. The date of the centrepiece is 1741/2. Crespin and Sprimont were certainly acquainted and part of the centrepiece may well be Sprimont's work. The figures balanced on the shell sauceboats as if in the act of leaping from them are suggested as a Triton and a Nereid, and related to baroque fountain sculpture. The centrepiece has been taken apart since 1984, and part of it proves to be the work of a Turin goldsmith.[4] Nevertheless, the case for Sprimont's involvement has grown stronger, although technical examination disproves the attribution of other Crespin-marked pieces to Nicholas Sprimont.

A set of six silver shell-shaped sauceboats by Sprimont, together with four stands, the stands only being hallmarked for 1746/7, and with ladles *en suite*, are now in the Jessie and Sigmund Katz Collection at the Museum of Fine Arts, Boston [fig. 2.3]. The stands clearly foreshadow those of similar shape which Sprimont subsequently made in porcelain. The earliest in this material occur *c.* 1750, and the form continued in use throughout the existence of the Chelsea Porcelain factory.

It may be of use at this point to repeat an explanation of the meaning of a maker's mark on eighteenth-century silver that Hilary Young gave when discussing

'Nicholas Sprimont, the Undertaker of Chelsea' in his recent work *English Porcelain 1745–95*.[5]

The presence of a silversmith's work on a piece of plate proves only that the holder of that mark sponsored the silver at the time of assay, not that he or she necessarily fashioned it and still less that the sponsoring silversmith actually designed it. Nevertheless, the evidence of the markedly individual treatment of rococo motifs and conceits in Sprimont's silver, taken together with the survival of a beautifully controlled pen and ink design signed by him, strongly suggest that Sprimont himself was involved in the design of at least some of the plate that bears his mark.

Pieces so marked are not 'fakes' in the modern sense of the term.

Sprimont's magnificent tea-kettle on a stand, described and illustrated by E. Alfred Jones in 1909,[6] was then in the Anitchkoff Palace in St Petersburg. It was hallmarked for 1745/6. Mr Jones described it as having '… a dragon spout, the wings spreading over the front – a laughing Chinaman on the cover, the panels on one side embossed with the scene of a tea-party, on the other a pastoral scene with Chinese figures in relief.'

In 1924 Dr Bellamy Gardner discovered a white porcelain figure of a robed standing Chinaman leaning over a small rectangular table with a teapot on it. He realised that it derived from François Boucher's 'Decoration Chinoise' in the *Louvre Inventaire Général*, Vol. II, No. 1415, and that it was only part of a group, the whole of which was reproduced on the side of Sprimont's silver tea-kettle. Here then, Dr Bellamy Gardner supposed, the same source served Sprimont as inspiration in both silver and porcelain. However, the porcelain Chinaman was of Bow origin, from a rare group which represents the Element of Fire. The companion group of Air is the only other Element of this series known in Bow porcelain, and an example which suffered damage in the kiln is in The British Museum.

An imposing silver cake or bread basket made by Sprimont and dated 1745 is in the Ashmolean Museum in Oxford. It is decorated with female classical heads at either end, and with sheaves of corn, and is engraved in the bottom with the arms of Skrymsher or Scrimshire.

By 12 September 1744, as we have seen, Sprimont had become sub-tenant of 'Mr Supply's House' in Church Lane East, Chelsea. Two days afterwards he stood as

Fig. 2.4 Portrait of L.F. Roubiliac by Adrien Carpentiers, 1762. National Portrait Gallery, London

godfather to Sophie Roubiliac, daughter of the sculptor Louis François Roubiliac [fig. 2.4] and his first wife Catherine, at the Huguenot church in Spring Gardens, Charing Cross.

That the making of porcelain at Chelsea had already begun can hardly be doubted. Six months later there was enthusiastic notice of the manufacture in the issue of the *Daily Advertiser* dated 5 March 1744/5.

We hear that the China made at Chelsea is arriv'd to such Perfection, as to equal if not surpass the finest old Japan, allow'd so by the most approv'd Judges here; and that the same is in so high Esteem of the Nobility, and the Demand so great, that a sufficient Quantity can hardly be made to answer the Call for it.

The late Nancy Valpy found a notable early reference to Chelsea porcelain among family papers preserved at the British Library. The collection of Pelham Papers includes an account book kept by 'Samuel Burt, Steward' for the Duke of Newcastle's house-keeping and other personal expenses 1742–52 (Add. MSS. 33158) where the section headed Extraordinary Bills contains the following entry:

To Ballance of the Chelsea Acct. 4:15–   *Nov. 17th 1746 (f.38)*

This is probably the earliest surviving financial reference to the sale of Chelsea porcelain.

Mrs Valpy also found among the Pelham Papers a Ledger of the Duke of Newcastle's Expenditure (Add. MSS. 33163) which among many entries for China bought from various dealers includes:

To (Cash) p^d Spermont for China   36:9–   *Sepr 30 1751)(f.30v)*

and also on the same day,

To Ditto p^d Spermont for Ornaments for Deserts   *6:14:–*

and the following month, on 10 October,

To Ditto p^d Spermont for China   *16:18:6 (f.63v)*

Fig. 2.5 South-east corner of old Lawrence Street in 1882. Watercolour by J. Crowther. London Metropolitan Archives

Fig. 2.6 Ordnance Survey plan of Chelsea 1976 with factory sites superimposed.

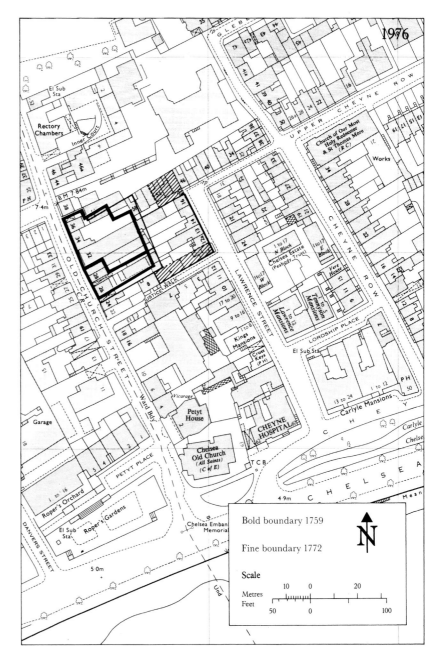

Sprimont did not finally leave his address in Compton Street, Soho, until Christmas 1748, according to the Rate Books. From at least September 1744 until the end of 1748 therefore, it seems that he must necessarily have been engaged in his business as a silversmith as well as in that of the infant porcelain factory.

A newspaper notice in the *General Advertiser* of 29 January 1750/51 refers to Charles Gouyn 'late Proprietor and Chief Manager of the Chelsea-House' as supplier of Chelsea porcelain to a dealer in St James's Street. This was for long the only known reference to Charles Gouyn as 'Proprietor' of Chelsea. He was a jeweller with a shop in Bennet Street at the top of the western side of St James's Street. Whether he was in fact the most important figure in the earliest years of the Chelsea porcelain undertaking remains to be discovered. In all probability, however, his main interest was financial, and his association with the business similar to that of Alderman George Arnold with the Bow factory; Arnold was described in his obituary notice in the *London Daily Advertiser and Literary Gazette* of 25 June 1751 as 'one of the principal Proprietors of the Porcelain Manufactory at Bow' when he was in fact rather one of its chief financial supporters, though a nominal member of the founding consortium of five partners.

Fig. 2.7 Plan of Mr Supply's and Mrs Phillips' premises, drawn from the measurements given in the Middlesex Deeds Register, 1759, vol. 1, no. 444 and 1759, vol. 3, no. 9.

Fig. 2.8 Plan of entire factory complex, drawn from the measurements given in the deeds for the previous plan, and also from those given in the Middlesex Deeds Register, 1772, vol. 5, no. 54.

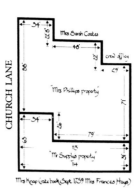

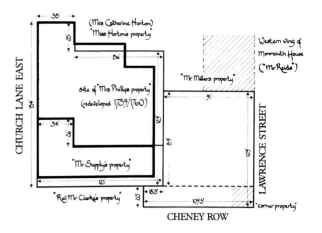

The means by which the Chelsea Porcelain factory was first financed, the identity of a certain 'riche particulier' referred to by Rouquet in 1755,[7] and the rumoured interest of William, Duke of Cumberland, in the factory, are matters which will later be mentioned at greater length. Here it is sufficient to say that having apparently commenced the manufacture in Mr Supply's house *c.* 1744, by 1749/50 the enter-

Fig. 2.9 Monmouth House in the early nineteenth century, from an etching by R.B. Schnebberlie. London Metropolitan Archives

prise was proving so successful that it became necessary to move to larger, purpose-built premises facing on to Lawrence Street, and to incorporate with them for eight or nine years following the old original factory as well as the property adjoining it to the north in Church Lane East known as 'Mrs Phillips' House' [see figs 2.6–8].

A factory showroom had been opened at least from 1747 in the double house comprising the eastern half of the Monmouth House complex [fig. 2.9] at the top of Lawrence Street, which had been built at the beginning of the century and later was converted into four dwelling houses.[8] The two in the eastern half became one house in 1717 and this was rated at £40 throughout the eighteen years of Sprimont's tenancy, *c.* 1747–65.

The Lawrence Street works seem to have come into operation towards the end of 1749, a supposition supported by the Rate Books; and the sales of porcelain to the public, which had been suspended for a year from March 1749, recommenced in the spring of 1750.

The use of an anchor as the Chelsea factory mark instead of the Triangle mark appears to have been employed from this time, and in its first form, as a 'Raised Anchor' applied on a small pad of clay, continued from *c.* 1750 to 1752. It was *c.* 1752 that Sprimont addressed his anonymous plea to the government to assist the Chelsea manufacture by curbing the import of porcelain from Meissen.

For the next few years everything appears to have gone well with Nicholas Sprimont, who was plainly closely involved with every aspect of the factory's management, from attracting the interest of influential people to the foundation of a training school for young painters and designers. He was helped by Sir Everard Fawkener, whose efforts enabled the Chelsea undertaking to borrow items for copying from the collection of Meissen porcelain which was deposited at Holland House and belonged to Sir Charles Hanbury-Williams (1708–59), English ambassador to the Saxon Court in Dresden.

It was in 1756 that the first hint of trouble occurred, when after a dozen years of hard work as a silversmith and then as a porcelain maker, Sprimont's health began its long decline. The trouble, which came on him at the age of about forty, was diagnosed by F.S. Mackenna as 'chronic gout, complicated by a nephrosclerosis with accompanying obesity' with death finally brought on by thrombosis.[9] It is always difficult to diagnose which particular illnesses people in past times actually suffered, but in Sprimont's case kidney trouble certainly seems a possibility.

CHAPTER 3

Foundation of the Porcelain Business

c. 1744–9/50

and Chelsea Triangle Porcelain

Fig. 3.1 Strawberry dish, polychrome with butterflies. Width 12.4 cm (4⅘ in). Mark: an incised Triangle. *c.* 1745–9. The British Museum

The mention of 'Sprimont' as sub-tenant of Mr Supply's house in Church Lane East in the Hand-in-Hand fire insurance policy issued for the premises on 12 September 1744[1] is the first suggestion we have that Nicholas Sprimont was already in Chelsea and presumably already interested in porcelain-making there. There is little doubt that Mr Supply's house was the seat of the first phase of the Chelsea Porcelain factory. When Henry Porter, who became ground landlord of the entire factory complex, bought Mr Supply's house from its actual owner, John Offley of Wichnor in Staffordshire, in September 1751, the Indenture recorded in the Middlesex Deeds Register[2] described it as '… all that messuage, house or tenement situate … in Church Lane in Chelsea … with the Coach house and stable *now converted into a room for other use* and the Outbuildings gardens ground and other the premises thereto belonging and Adjoining …'. When 'Outbuildings' are mentioned in the Rate Books in connection with premises rated to Sprimont, or after 1770 to William Duesbury of Derby, or his foreman Robert Boyer, the word is a synonym for factory buildings or kilns, and it is presumably so in the case of this Indenture of 1751.

The earliest productions of the Chelsea factory are the Triangle pieces, so called because the factory mark incised on many of them was a simple equilateral triangle, an alchemical sign signifying 'Fire'; the association is obvious. If Charles Gouyn was indeed an interested party in the early years of the Chelsea factory, these are the items produced under his 'Proprietorship'.

Chelsea, like other eighteenth-century English porcelain factories, produced a number of variations in the recipes for its porcelain. At this early date porcelain-making was an empirical, not an exact, science, and various factors had to be taken into account by the makers. The body had to be suitably plastic for good throwing and modelling, not 'short' (i.e. without much plasticity) so that it would tear. It had

Fig. 3.2 Crayfish salts. Left: width 11.1 cm (4⅖ in); mark a Red Anchor; *c.* 1755–6. Right: 10.5 cm (4⅖ in); mark an incised Triangle; *c.* 1745–9. The British Museum

to withstand the heat of the kiln without melting and thus obliterating fine detail. A recipe which answered well for standard household items would not necessarily suit for ornamental pieces, and so on. The earliest body used at Chelsea was notable for a large admixture of lead; this would in fact have derived from the incorporation of glass cullet, lead being an important addition in contemporary glass-making. Crushed glass was a major ingredient in early Chelsea porcelain which has been described as 'In essence … a nonfusible clay suspended in a glassy substance'.[3] The glaze added after the initial firing was also lead-based, and on the early Triangle pieces appears slightly cloudy. The wares are warm in tone, and show 'pin-holes' of brighter translucency when held against a light. Later in the Triangle years tin-oxide was added to whiten the glaze, in the same way as was done by the French at Chantilly.

From *c.* 1744 to 1747 or 48, Nicholas Sprimont was still attached to his silversmith's business in Soho, as well as being involved in porcelain-making. As we have seen in Chapter 2, some of his silver pieces find their exact counterparts in Chelsea Triangle porcelain, and among these are the salts with a life-sized crayfish on a rocky base which also supports the shell-shaped container [fig. 3.2]. A pair of these crayfish salts in the white, which were once in Horace Walpole's collection at Strawberry Hill, are now in The British Museum; one of them has the number 3 incised, as well as the Triangle mark. An example with the Triangle mark in blue underglaze is at

Colonial Williamsburg.[4] The pair at The British Museum are thought to have been sold undecorated, as was usual with those of Triangle date; but pairs of 'crawfish salts' were made in the early Red Anchor years and some are listed in the catalogue of the Chelsea yearly sale of 1756. Crawfish salts of Red Anchor manufacture can also be identified by the paste and glaze, even when unmarked, and among them are examples either wholly or partly decorated in enamel colours. Shallow oval shell-like dishes, rather akin to salt cellars and raised on a pedestal sometimes decorated with applied berries and leaves, are another typical production of the Triangle period, and are often called 'Strawberry dishes' [figs 3.1, 3.3–4]. Simple flowers and naïvely painted small insects are found on some, usually employed to hide blemishes and firing faults. Several of these dishes are known which are decorated on the inside with early essays in the botanical style, deriving from Meissen, as well as with insects, including butterflies.

Among other items of the Triangle period which make use of shell forms (perhaps the most typical components of rococo design) are salt cellars in which a single porcelain shell is balanced on a base formed of rockwork and smaller shells. Also known, though rare in Chelsea porcelain, are centrepieces of three shells similarly supported, and arranged to surround a central knot of coral stems. This is a type produced in large numbers at Bow.

From the Raised Anchor period onward (post 1750) Chelsea dishes and plates were regularly produced with edges shell-moulded in the same way as Sprimont's

Figs 3.3 & 4 Shell-shaped dish on a rockwork base decorated with applied strawberries and foliage in natural colours. Painted inside with a spray of flowers and foliage in 'botanical' style, and both inside and out with tiny scattered flowers and insects, many arranged to hide a blemish. Length 12.5 cm (4⅞ in). Mark: an incised Triangle. *c.* 1745–9. Private collection

Fig. 3.5 above left Teapot, moulded in the acanthus or 'Strawberry leaf' pattern. *Faux bamboo* handle. Width 16.1 cm (6⅖ in). No mark. *c.* 1745–9. The British Museum

Fig. 3.6 above Coffee-pot, moulded in the acanthus or 'Strawberry leaf' pattern. *Faux bamboo* handle. Height 24 cm (9⅖ in). No mark. *c.* 1745–9. The British Museum

Fig. 3.7 left Rare teapot, moulded in the acanthus or 'Strawberry leaf' pattern, with painted polychrome decoration of butterflies and flowering plants over glaze. *Faux bamboo* handle. Width 16.1 cm (6⅖ in). Mark: an incised Triangle under glaze on base. *c.* 1745–9. Private collection

silver stands for the shell-shaped sauceboats now in the Katz Collection, and are found with various types of enamel decoration. They obviously proved to be a favourite design among the factory's customers.

A well-known all-over moulded design in Triangle wares is the 'Strawberry leaf' or acanthus pattern. Its complex but strongly ribbed swirling forms seem to fit themselves tightly to the shapes they cover [figs 3.5–7]. Examples can be found both in the white and with light polychrome decoration, often with flowers and insects scattered over with no relation at all to the moulded design. The moulded raised flowers and foliage of the teaplant pattern, a familiar decoration on coffee-pots and beakers of the Triangle period, can likewise be found in the white, or with the trailing sprays picked out in bright colours. The teaplant moulding is almost certainly derived from repoussé silverware. The forms of these moulded wares include coffee or chocolate pots, teapots, sugar boxes, a few surviving saucers, teabowls, beakers [fig. 3.11] and two sizes of milk or cream jugs.

Jugs of the Triangle period occur in several designs including variations of a lobed baluster shape which again probably derives from silver. The best known form, however, is certainly that referred to as 'Goat-and-Bee'. It is supposed to be of silver origin and may have been the creation of Sprimont, though it has been suggested that it was taken from a silver jug by Edward Wood, at one time thought to have been made in 1735.[5] It is now believed that all known silver examples of Goat-and-Bee jugs are in fact fakes. At any rate, quite a large number of Goat-and-Bee jugs were made in the Triangle period, judging by those

Figs 3.8 & 9 'Goat-and-Bee' jug, with 'Chelsea 1745' and a Triangle incised beneath. Height *c.* 11 cm (4⁵⁄₁₆ in). The British Museum

Fig. 3.10 Sauceboat with moulded floral swags, after a silver prototype of Sprimont's own making, 1744/6, and now in a private collection in North Carolina. Height 11.9 cm (4¹¹⁄₁₆ in), length 20.3 cm (8 in). Mark: an incised Triangle under glaze on base. *c.* 1745–9. Colonial Williamsburg Foundation, Virginia

Fig. 3.11 Beaker, moulded in the acanthus pattern, with painted decoration of tiger, prunus, bamboo and rocks; with chrysanthemum sprig inside. Height 7 cm (2¾ in). No mark. 1745–50. Private collection

which survive. They are usually marked with the incised Triangle, but a famous example in The British Museum [figs 3.8–9] also has 'Chelsea' and the date '1745' incised beneath, and there is another, similarly marked, in the Fisher Loan at the Fitzwilliam Museum, Cambridge. F.S. Mackenna owned one with a date which he read as '1743', though this reading has been questioned by J.V.G. Mallet, who thinks that the incised line that has been read as the top stroke of the date's final digit may have been caused before firing by some accidental means.[6] There are examples which have the word 'Chelsea' and no date.

The influence of a silver original is obvious in the design of some pedestal sauceboats of Triangle porcelain which are moulded with festoons of flowers in relief, and which also have added enamel decoration of scattered flowers and insects [fig. 3.10]. Double-handled sauceboats are known too, with a pedestal foot but of plainer design without repoussé-type moulding. On pieces such as this are found the earliest examples on Chelsea porcelain of Kakiemon-inspired designs. One such sauceboat illustrated by Glendenning and MacAlister[7] and also by F.S. Mackenna[8] is decorated with the tiger and banded hedge pattern, and a bag-shaped vase with flared mouth and marked with an incised Triangle beneath, in the Untermyer Collection, is also decorated with this pattern.[9] Kakiemon decorations are usually considered to be among the later productions of Triangle Chelsea.

As T.H. Clarke pointed out,[10] a certain amount of French influence is discernible in Chelsea porcelain, even so early as the Triangle period. A pair of tall, slightly fluted vases with brown-edged wavy rims, which are decorated in a naturalistic 'botanical' style with rose blooms and butterflies, are illustrated both by him and by F.S. Mackenna.[11] Their decoration seems very close to some from Vincennes, and the wavy rims also have something French about them. Clarke points out that the early botanical flower painting which occurs inside some of the Chelsea strawberry dishes is very similar in both style and execution to that of Vincennes, but he does concede that both Chelsea and Vincennes could in fact have been copying independently from Meissen.

Some Chelsea shapes, however, have direct French parallels, though only in a very few cases as early as the Triangle period. One such is a lobed form of octafoil beaker and saucer, usually decorated with sprays of flowers, which is very close in design to similar pieces from Vincennes. Other early Chelsea pieces with French prototypes are the teapots and tea caddies in the form of a fat little Chinaman, smiling and wearing a lid in the guise of a hat [fig. 3.12]. The teapot spouts are formed either as a snake or as a parrot held by each 'magot' figure in his lap. These find their originals at St Cloud. The two Chelsea teapots known which are formed as

Fig. 3.12 Teapot in the form of a Chinaman with snake (mismatched lid). Height 17.5 cm (6⅞ in), width 19.3 cm (7⅗ in). Mark: an incised Triangle. *c.*1745–9. The British Museum

Fig. 3.13 Teapot in the form of a guinea-fowl (handle restored). Height 14.1 cm (5½ in), length 18.5 cm (7¼ in). Mark: an incised Triangle. *c.*1745–9. The British Museum

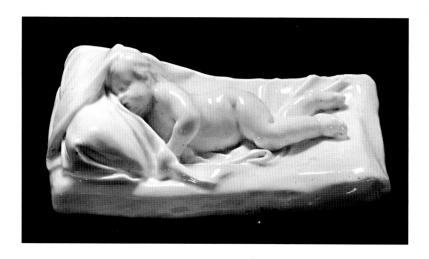

Fig. 3.14 Figure of a sleeping nude child, with 'June ye 26th: 1746' incised beneath. After a bronze original attributed to Il Fiammingo (b. 1597). Length 15 cm (6 in), width 9 cm (3½ in). The British Museum

Fig. 3.15 Front and back views of a figure of Ceres, undecorated, thought to be the work of Joseph Willems. Height 29.9 cm (11¾ in). No mark. *c.*1749. Private collection

a naturalistic guinea-fowl caught in a rose bush [fig. 3.13] are not true Chinoiserie as Clarke suggests, but perhaps derive from an oriental prototype.[12]

Ornamental pieces of the Triangle period are rare, and only a few examples of each figure still exist. They include models of animals and birds and a limited number of human figures. Bronzes or small statuary may have provided some patterns for the Chelsea factory, but two Triangle figures certainly derive from Chinese white glazed porcelains made at Dehua. One is a squat smiling corpulent Chinese figure, reminiscent of the two Chelsea Triangle teapots in the form of Chinamen, and probably representing the Buddhist Pu-Tai Ho-Shang, a holy man of about 900 BC. This figure also occurs adapted to be an incense-burner. The other is a simple seated draped figure of the goddess Kuan Yin directly copied from the Chinese. Another figure in Triangle porcelain of Chinoiserie rather than Chinese derivation is that of a fisherman sitting on top of shell-encrusted rocks[13] which was copied from a drawing by François Boucher. It is over 20.4 cm (8 inches) high; F.S. Mackenna suggests that it was designed as a support for a clock. A figure, almost certainly inspired by a plaster copy of a bronze original, of which two examples are known, is that of a sleeping child lying on a mattress [fig. 3.14]. The first, in The British Museum, bears underneath the incised inscription 'June ye 26th: 1746'; the other is undated. This little figure was modelled originally in the early part of the seventeenth century by the Flemish sculptor François Duquesnoy, who spent most of his life in Italy, and was popularly known as Il Fiammingo. It was one of a series of small bronzes, which were his most influential works. A boy seated with a reed pipe, and a pair of models of a boy seated on rocks, may also be derived from Il Fiammingo.

An early pair of Sphinxes, wearing neck ruffs, frilled head-dresses and lying on upward-slanting scrollwork bases, were formerly in the Allman Collection. They date from *c.* 1747, and one has an indistinct Triangle incised under the base. They probably pre-date the arrival of the modeller Joseph Willems at Chelsea, and may well have been designed by Sprimont himself. J.V.G. Mallet points out that 'pieces of his silver show a similar use of rococo scrollwork and the same nervous sensibility of spirit'.[14]

Other Triangle figures with human (or divine) subjects are a version of Milton standing beside a plinth, probably derived from Scheemaker's memorial in Westminster Abbey; a 'Map seller' from the *Cries of Paris* by Bouchardon; and a Ceres holding a wheatsheaf and crowned with ears of corn. The figure of Ceres [fig. 3.15] has a monumental aspect and may be one of the earliest works of Joseph Willems at Chelsea.

The beautiful group of the Rustic Lovers [fig. 3.16] in The British Museum carries the Crown and Trident mark in underglaze blue.[15] That this mark belongs to Chelsea and is contemporary with the Triangle mark is proved by its application over the Triangle on one particular strawberry-leaf moulded teabowl as well as to other wares indistinguishable in any way from Triangle-marked pieces.[16] Two figures only are known which carry the Crown and Trident mark: one the group just mentioned, the other a model of a recumbent greyhound, in the Victoria and Albert Museum (C13–1972). A larger pair of a rough coated retriever and a greyhound, also in the Museum, carry no mark, and a second version of the Rustic Lovers with slight differences in detail, which is in the Katz collection, is also unmarked. The significance of the mark is not known, but it has been suggested that it might have been used on pieces sold by Richard Stables' shop in St James's Street, which was at the corner of Crown and Sceptre Court.

The use of the underglaze blue for the Crown and Trident mark leads one naturally to suppose that at Chelsea the colour was also employed for decoration. This was so, but few examples of wares thus decorated survive from any of the Chelsea periods. The whole output of blue and white porcelain from Chelsea may have been greater than is now believed; those pieces which survive seem to range in date from 1745 to 1755. However, several inventories of china belonging to the Earl of Bristol have been found. That of 1767 contains a list of blue and white Chelsea wares being used in a noble house which does seem to suggest that Dresden was for best and Chelsea for ordinary use. The listed breakage of the blue and white Chelsea plates in 1767 was considerable, twenty-nine out of a total of forty-seven.[17]

From the Triangle period we have the handsome, fluted, Triangle-marked silver-shape cream jug [fig. 3.17], now in the Cecil Higgins Museum at Bedford, which came to light in the attics of a local house; a Goat-and-Bee jug with a blue bee;[18] and a flared beaker painted with insects and a flowering rose spray in an oddly bright blue, and carrying the Crown and Trident mark. This beaker was sold at Christie's in June 1978 and is now in a private collection in Australia.[19]

Two or three bird models, including a pair of finches perched on stumps, after Vincennes, a pair of tawny owls and a canary, as well as several animal models, were made in white Triangle porcelain. The animals include two versions of a squirrel eating a nut [fig. 3.20], one of which also occurs with polychrome decoration; these are probably after a Meissen original. There are also three examples of a model of a recumbent pug dog, two facing to the right and one to the left. One of the right-facing pugs is picked out in enamels and has two sprays of flowers enamelled on the base [fig. 3.21]; the others are in the white. These are large models, varying between 26.7 and 29.2 cm (10½ and 11½ inches) in length. The white left-facing pug is now in the Victoria and Albert Museum, and the coloured model was

Fig. 3.16 Group of the Rustic Lovers, modelled by Joseph Willems. Height 22.3 cm (8¾ in). Mark: a Crown and Trident in underglaze blue. *c.* 1749–50. The British Museum

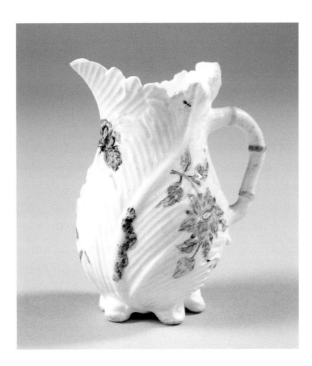

Fig. 3.17 A rare fluted silver-shape cream jug, with 'botanical' floral decoration in underglaze blue. Only two other jugs of exactly similar form are known. Height 12.1 cm (4¾ in). Mark: an incised Triangle beneath the base, *c.* 1745. Cecil Higgins Art Gallery, Bedford

Figs 3.18 & 19 Cream jug, moulded in the acanthus pattern, uniquely decorated in polychrome with flower sprays, moths and insects. *Faux bamboo* handle. Height *c.* 8.5 cm (3⅜ in). Mark: a Crown and Trident in underglaze blue. 1745–9. Private collection

Fig. 3.20 Figure of a squirrel. Height 13.5 cm (5⁵⁄₁₆ in). No mark. *c.* 1746. The British Museum

sold in 1986 from the Rous Lench Collection. A smaller pug on a marbled base was also at Rous Lench.

T.H. Clarke discovered and first published the fact that the large Chelsea pug model was in fact taken from a terracotta designed by the contemporary sculptor L.F. Roubiliac, and that it represented none other than Trump, the famous dog belonging to William Hogarth. All that is known about the versions of the model of Trump is set out and fully discussed by J.V.G. Mallet in an article reprinted from the Victoria and Albert Museum Bulletin in 1971.[20] Roubiliac's terracotta was sold in 1789 after the death of his widow. Although at one time it was thought that Roubiliac provided a number of models for Sprimont's factory, the figure of Trump is in fact the only one for which he was undoubtedly responsible. Roubiliac allowed the sale of plaster casts of his Trump, and it could have been from these that the Chelsea versions were reproduced. Although a similar marble figure of Trump mounted on a base of dark Purbeck marble [fig. 3.22], and probably used as a paperweight, has been discovered, expert opinion gives it a date of *c.* 1790. It was not made by Roubiliac.

In 1996[21] Malcolm Baker told the English Ceramic Circle of a letter found in the William Salt Library in Stafford.[22] It was written on 7 May 1745 by Sir Theophilus Biddulph in London to an unnamed correspondent (probably a relative named John Byrche) in Staffordshire. It deals with the progress of Roubiliac's first major monument, commissioned by Byrche *c.* August 1744 and to be erected in Worcester Cathedral in memory of Bishop Hough. There was some uncertainty about the inscription and Biddulph, who was a relation of both Hough and Byrche, had been

asked to visit Roubiliac to discuss the matter. The monument was to include a bas relief on the side of Hough's sarcophagus as it was represented in the design; and the relief was to illustrate Hough's splendid refusal to surrender the presidency of Magdalen College, Oxford, when he was brought before James II's commissioners. Biddulph told Byrche that the relief was 'to be in Chelsea China'.

This was in the earliest years of the Chelsea factory, only two months after the appearance of Sprimont's first advertisement. In the end Roubiliac himself carved the bas relief in marble, but Malcolm Baker reflects on Biddulph's 'telling remark, not about Roubiliac's involvement in the *production* of Chelsea porcelain, but rather about his response to what was being produced at Chelsea and its potential ... the way in which porcelain was perceived and appreciated is as much a part of the history of ceramics as its production.'

So far as enamel decoration on the Triangle productions is concerned, it was used sparingly and with *naïveté* in the earlier years. As we have seen, small flower heads and small insects were scattered haphazardly on the early shell dishes and some useful wares, being often employed to cover up blemishes in the glaze or even firecracks in the body. Raised moulded flowers and leaves were picked out in bright colours of red, blue, green and yellow, with black and brown [see figs 3.23–4, 4.1]. Figures were generally left undecorated with fired enamel colours, except for the few examples already mentioned here; though in some cases traces of unfired pigment have been discovered in the crevices formed by folded drapery. Early semi-botanical painting and Kakiemon designs are the most important types of decoration to be applied to wares during the earliest years of the Chelsea Porcelain Manufacture [see fig. 3.25].

Fig. 3.21 Figure of Hogarth's pug, Dog Trump, after a lost terracotta original by L.F. Roubiliac, the only decorated example of the three which are known. Length 28 cm (11 in). *c.* 1745–9. Private collection

Fig. 3.22 Marble figure of Hogarth's pug, Dog Trump. Length of base 16.5 cm (6½ in). *c.* 1790. Private collection

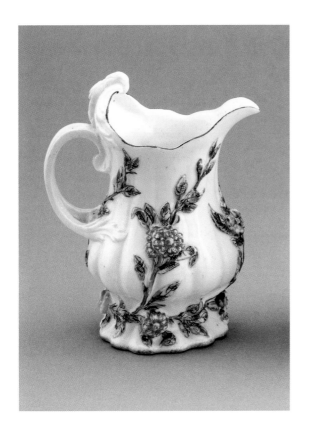

Fig. 3.23 far left Tea-plant moulded cream jug. Height 10 cm (4 in). No mark. *c.* 1745–9. The British Museum

Fig. 3.24 left Tea-plant moulded sucrier and lid, the only recorded polychrome example. Height 12.7 cm (5 in). No mark. 1745–9. Private collection

Fig. 3.25 below Fluted lobed beaker decorated with Kakiemon-style design of a Ho-Ho bird perched on rockwork (Sir Joshua Reynolds pattern); and a flared and fluted coffee cup with a scroll handle, painted with a loose bouquet of European flowers, both *c.* 1750. Also a lobed tea-plant moulded beaker decorated in the *famille rose* palette; the interior with minutely scattered foliage and an insect. *c.* 1745–9. All three are 7.5 cm (2¹⁵⁄₁₆ in) in height. Private collection

CHAPTER 4

Mr Supply's House

Reading between the lines of the newspaper entries, the Middlesex Deeds Registers and the Rate Books, it can be seen that Sprimont's business was closed for nearly a year between March 1749 (NS) and April 1750. This abeyance was almost certainly brought about by the need to expand and reorganize a growing business, and to establish the Chelsea Porcelain factory on its main site on the north-western part of Lawrence Street.

Before the system of annual public auction sales of Chelsea porcelain was established in 1754, the outlets for the factory production were first the factory warehouse, situated, it seems, in Monmouth House East, and secondly the West End warehouse, which from Midsummer 1751 to Midsummer 1755 was in Pall Mall; and then until the spring of 1758 'over against the White Bear in Piccadilly'. Both dealers and the public could buy from these two sources; of course much of the porcelain was re-sold, either by china shops, or through auctions of dealers' goods, which occurred in the larger towns in various parts of the kingdom. This notice from the *Edinburgh Evening Courant*[1] of Thursday 13 February 1752 is typical.

> There is sold by Auction, at the large Room second Storey below Mr Wilson's Vintner in Writers-Court, Edinburgh, a large and curious COLLECTION of CHINA, such as Dishes, Plates, Trenchers, Mugs, Coffee Pots and Flower ditto, full Sets of Tea Table China, and great variety of Images, and ornamental ditto, from Chelsea and New-Canton, with several other pieces of China too tedious to mention: great Choice of Paintings, Prints and Maps; Gold, Silver and Pinchbeck Watches … etc. … etc.
>
> NB Gentlemen and Ladies that have any Curiosities, or any other sorts of Goods to dispose of, may send them to JOHN GIBSON Auctioneer. The Sale to continue till all be sold off…

On 21 and 24 February 1749 (NS) through the medium of the *Daily Advertiser* the 'Undertaker of the Manufactory of China Ware' acquainted the 'Publick, that he has

Fig. 4.1 Moulded, ribbed cream jug with applied painted strawberry plants around the foot and garlands around the upper handle terminal, painted with insects and flowers. Height 13.4 cm (5¼ in). Mark: an incised Triangle. *c.* 1745–9. The British Museum

prepared a large Parcel of that Ware, consisting of Tea and Coffee Pots, Cups and Saucers of various Forms, besides several other Things as well for Use as Ornament, which he proposes to offer to Sale on Tuesday next, the 28th instant, at the Manufactory at Chelsea, from which time the Warehouse will be open constantly and Attendance given.'

The demand must have been phenomenal. Only three days later, on 3 March, again in the *Daily Advertiser*, Mr Sprimont had to declare 'that the favourable Reception and general Approbation his China-Ware has met with, makes it necessary for him to suspend all further Sale thereof at his Warehouse after tomorrow, that he may have Time to make a sufficient quantity of such Things as he has observed to be most agreeable to the Taste of those who have done him the Honour to look at his Performance...'

The suspension apparently lasted for the rest of the year. About Christmas time Sprimont gave notice that he hoped to be 'in a condition to offer a considerable Parcel' in March next.

On 9 January 1750 (NS) the *Daily Advertiser* published a notice enumerating the goods which Sprimont hoped to have in his forthcoming sale.

> The Manufacturer of China Ware at Chelsea ... has been employed ever since his last Sale in making a considerable Parcel ... it will consist of a Variety of Services for Tea, Coffee, Chocolate, Porringers, Dishes and Plates, of different Forms and Patterns, and of a great Variety of Pieces for Ornament in a Taste entirely new.

The entries in the Rate Books imply that Sprimont's business was associated with the little house on the corner of Lawrence Street and Justice Walk, and the land adjacent to it, from Midsummer 1749. This was the point at which the Lawrence Street factory was established. During 1749 new factory buildings were erected on this piece of virgin ground north-west of the Corner House and the manufacturing apparatus was transferred there from Mr Supply's house. This was listed as 'Empty' in December 1750, though by 1751 it had reverted to the normal £30 rate, and was rated as usual, again under Sprimont's name.[2]

By the end of 1750 the deeds transferring Mrs Phillips' house and the corner property in Lawrence Street (both formerly parts of the estate of John Offley, the Staffordshire land owner whose mother had been Margaret Lawrence) to Henry Porter were all signed and sealed. A few months later, in May 1751, Henry Porter transferred Mrs Phillips' house to his nephew Isaac Porter, but it seems to have made no difference; both properties in Church Lane East were held in tandem, apparently from 1750 until the spring of 1759 alongside the Lawrence Street works, and both were in the occupation of Sprimont.

The naïve and rustic charm of some of the St James's ('Girl-in-a-Swing') class of figures and 'toys', for long accredited to Sprimont's Chelsea factory, has often been remarked upon.[3] However, a certain simplicity in some of the modelling akin to that found in earlier Staffordshire salt-glazed and lead-glazed figures was at one time called in aid to support the idea that the St James's potters were Staffordshire men who seceded from Sprimont's factory and founded an undertaking of their own somewhere in Chelsea, and prior to 1754.[4] This theory is based on an account given by Simeon Shaw whose *History of the Staffordshire Potteries* was published in 1829, some eighty-odd years after the event. He recorded that 'Carlos Simpson, 63 years of age, 1817, was born at Chelsea; to which place his father Aaron Simpson went in 1747 along with' several other named pottery workers from Burslem, including the turner Samuel Parr, 'to work at the Chelsea China Manufactory.'[5] Only the names of Simpson and Parr have been found in any relevant document so far. Samuel Parr removed to Chelsea *from Bow* in 1754, and the baptism of Carlos, 'son of Aaron and Elizabeth Simpson' is recorded at Chelsea on 4 December 1754. After leaving the Chelsea factory where they were 'the principal workmen' and setting up a factory on their own account 'at Chelsea', Shaw said that the Staffordshire men 'were in some degree successful' but then disagreeing amongst themselves they returned to Burslem.

In 1987 I suggested that from 1751 to 1759 'Mr Supply's House', the original Chelsea factory, was used, following the building of the Lawrence Street works *c.* 1749, to train Nicholas Sprimont's 'nursery of thirty lads, taken from the parishes and charity schools, and bred to designing and painting'. These thirty trainees (possibly taught by at least some Staffordshire potters) would have been included in the total of about a hundred workers at Chelsea during the early 1750s. Such a scenario could have been the origin of Shaw's assertion that migrant Staffordshire workmen set up their own factory in Chelsea. Supportive of my suggestion is the fact that throughout the 1750s Sprimont paid the rates for 'Mr Supply's House', something he would never have done if it were occupied by a rival undertaking.

Whatever the truth, it is now clear that a second factory actually sited *in* Chelsea was certainly not responsible for the charming class of figures, bijouteries and the few useful wares of porcelain formerly classified as 'Girl-in-a-Swing', alias a second Chelsea manufacture. This whole question will be further discussed in the following chapter.

The earlier years of the 1750s were a most prosperous time for Sprimont. The use of an anchor as the factory mark can be assumed from *c.* 1750 when he 'built, erected, stablished' the main part of his manufactory in Lawrence Street; and we can consider Raised Anchor marked porcelain the first type to be produced on the new Lawrence Street site.

CHAPTER 5

Charles Gouyn, his Factory and St James's Porcelain

In June 1993 Bernard Dragesco surprised and amazed everyone interested in eighteenth-century ceramics by distributing to all who attended the International Ceramic Fair in London his monograph entitled *English Ceramics in French Archives*. Monsieur Dragesco had been alerted by Madame Tamara Préaud, Director of the archives of the Manufacture Nationale de Sèvres, to the existence at Sèvres of three Notebooks, and in Caen City Library to that of a large collection of notes and essays, all written by Jean Hellot (1685–1766), an important French scientist. He was 'Pensionnaire Chymist' of the Royal Academy of Sciences in Paris, and, from 1740, a Fellow of the Royal Society in London. He was also invited by command of Louis XV to oversee the production of porcelain at Vincennes after the death of the factory's head, Orry de Fulvy, and stayed on as 'Academicien Chimiste' at Vincennes from 1751, through the removal to Sèvres in 1756 until his own death ten years later. Madame Préaud had realized the relevance of some of Hellot's material to the study of English ceramics, and kindly agreed that Monsieur Dragesco should publish it.

Hellot's manuscripts at Caen contain seven pages dealing with English porcelain and pottery making. The information they give was provided by Jacques Louis Brolliet, a Swiss who was expert in gilding glass and porcelain, and who professed to be able to make China himself,[1] as is shown by an advertisement in *Jackson's Oxford Journal* of 11 January 1755.

JAMES BROLLIET
Proprietor of the China Manufactory at Oseney-Mill
near Oxford

In order to convince the Publick that the scandalous and malicious reports that have been propagated to his Prejudice are without the least Foundation, Hereby begs Leave to inform Gentlemen and Ladies, That he will burn China of his own making at Oseney-Mill aforesaid, on Wednesday next the Fifteenth of the Instant, from Nine o'Clock in the Morning till Twelve,

Fig. 5.1 Dancing Girl and Boy figures, St James's Factory. Height of boy 14.9 cm (5⅞ in). No mark. *c.* 1750–59. The British Museum

where all those who are pleased to honour him with their Company will receive proper Satisfaction.

N.B. Gentlemen and Ladies are desired not to handle the China before it is burnt.

Ms Mellor of Oxfordshire Museum Services was kind enough to send me a copy of a further advertisement of Brolliet's she had recently discovered which suggests that some of those who accepted his first invitation were not altogether convinced that he was indeed able to make porcelain as he had claimed. It was published in the same *Oxford Journal* on 25 January 1755:

Gentlemen and Ladies who are desirous of seeing a specimen of the China made by James Brolliet at Oseney near Oxford, are desired to apply to Mr Bernard Gayse, Confectioner behind All Saints Church; where they will receive proper satisfaction that the scandalous reports which have [been] spread by some evil-minded Persons, are malicious and groundless, and that this China is, absolutely of his own Manufactory.

(All Saints Church is now Lincoln College Library fronting on to the High Street, Oxford.)

Although the first of these two notices was found more than a decade before the publication of Bernard Dragesco's monograph, it was not generally known until 1994 when it appeared in Mrs Valpy's posthumously-published paper on 'Charles Gouyn and the Girl-in-a-Swing Factory'. Dr Bernard Watney had first drawn it to her attention.[2]

There seems little doubt that although he was a man with ability, Brolliet had a varied and chequered career. On his first visit to England *c.* 1755, he appears to have become acquainted with a number of English factories which he later mentioned to Hellot in 1759, 'Schtaffshire' (presumably Longton Hall), 'Darbschire' (Derby), 'Ouestershire' (Worcester), and 'Baw' (Bow), also 'Brumjon' (Brummagem/Birmingham) and 'Schelsea'.

Although a number of people he met had doubts about Brolliet's capacities, Hellot thought well of him and had actually employed him for about two years in the mid-1750s, as he says in a letter to the director of the factory at Sèvres, written as a reference for Brolliet on 3 February 1759. Between his first visit to England in 1755 and 1759 Brolliet had also managed to travel to Canada, fought and been wounded at the siege of Louisbourg there, and been brought back to England (probably in the autumn of 1758) as a prisoner. Being fluent in English, German, Dutch and Italian, he pretended to be a German, and thus was able further to visit several English ceramic factories, Chelsea among them. Then with the help of Simon François

Ravenet, the noted engraver, he escaped to France where he revisited Hellot and gave him many fascinating details about English porcelain-making.[3]

After describing the round tower-like kilns of his former pottery at Oxford, and that at Chelsea (each of which had six or eight fire-mouths, the usual form in Staffordshire), Brolliet continued as follows:

> This is how is built the kiln of *Chelsea*, of which the porcelain factory is near the church. It was first established by Mr Gouïn, brother of a Paris Jeweller of that name, born at Dieppe in the so-called Reformed Faith. His paste was compounded by d'*Ostermann*, a German, chemist and artist of *Dr Ward*, a famous empiric. Mr Gouïn left, with the loss of part of his funds, and makes at his house in St James's Street, very beautiful small porcelain figures. The present (1759)[4] undertaker of the *Chilsea* [*sic*] factory is one named Sprémont, from Liège. The turner was a Frenchman named Martin. He left *Chelsea* and went to *Lambeth*, to work for Jacson,[5] a faience-maker. The modeller is one named *Flanchet*, a pupil of Mr Duplessis. The draughtsman is named *Du Vivier*: he is Flemish.

Fig. 5.2 A bonbonnière in the form of an egg, with gilt metal mounts and painted with a bouquet and spray of flowers, St James's Factory. Height 5.6 cm (2⅕ in). No mark. *c.* 1750–53. Private collection

On 9 April 1750, as Mrs Valpy discovered, Nicholas Sprimont had first published a notice in the *Daily Advertiser* specifically disclaiming any further connection with the 'Chelsea-China-Warehouse' in St James's Street.

> As the Proprietor of The Chelsea Porcelaine finds that a great many of the Nobility and others think, that the former Place in St James's Street, call'd the Chelsea-China-Warehouse, belongs still to him; this is to give notice in general that I am not concern'd in any Shape whatsoever, in the Goods expos'd to Sale in that Shop. N. Sprimont.[6]

The inference is of course that Sprimont had had a personal interest in the shop and had been marketing the Chelsea wares there previously – that is, until Charles Gouyn the jeweller left the Chelsea undertaking *c.* 1748.

Mrs Valpy in the same article shows exactly which was the shop in question; she gives a short notice which first appeared under the heading 'London' on 18 and 24 April 1746 and stated that:

> The Chelsea China will be constantly brought from the Manufactory to Mr Stables's, the Corner of Crown-and-Scepter-Court, St James's Street, for the Conveniency of the Publick, who may there be supplied in like manner as at Chelsea.'

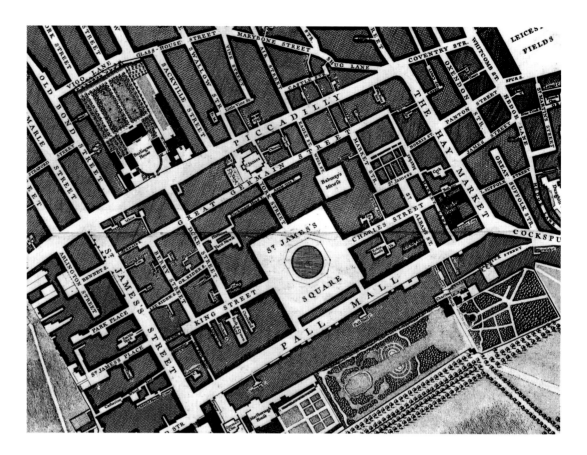

Fig. 5.3 The St James's area, from John Roque's map of 1744. Guildhall Library, Corporation of London

An extract from John Roque's map of 1744 [fig. 5.3] shows that 'Crown-and-Scepter-Court' was situated on the east side of St James's Street, immediately south of Little Germain (Jermyn) Street, which connected Great Germain Street with the main throughfare. Richard Stables was first recorded at this address in the Watch Rate Book in June 1737 and continued there until June 1755.[7] On the opposite side of St James's Street was Bennet Street, where Charles Gouyn – who, it will be remembered, was advertised in January 1750/51 as 'late Proprietor and Chief-Manager of the Chelsea-House' – had his retail jewellery business from 1736–83.

As Bernard Dragesco points out, Brolliet's report confirms the statement in the *General Advertiser* of 29 January 1751 (NS) inserted by 'S. Stables', then Manager of the 'Chelsea China Warehouse' in St James's Street, in reply to Nicholas Sprimont's previous numerous and emphatic notices in the press that he and his Manufactory at Chelsea were 'not concerned in any Shape whatsoever with the Goods exposed to Sale in St James's Street, called the Chelsea China Warehouse'. Mr Stables continued:

… in common justice to N. SPRIMONT [who signed the Advertisement] as well as myself, I think it incumbent, publicly to declare to the Nobility,

Gentry, etc. that my China Warehouse is not supply'd by any other person than Mr *Charles Gouyn*, late Proprietor and Chief Manager of the Chelsea-House, who continues to supply me with the most curious goods of that Manufacture as well useful as ornamental...

What has been overlooked recently is Sprimont's much earlier advertisement in the *Daily Advertiser* of 3 March 1748/49 (only two earlier than this are recorded) which was discovered many years ago and published by Dr H. Bellamy Gardner as far back as 1928 in the very first volume of the *Transactions of the English Porcelain Circle*. In it Sprimont states categorically '... that he has no sort of Connexion with nor for a considerable Time past has put any of his Ware into that Shop in St James's Street which was the Chelsea China Warehouse'.

In other words, Sprimont says without equivocation that none of his own porcelain has gone into that shop known as the Chelsea China Warehouse in St James's Street since (at least) September 1748 (assuming that 'a Considerable time past' means 'at least six months' – though it could well be a year). It does certainly imply, however, that no porcelain of Sprimont's at all was sold in St James's Street throughout 1749 and that what was then offered there must either have been Chelsea Triangle porcelain, removed by Gouyn when he left the original Chelsea partnership, or porcelain made somewhere else under Gouyn's aegis, and sold under the continuing name of 'Chelsea' to please potential customers.

In the second case he would have been selling under a trade description to which he had no longer a right, even though he may have felt so. If Brolliet's statement in 1750 that the Chelsea factory was first established by 'Mr Gouïn' (*c.* mid-1740s) is correct, one can well understand Gouyn's chagrin, after a quarrel which forced him to leave 'with the loss of part of his funds'.

Whether the quarrel was occasioned by the intervention of the Fawkener brothers as funders or 'proprietors' of the Chelsea factory, or whether Gouyn quarrelled with Sprimont over the type of design of wares to be produced, we may never known. What is certain is that he apparently continued to make 'very beautiful small porcelain figures' as late as 1759.

The word 'make' in this context may refer to the mounting of scent-bottles, snuff-boxes, and seals with gold fittings. An important point to be considered is whether, in his St James's premises just off the main throughfare at No. 3 Bennet Street, Gouyn did actually design and fire his porcelain pieces. If in fact he was simply applying their mounts, as a jeweller, where in Bennet Street were his porcelain kilns? Nancy Valpy argued cogently that even a small porcelain-making business would have been unacceptable in St James's because of the nuisances of manufacture and the risk of fire in so developed and aristocratic an area. She pointed out that from 1747 to 1777 Gouyn paid rates on premises in Brick Street (the lower part of

Fig. 5.4 Naturalistically painted figure of a Goldfinch on a tree stump painted with flower sprigs, St James's Factory. Height 15.4 cm (6¹⁄₁₆ in). Pad marks beneath. No factory mark. *c.* 1754. Private collection

Fig. 5.5 Four seals, St James's Factory. Height of Dalmatian 2.6 cm (1 in). *c.*1750–59. Private collection

Fig. 5.6 Combined étui, scent-bottle and seal, St James's Factory. Height 11.5 cm (4½ in). *c.*1750–59. The Victoria and Albert Museum, London

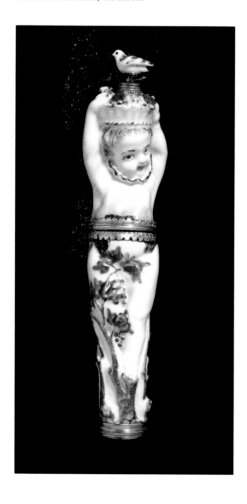

which was then called Engine Street), a narrow lane which led out of Piccadilly on the north side about half a mile west of St James's Street. Swinging left a short way up, Engine/Brick Street ran into Old Park Lane, then known as Tyburn Lane. Most of the properties in Brick Street were stables or small tenements; after the left-hand bend some of those on the north side backed on to open ground. A brickfield gave its name to the lane; one wonders whether, perhaps, Gouyn's factory employed its site for a similar smoky process?

From the latter half of 1771, when Messrs Drummonds of Charing Cross became his bankers, until his death in 1785, the ledgers show that Gouyn paid an annual charge each January or February to Sir Fitzwilliam Barrington (presumably Viscount Barrington, whose house was No. 16 Cavendish Square). The amount was usually about £38. In 1779 only, the greatest sum of £40 was paid to Mr Hamming, possibly Viscount Barrington's agent.[8]

Were these payments made in respect of rent for the Brick Street property? It is an interesting speculation. The last payment of the series, also the smallest at £37. 19. 6., was made to 'Sir Fitwm Barrington' in 1780. Gouyn left Bennet Street in 1783, and apparently moved to King Street, Soho, where he died on 7th January 1785.

Although Gouyn's porcelain manufactory may have ceased operation some time after 1760, it was probably not as late as 1777 when he ceased paying rates on the premises in Brick street. As Mrs Valpy suggests, they may also have been used as the jeweller's workshop. That, however, he kept some association with porcelain shows in the codicil to his will. As Dr Bellamy Gardner revealed in a paper given to the English Porcelain Circle in 1929, Gouyn made his will on 8 April 1782; a codicil was added on 29 September 1784. In it he bequeathed to his (second) wife Elizabeth (Pass) 'all my china, ornamental and stock-in-trade'. For many years it has been the practice of retail jewellers to stock a certain amount of (usually ornamental) china; and this is perhaps a legacy from the eighteenth century, when jewellers such as Gouyn and Nicholas Crisp of Vauxhall were so closely identified with the manufacture and sale of porcelain.[9]

Gouyn's bank records also reflect his association with some members of the ceramic fraternity. For instance, between October 1771 and January 1776 he made eight payments to 'Thomas Hughes' – probably Thomas Hughes (II) the porcelain decorator ('enameller') of St Pancras. They ranged in value between £30 in January 1774 and 10 guineas in March and September the same year, as well as the previous October. The total was £130 8s.

Between December 1773 and February 1784 Gouyn's payments to 'Mr Williams' (Thomas Williams, Chinaman?) totalled £454 6s.

On the other hand he received *from* 'Jenkin Jones' between December 1776 and December 1784 no less than £927 12s. Most of this sum was made by Jones in two payments each of £350 in March and December 1784. In 1781 Gouyn had paid 'Mr Jones' £100 and on 31 August the following year £120 to 'Jenkin Jones'.

At this late period Jenkin Jones was a 'Chinaman' and had been 'On the Terras St James's Street' at least from 1761.[10] However, the accounts of the Marquis of Rockingham show that at least in 1753 and 1754 Jones had been acting as sales accountant for Nicholas Sprimont himself at the Chelsea factory warehouse.[11] Many years later he gave up his own business in St James's Street; Mrs Valpy discovered the notice of 14 April 1790 in the *Daily Advertiser*. Perhaps influenced by Charles Gouyn, Jenkin Jones had by then become a jeweller.

> To be sold by Mr Compton at the Great Room, in King Street, St James's Square, this and six following Days, THE capital, extensive and valuable Stock in Trade of Mr JENKIN JONES, Jeweller, of St James's Street, quitting the Business; consisting of Pearls and Diamonds, antique Gems and a Variety of Gold Toys etc. an Assemblage of fine Dresden Desserts, Tea and Coffee Sets, Dejeunes, Cabinet and Caudle Cups etc. matchless Curiosities, rare old Japan.[12]

The 'Girl-in-a-Swing' pieces – figures, wares, miniatures or 'toys' – now believed to have been made at Charles Gouyn's 'St James's' factory, are identified primarily by the porcelain paste of which they are made, and only secondarily by similarities of form and modelling.

The paste, as already mentioned, is not altogether unlike that of Sprimont's Triangle pieces, but it is noticeably dense, cool in appearance, and has a close-fitting, clear glaze containing a tinge of green. Analyses from several sources published as an appendix to their paper by Lane and Charleston[13] show a silica content of well over 60 per cent in St James's porcelain; but the most noticeable feature of the analyses is the high content of lead oxide, about 16 per cent, i.e. almost double that of Triangle Chelsea. This will have been due to the incorporation of large quantities of lead glass cullet in the recipe. It would not have been an easy paste to control in the kiln, and the slip-cast figures were formed so that projections which might sag or slump during firing could be avoided.

It is a moot point whether one or more modellers were engaged in making the St James's pieces. The style is distinctive, and a diagonal sweep in the composition of the figure groups is noticeable, especially in pairs which could be adapted as supports for candle nozzles, and therefore likely to complement each other from the opposite ends of a mantelpiece. The figures appear elongated, abstracted from, rather than exactly representing, a human body; a simplicity which in some cases is reminiscent of early Staffordshire figures in salt-glazed or lead-glazed earthenware. The heads are distinctive also, with a straight-nosed

Fig. 5.8 Taper-sticks, Autumn and Winter, St James's Factory. Height 10.2 cm (4 in). *c*.1750–59. The Potteries Museum and Art Gallery, Stoke-on-Trent.

Fig. 5.9 Pair of ornamental taper-sticks, St James's Factory. Height 10.2 cm (4 in). *c*.1750–59. Museum of London

'Grecian' profile, short upper lip and pointed chin. Deep-set eyes, with emphasized upper lids and indented pupils, make an effect without the need for any added enamel colouring. Hands and feet are small and delicately modelled.

The bases for the figures include irregular shapes with some imitation of natural ground, and simple rectangular pads; but a characteristic form is a hexagonal bevelled base with alternating convex and concave edge curves [fig. 5.9]. This can also be seen on a pair of taper-sticks with figures representing Autumn and Winter [fig. 5.8] in the Potteries Museum and Art Gallery, Stoke-on-Trent;[14] and also on a model of a finch in the Victoria and Albert Museum. Small curved impressions, like those of a finger nail, on bases, are another characteristic of St James's figure modelling.

As human figures of the St James's type are not anatomically exact, but rather stylized, so are the animal models. Their eyes bulge, and have indented pupils [fig. 5.10]; this feature is also to be found in the Chelsea pair of greyhound and retrieving setter of the Triangle period discussed by J.V.G. Mallet,[15] as well as in the single, smaller recumbent greyhound marked with the underglaze blue Crown and Trident, and a goat being milked by a putto, both in the Victoria and Albert Museum. J.V.G. Mallet feels that all these Chelsea pieces may have been modelled by Sprimont himself.

The famous small St James's model of a Dancing Girl [fig. 5.1] (partnered by a separate Boy with a Hurdy Gurdy) is likely to have been based on a Meissen model of a Dancing Girl created by J.J. Kändler *c.* 1745. The pose is identical; only details of sleeves, neckline and head ornament have been simplified.[16] If the Meissen model was borrowed for copying from Sir Charles Hanbury-Williams' collection at Holland House in 1751, this gives us a clear date for the Chelsea Dancing Girl wearing a hat in Raised Anchor porcelain; the same model being produced, hatless, a little later by the St James's factory.

A few of the St James's models differ little from Chelsea productions either in form or in ornament. For instance, the St James's version of the Rustic Lovers [fig. 5.11] in the National Museum of Ireland in Dublin reproduces the salient features of the Chelsea Triangle version in The British Museum; but in a smaller and simplified form. The several examples of a St James's finch [fig. 5.4] perched on a stump (some facing left, two

Fig. 5.10 Figure of a Hound Bitch, St James's Factory. Pair to a Dog in the Museum of Fine Arts, Boston. Height 11.5 cm (4½ in). *c.* 1750–59. The Victoria and Albert Museum, London

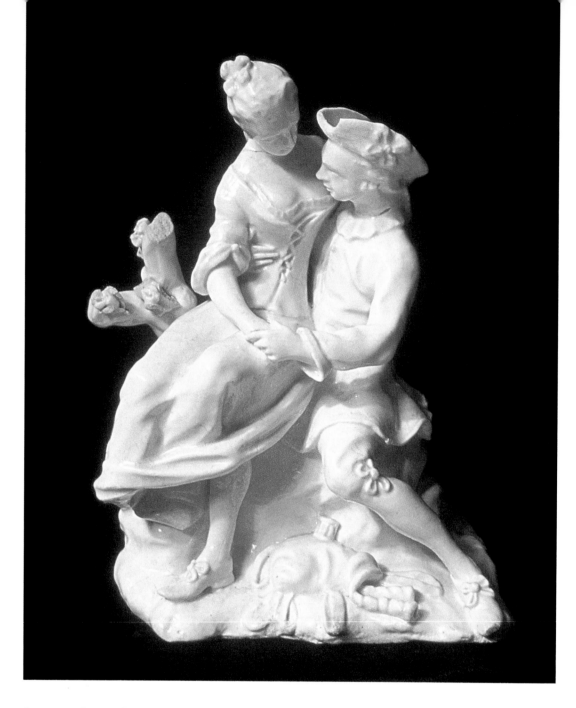

Fig. 5.11 Group of Rustic Lovers, St James's Factory. Probably after the similar group modelled in Triangle porcelain. Height 17.3 cm (6¹³/₁₆ in). *c.*1750–59. National Museum of Ireland, Dublin

facing right, and another also facing right with a wing displayed) are also remarkably similar to recognized Chelsea models.

Some thirty different models of St James's groups and figures are now known, one of the more recently discovered being a group of the Holy Family in the white which was the subject of an article by Patrick Synge-Hutchinson in June 1968.[17] The piece is slip-cast, and was inspired almost certainly by an engraving by François de Poilly the elder of a painting by Raphael, *The Small Holy Family*, which is now in the Louvre. Another religious figure, of the Mater Dolorosa, was perhaps copied from an

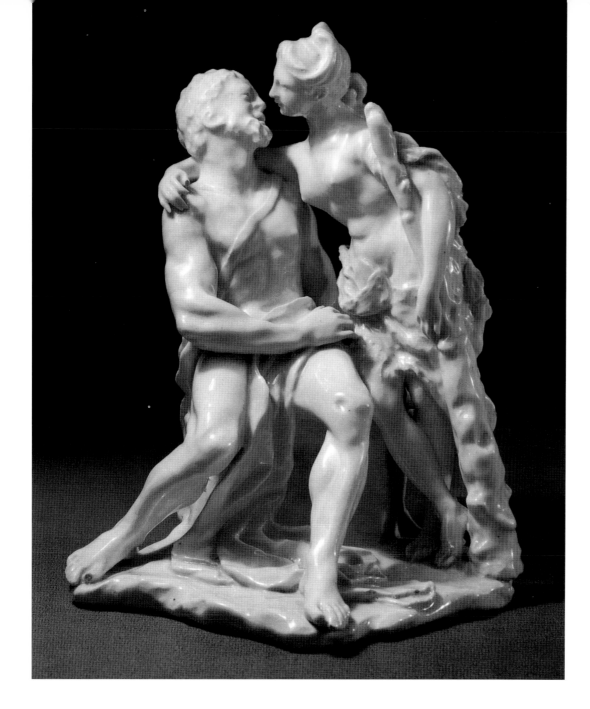

Fig. 5.12 Group of Hercules and Omphale, St James's Factory. Taken from an engraving by Laurent Cars after the picture by François Le Moyne painted in 1724. Height 22.9 cm (9 in). *c.* 1750–59. Fitzwilliam Museum, Cambridge

ivory. Two examples are recorded, one in the white in The British Museum and a coloured version sold at Phillips in 1985.

Engravings were obviously often used as a source of design by those who produced the St James's pieces. Another famous group, of Hercules and Omphale [fig. 5.12], was probably adapted from an engraving by Laurent Cars after a picture painted in 1724 by François Le Moyne, though Bernard Watney pointed out that it seems closely related to an early seventeenth-century bronze group '*Mars, Venus and Amor*' by Hubert Gerhard (1540/50–1620), who had earlier worked in the studio of

Fig. 5.13 Group of Lovers with a Lamb, St James's Factory. The decoration is probably later. Height 12.6 cm (4¹⁵⁄₁₆ in). *c.* 1750–59. Tullie House Museum & Art Gallery, Carlisle

Fig. 5.14 Group of a gentleman presenting a bird's nest to a lady, St James's Factory. This is the only recorded example of the group. Height 16.8 cm (6⁹⁄₁₆ in). *c.* 1750–59. Fitzwilliam Museum, Cambridge

Giovanni da Bologna (1529–1608) in Florence.[18] The work of the Venetian engraver Jacopo Amiconi, who was in England between 1729 and 1739, provided some printed designs on both Worcester porcelain and Battersea enamels, and his engravings of scenes emblematic of the Elements were translated into the St James's porcelain groups of 'Water' and 'Air'.[19] In the first, a standing young man is presenting a large (missing) fish to a girl with other fish in a basket beside her; in the second, Amiconi's design had to be substantially modified as the young man was half-way up a ladder, a scene very difficult to reproduce in porcelain. Instead he sits awkwardly, cross-legged on the ground, holding a large bird in his lap with a smaller one beside him, while the standing girl, holding a bowl or handleless basket, looks on. Both standing figures from these groups were also issued as single pieces on hexagonal bevelled bases. Two candlestick groups with a sleeping girl on the one hand and a youth with his finger to his lips on the other, of which coloured examples are in the Untermyer Collection, were taken from an engraving 'The Dying Nymph' by George Bickham, which was published in the *Musical Entertainer* in 1739.

A pastoral scene by François Boucher was most probably the source for a group of a lady receiving a bird's nest from her kneeling lover [fig. 5.14]; and Boucher may also have prompted the paired groups of 'Lovers with a Lamb' [fig. 5.13], and 'Lovers with a Dove'. The source of the paired groups of classical origin, 'Ganymede and the Eagle' [fig. 5.15] and 'Europa and the Bull' [fig. 5.16], has not yet been discovered, but was possibly also French.

A documentary group of Britannia lamenting the death of Frederick, Prince of Wales, an event which occurred on 31 March 1751, is important because it enables us to associate some of the St James's pieces closely with the earlier years of the sixth decade of the eighteenth century. Britannia sits holding a handkerchief to her face, down which a single delicate tear is coursing. On her right is her shield, moulded with the Union flag, and her left arm supports an oval moulded cameo of a profile bust of the Prince. The British lion lies recumbent before it, parallel to the side of the simple pad base. The lion in the example at the British Museum [fig. 5.18] is a lumpy, cheerful beast, but that in the group in the Untermyer Collection and in another at Birmingham City Museum and Art Gallery are fine and realistic animals, possibly copied from a bronze original. A different model of mourning Britannia was made in Chelsea Raised Anchor porcelain [fig. 7.34].

Fig. 5.15 Group of Ganymede and the Eagle, St James's Factory. Made as a pair to the group of Europa and the Bull; one of six examples recorded. Height 14.4 cm (5⅝ in). *c.*1750–59. The Victoria and Albert Museum, London

Fig. 5.16 Europa and the Bull, St James's Factory. Height 14.9 cm (5⅘ in). No mark. *c.*1750–59. The British Museum

Fig. 5.17 Group of Fox and Crane, St James's Factory. This is the only example known of this group. It may derive from an illustration in the *Weekly Apollo*, 1752. Height 14.1 cm (5½ in). *c.*1752. Museum of Fine Arts, Boston

Fig. 5.18 Britannia lamenting the death of Frederick, Prince of Wales, which occurred in March 1751, St James's Factory. Height 18.5 cm (7¼ in). *c.*1751. The British Museum

A Fable group of the Fox and Crane is another St James's piece which ties in closely with a date in the 1750s, since it derives from an engraving in an issue of the *Weekly Apollo* of 1752. Only one example of this group is known, now in the Boston Museum of Fine Arts [fig. 5.17].

A few more models remain to be mentioned. The 'Girl-in-a-Swing' herself appears twice, in the Victoria and Albert Museum [fig. 5.19] and in Boston. Both figures are in the white. The girl sits on her swing, slung between two tree stumps which sprout typical oval serrated leaves and a number of nozzles for the insertion of the stems of porcelain (or real?) flowers. The characteristic modeller's nail marks are clear on the simple pad base. The family likeness between the Girl and Britannia is remarkable.

Fig. 5.19 Figure of the Girl-in-a-Swing, St James's Factory. Height 15.9 cm (6¼ in). *c.* 1750–59. The Victoria and Albert Museum, London

Within the last decade a previously unrecorded St James's figure of Leda and the Swan has come to light (fig. 5.7), reputedly found in a cupboard in a house in East Anglia. It has echoes of Chelsea in the figure of Leda, but has no attendant Cupid, and the swan on Leda's right is rather awkwardly formed. It is the only example of this St James's model known, and is now in the British Museum, sold to them thanks to the late Mrs Sheila Davis.

Mention of a small number of other figures concludes the list of this class of St James's productions. These are an enamel-decorated pair of male and female vintners in the Untermyer Collection, he with a pannier of grapes and she leaning against a tree trunk, with a bunch of grapes in one hand. They derive possibly from Meissen.

A rare model of a barefoot lady standing beside an altar of sacrificial flame may represent 'Amitié', and be adapted from a Vincennes copy of a sculpture by Falconet. She is uncoloured, as are the single pair of seated hounds (reminiscent of those produced *c.* 1750 at Bow), of which the Dog is in the Boston Museum of Fine Arts and the Bitch [fig. 5.10] in the Victoria and Albert Museum.

Closely allied to the St James's figures are, of course, the miniature items for which the class is still perhaps best known. A large number of these are scent-bottles of varying figural and fantastic forms. In 1966 Kate Foster read a paper to the English Ceramic Circle in which she divided the scent-bottles into two separate categories, each group being marked by particular characteristics.[20]

In the first category, which she designated as 'Girl-in-a-Swing' bottles, she included nearly forty bottles which she listed in detail. She stated that:

> The paste used in their manufacture is of a greyish-green tone and can certainly be very closely compared with the groups and figures bearing the same attribution. The figures are painted freely, but in minute detail, with full sprays of flowers, among which there appear, almost without fail, a yellow and a pink rose. This decoration appears on the clothes of the figures, on the upper side of the concave bases, and also on the underside, sometimes accompanied by small sprays of cherries; the hair, if any, is in grey streaks, the tree trunks are brown and the serrated leaves are green-brown … When mounted these bottles all bear finely chased gold mounts at the collar and foot …

Kate Foster also pointed out the close similarity of the painting on these bottles with the decoration on pieces of Chinese porcelain called 'London decorated', and emphasized that there was more than a purely stylistic resemblance. The small porcelain casket now in the Victoria and Albert Museum, which contains four cut-glass scent-bottles and which is mounted with gold and painted with the 'London decorated' type of floral sprays, is allied to the first 'Girl-in-a-Swing' group of scent-bottles identified by Kate Foster. So also is a cylindrical étui, painted similarly with bouquets, scattered fruits and flowers, which has stamped gold mounts embellished with scrolls and flowers, and was sold at Christie's, lot 150, on 20 October 1986.

In the second group Miss Foster included nearly fifty models of scent-bottles which she distinguished from her first group by details of the decoration, and by the addition of French mottoes on the base. In models common to both groups those in the second are generally considerably smaller in size than those in the first.

In the decoration of the second group hair is painted a bright chestnut brown; eyes are outlined, and blue-green leaves sometimes appear growing immediately out of short tree trunks or from no trunk at all. A vivid turquoise is a characteristic colour, and the colouring of the clothes on some models identical. Single-bloom small pink roses abound instead of mixed bunches of garden flowers; and a single pink rose is often found on the underside of the concave bases, sometimes enclosed in a wreath of stiff green leaves. The mounts are not of gold, but of plain gilt metal.

Rather than ascribing these bottles to two different makers as Miss Foster's book suggests, I would argue that they are both of Charles Gouyn's St James's manufacture. There is no reason why the first, finer group of larger bottles should not have been decorated outside the factory, as their affinity with the 'London decorated' Chinese porcelain suggests. Kate Foster concludes that the bottles in the second category were a cheaper line, made to appeal to a wider market than those more expensively mounted in gold, and with this I entirely concur.

One of the most amazing of all silver and silver-gilt caskets, set with more than thirty panels of St James's porcelain, appeared at Christies as lot 16 in an 'Important Sale of Silver & Objects of Vertu …' on 8 December 1994 [fig. 5.21]. It was an extraordinary artefact, a truly outstanding example of full rococo taste, described in the Catalogue as 'A Magnificent Rococo Silver, Silver-gilt, "Girl-in-a-Swing" Porcelain and Polished Steel-mounted Dressing-table Casket surmounted by an Arched Triple Looking-Glass with Folding Doors, *c.* 1755, perhaps [made at] the St James's factory of Charles Gouyn.' The Casket itself was 27 cm (10⅝ inches) wide; the mirror 35 cm (13¾ inches) high and the height overall 45 cm (18 inches).

Its contents had come from several sources. Three rectangular porcelain boxes, one larger, two of matching smaller size, were all of Sprimont's Chelsea porcelain, enamelled with flowers and elaborately mounted in gold. Matching them was a Chelsea porcelain gold-mounted 'carnet' (or note pad), its porcelain covers hinged; and the clasps joined by a reeded gold pencil.

Besides these, the contents included a circular snuff-box of St James's porcelain painted with flowers, mounted in gold and with the cover hinged. There were also two gold-mounted étui scent-bottles of St James's porcelain, one formed as a bunch of apple-blossom, the other as a bunch of pink and white Sweet William; a pair of St James's gold-mounted sunflower scent-bottles and stoppers, the stoppers formed one as a butterfly and the other as a bouquet; two gold-mounted St James's type scent-bottles and stoppers, both bottles modelled as a nymph in a loose dress with a basket of flowers in her lap, sitting before a rose-bush on a green mound; as well as two more of St James's type, one modelled as Cupid by a rose-bush, the other as a putto sitting by a rose-bush on green rockwork, holding two doves and with a dog at his feet.

There were also a Meissen porcelain thimble, two gold-mounted cut-glass scent-bottles; two gold-mounted cut-glass bonbonnières, several steel manicure implements, a gold-mounted steel bodkin and a pair of polished steel scissors with reeded oval gold handles.

Fig. 5.20 Scent-bottle modelled as a squirrel, the head forming its stopper. The squirrel sits holding a nut between its paws; the domed base is decorated with a pansy and two cherries, the underside with a flower spray. The hinged lid is fitted with a mirror. St James's Factory. Height 6 cm (2.4 in). *c.* 1750–59. Private collection

As the auctioneers suggested, 'the presence of the hitherto unrecorded "Girl-in-a-Swing" rococo plaques made specifically for it, and the contents including "Girl-in-a-Swing" scent-bottles and étui strongly point to Charles Gouyn of Bennet Street, St James's as the assembler ...' Whether he was the actual maker of the casket and mirror frame is a moot point. The creation of such a piece would have been enormously expensive, and one can say with almost complete certainty that it must have been a specific, and possibly even a royal, commission.

Every available record was searched by the auctioneers to discover the casket's provenance; the only possibly relevant reference that could be found was in the announcement of the sale of the late Sir Everard Fawkener's property in the *Daily Advertiser* on 17 February 1759. The six-day Sale, 12–19 February, conducted by Mr Ford 'at his great Room in the Haymarket' included '... a most beautiful JEWEL CABINET mounted in Gold, with Gold Equipage for the Toilet etc.', but we cannot know for certain that the casket sold in the 1990s had once belonged to Sir Everard.

Having so spectacularly reappeared, the casket was bought by a London dealer, vanished into the firm's vaults, and from thence into the Dallas Museum of Art, Texas – like the passing of a comet. One feels grateful at least to have had the opportunity to see, and to wonder at so extraordinary a piece and its attending 'tail' of delightful miniature artefacts.

In 1948 F.S. Mackenna first made the suggestion that, as well as figures and 'toys', useful wares of St James's type were probably also in existence.[21] His perspicacity was fully justified; the first such piece identified was a tall, slightly flared handleless cup in his own collection, decorated with a bouquet of mixed flowers. The decoration was remarkably like that on two similar but lobed Chelsea cups, one of the Triangle period, the other perhaps of Raised Anchor dating. The cup of simple shape was at first accepted by F.S. Mackenna as Chelsea, 'but almost from the outset I was unhappy with this attribution ... Now it will be recalled that this was originally exactly the position regarding the Swing Girl figures; Chelsea and yet somehow not quite.'[22]

In fifty years the number of recognized useful pieces of St James's type, though still not large, has expanded quite considerably. Only two of them are entirely undecorated. These are both tea caddies, 12.7 cm (5 inches) high and of tall, lobed 'melon' form, girdled with intrinsically moulded swags looped through moulded rings. A knot of three-dimensional strawberries and leaves surmounts each of their slightly domed lids. One of these caddies is in the Schreiber Collection at the Victoria and Albert Museum, the other at Colonial Williamsburg.

Two sugar boxes and lids of double-ogee form similarly crowned with knots of strawberries and leaves have also appeared, and one is now in the Victoria and Albert Museum [fig. 5.22].[23] Both are enamelled with floral sprays and with a beetle on the lid. They are somewhat similar in shape to two silver tea caddies and a sugar box

Fig. 5.21 A rococo silver, silver-gilt, St James's Factory porcelain, cut-glass and polished steel-mounted dressing-table casket surmounted by an arched triple looking glass. Height overall 45 cm (18 in). *c.* 1755. Dallas Museum of Art, Texas

Fig. 5.22 Sugar box and lid, St James's Factory. The shape resembles that of three silver tea caddies assayed by Nicholas Sprimont in 1744. Height 13.4 cm (5¼ in). *c.* 1750–59. The Victoria and Albert Museum, London

with Sprimont's mark and the date letter for 1744 in the Museum of Fine Arts, Boston.[24]

The Victoria and Albert Museum possesses a cluster of St James's wares, which include, besides those already mentioned, a hexagonal sauceboat, painted with flowers, and a large double-handled cup with its saucer. The handles on both cup and sauceboat are curiously angled, and not unlike those generally used seventy-odd years later, *c.* 1830, in conjunction with 'London Shape' tewares. Like the sugar box lids, sauceboat, cup and saucer are all finished with a brown edging on the rim.

Cups of St James's porcelain are not common. One of simple lobed form once in the Goldblatt Collection related not only to flared Chelsea cups of the Triangle period but also to some made at Vincennes. It was painted with five simple sprays of flowers in various colours, including pink and yellow, on the outside, and magenta daisy-like flowers within. This cup was one of three found in an antique shop in the north of England by Simon and Enid Goldblatt. It was labelled as of Derby origin. The handle form was a flattened loop attached at either side of the central third of the cup's depth, and there was a noticeable bump just before its lower end met the cup.[25]

A small gourd-shaped bottle, decorated with flowers, is a unique piece, and is in the Victoria and Albert Museum. Two cream jugs are there too, one slightly larger than the other and rising from a globular body to a flared mouth with a shaped edge, lined, like other pieces already mentioned, in a dark brown. It has a plain loop handle. The other jug, purchased in recent times by the Museum, certainly appears related to the rather larger creamers of lobed baluster form made in the Chelsea Triangle period. The simple sweep of its rim is again edged with chocolate brown, which is also used to colour the looped twig-handle. The jug is painted in scattered flower-sprays and flowers in a palette of pink, blue and yellow. It is tiny, only just over 8 cm (or 3 inches) high. One other St James's jug similar to this is recorded, moulded in the same way but decorated by the addition of a band of applied strawberries and serrated leaves round the foot. It was sold by Sothebys on 24 November 1970, and again from the Rous Lench Collection on 1 July 1986.

The shop which labelled the Goldblatt cup as 'Derby' was perhaps not altogether mistaken. Dr Bernard Watney pointed out in a paper published in the *Transactions* of the English Ceramic Circle in 1968[26] that a distinctive style of flower painting of which the hallmark is the inclusion of a pair of cherries in the decoration, and which he called Type B, occurs not only on English decorated Chinese porcelain but also on Worcester, 'dry-edge' Derby, and some St James's scent-bottles, as Kate Foster had realized. Some of the cheaper group of scent-bottles, mounted in metal instead of gold, Dr Watney continued, 'were decorated by another painter of the Type B school whose hand is also found on "dry edge" Derby figures'. This decoration may have been the work of unknown London enamellers, or perhaps amongst the earliest decoration executed by James Giles.

Dr Watney pointed out in a paper published in 1971[27] similarities between the modelling of St James's figures and some primitive-looking figures which he identified as very early productions of Derby. They included a Turk and his Companion with flat octagonal bases from the Rous Lench Collection, and four putti, two of them representing Spring and Summer. Details about them reminiscent of the St James's pieces include the way the putti are seated with knees apart and legs placed obliquely, as are those on certain St James's tapersticks; incised nail paring marks on the base of Summer and those of the Turks; and some similarities of form in the bases, though none are identical with St James's bases. However, details of features and hands are not the same as those of St James's pieces, though the figures are likewise slip-cast and composed of a glassy paste.

Dr Watney also drew attention to the marked similarity between three Derby cream jugs, including one incised 'D 1750', and the small St James's jug mentioned above. The wreath of coloured strawberries and leaves round the base of the 'D 1750' jug is reminiscent of those on the lids of the St James's sugar boxes.

One of the more recently published items of St James's useful ware is the small lidded pot [fig. 5.23] discovered by Dr Geoffrey Godden.[28] Like the cream jug in the Victoria and Albert Museum, it is only 7.7 cm (3 inches) high. It stands on a circular sloping foot, and the main part of the body is moulded with eight facets. The slightly domed lid is tiny, a 'mere inch or so' in diameter, and has a single five-petalled flower (one petal missing) as knop, surrounded by four radiating leaves. The painted decoration consists of a typical spray of flowers on the pot itself, with simple stalked flower heads scattered elsewhere on both pot and lid. It is a delightful little piece and, whether for use as a mustard pot or as an adjunct to a dressing table, so far as is known, unique.

Fig. 5.23 Small faceted pot and lid, with polychrome floral decoration and flower knop, St James's Factory. Height 7.7 cm (3 in). *c.* 1750–59. Geoffrey Godden; on loan to the Potteries Museum and Art Gallery, Stoke-on-Trent

CHAPTER 6

The Heyday of the Manufacture

c. 1750–56

Fig. 6.1 Portrait miniature of Sir Everard Fawkener, pastel, by J.E. Liotard. Private collection, through Ashmolean Museum, Oxford

Fig. 6.2 Large silver-shape dish, Fable decorated. Diameter 33.7 cm (13¼ in). No mark. c. 1755–8. Private collection

Although a certain amount of mystery even now surrounds the origin of the Chelsea porcelain factory in spite of the recent discovery of the documentary assertion by Jacques Louis Brolliet made in 1759 that it was founded by Charles Gouyn, we can now at least be sure, as I have shown, that Nicholas Sprimont was on the scene from c. 1744. With the transition of the main business of the works to the Lawrence Street site in 1749/50, Nicholas Sprimont's position as controller of the factory was confirmed; and it is probably at this point also that Sir Everard Fawkener [fig. 6.1] became chief financier of the undertaking, a position that had presumably been Charles Gouyn's until c. 1748/9.

The involvement of Sir Everard Fawkener and his brother William, Governor of the Bank of England, can be seen in their payments to 'Premonte' and 'Sprimont' which came to a total of £1495 between August 1746 and August 1748.[1] It was thus probably due to the Fawkeners that the newly-erected pottery on the upper western side of Lawrence Street was in occupation from the middle of 1749, its productions first coming on the market at the beginning of April 1750. However, there can be no doubt that the Chelsea Porcelain Manufacture was an undertaking that owed its existence first and foremost to Nicholas Sprimont. Although he had to rely upon others to provide the necessary finance, without his spirit and creative energy there would have been no Chelsea porcelain, no matter how many 'riches particuliers' had been available to finance it. Nicholas Sprimont *was* Chelsea, and in spite of the changes in style during the factory's two and a half decades of existence his was the guiding influence on everything that was produced there.

In the newspaper advertisements at this time Nicholas Sprimont refers to himself as both 'Proprietor of Chelsea Porcelain' and 'Manufacturer of China'. In a preliminary notice issued on 9 January 1750 (NS) in the *Daily Advertiser* he gave out that his forthcoming spring sale would 'consist of a Variety of Services for Tea, Coffee, Chocolate, Porringers, Dishes and Plates, of different Forms and Patterns, and of a great Variety of Pieces for Ornament in a Taste entirely new'. To begin with they

were obtainable only at the factory warehouse, conducted as previously in the double eastern half of Monmouth House at the northern end of Lawrence Street. Selling began at the warehouse on 2 April, and continued successfully throughout April and May. The following newspaper advertisement appeared in late April and early May.

> CHELSEA PORCELAINE will continue selling at the Manufactory there every day at Eleven o'Clock. As I have seen the forms most in the general Taste, I shall do all that is in my Power, to produce more of that sort, and make Additions to a great many of the new Shapes; which Things will be brought into the Sale-Warehouse every Day as finished. I take the Liberty to return my humble Thanks to all those who have been so good as to favour me with their Encouragement, and will endeavour to merit the Continuance of their favours.
>
> Note. The Quality and Gentry may be assured that I am not concern'd in any Shape whatsoever with the Goods expos'd to Sale in St James's Street, call'd the Chelsea-China-Warehouse. N. Sprimont.

Sprimont's references to his 'new Shapes' and to 'Pieces for Ornament in a Taste entirely new' have caused a good deal of speculation and interest among scholars in the field of English porcelain. In an article published in January 1981[2] I suggested that the latter were the models of 'Uncommon Birds' [see figs 6.3–4] taken from the plates in George Edwards' *Natural History of Uncommon Birds*, the first part of which was published in 1743. Similar individual bird models had already been produced at Meissen. The 'new Shapes', I suggested, were the Raised Anchor useful wares based on Japanese forms, the octagonal beakers, tea bowls and saucers, hexagonal teapots [see figs 6.5–6], double-leaf dishes and so on.

The notice of 9 April 1750 quoted in the previous chapter seems to indicate that the 'N. Sprimont' who signed it was by then a 'Proprietor' and presumably also the 'Chief Manager' of the 'Chelsea Porcelaine'. If, however, the word 'Proprietor' in fact indicates a financial backer, as has been supposed in the case of Charles Gouyn, who else was available to assist in raising the capital during these early years at the Lawrence Street site? The immediate answer is of course 'Sir Everard Fawkener', who, as I have said, probably paid for the Lawrence Street factory buildings (though not for their site). David Burnsall, the auctioneer, in 1776 stated his belief that for some years before 1757 Fawkener had been 'owner and proprietor of the houses, warehouses, kilns and other buildings used for the manufacturing of porcelain and in that year did decline such business in favour of Nicholas Sprimont ...'[3] That this was true is suggested by the fact that it was not until 1760 that Sprimont first insured the factory buildings, and did so in his own name.[4]

Fig. 6.3 Crested bird (Topknot bird?). Height 16.5 cm (6½ in). Mark: a Raised Anchor. *c.*1750. The Victoria and Albert Museum, London

Fig. 6.4 Figure of a Guan after the print in George Edwards' *Natural History of Uncommon Birds*, vol. 1, pl. 13, London 1743. Mark: a Raised Anchor painted in red, applied to the tree stump beneath the bird's tail. Height 21.6 cm (8½ in). *c.*1750–52. Colonial Williamsburg Foundation, Virginia

Fig. 6.5 Hexagonal teapot with Kakiemon pattern of Phoenix and Banded Hedge (lid a replacement). Height 14.6 cm (5¾ in). No mark. 1750–52. Private collection

Henry Porter was certainly another 'Proprietor' in the sense of financier; as has been said he purchased the old houses and plots of land utilized by the factory in Church Lane East and Lawrence Street between September 1750 and September 1751 (though they had been in the occupation and use of Sprimont for some while already). His nephew Isaac Porter, 'Gentleman, of St James's', probably also had a financial interest in the business as it was his money which was used to purchase Mrs Phillips' house in Church Lane in November 1750, and it was for this reason that his uncle assigned the house to him by deed-poll in May 1751.[5]

William Augustus, Duke of Cumberland (1721–65) [fig. 6.7], the second son of

Fig. 6.6 Transitional teapot, Fable decoration. Height 12.2 cm (4¾ in). *c.* 1752–3. Potteries Museum and Art Gallery, Stoke-on-Trent

King George II and Queen Caroline, has sometimes been credited with possessing a very close financial connection with the Chelsea Porcelain factory. On 9 June 1751 Sir Charles Hanbury-Williams, the British Envoy to the Saxon Court in Dresden [fig. 6.8], wrote to his friend Henry Fox at Holland House in Kensington, where a quantity of Meissen porcelain, presented to Hanbury-Williams by Augustus III, King of Poland and Elector of Saxony, was stored. Hanbury-Williams evidently thought that Sir Everard Fawkener, the Duke's secretary, rather than the Duke himself, was connected with the Chelsea factory.

I receivd a letter about ten days ago from Sir Everard Fawkener, who is, I believe, concernd in the manufacture of China at Chelsea. He desird me to send over models for different Pieces from hence, in order to furnish the Undertakers with good designs: and would have had me send over fifty or threescore pounds' worth. But I thought it better and cheaper for the Manufacturers to give them leave to take away any of my China from Holland House, and to copy what they like. I have therefore told Sr Everard, that, If he will go to your house, you will permitt him, and anybody He brings with him, to see my China, & to take away such pieces as they may have a mind to Copy. I find also that the Duke is a great encourager of the Chelsea China, and has bespoke a set for his own Table.

On 12 August following Sir Everard himself wrote to Hanbury-Williams to thank him for the facility he had given the Chelsea factory, and to make some pertinent queries about the wholesale prices obtaining at the royal factory at Meissen. His letter is worth quoting in full.[6]

Lond. the 12th Aug. 1751

Sir,

I owe you many ack^ments, as well for the very obliging manner in which you have been pleased to comply with my request in favour of the Porcelain Manufactory at Chelsea, as for late kind letter, but as I have been out of town, I have chosen to defer them till I could give you some acc^ts of the use which has been made of your generous contribution to its advancement. I found on my return to Town that many imitations are made, as well in some forms as in paintings. This is of the greatest consequence to this new manufacture, as that of Dresden has not only the advantage of a longer establishment, & of all the support of a Royal expence, by w^h a number of the best artists in the way they want are drawn thither, but there exists at Dresden the greatest collection of old china in Europe, from whence many excellent patterns are to be had.

I have been desired to move you for a further favor in the behalf of this new manufacture, when I should return thanks for that advantage receiv'd, which is, that you would be pleased to let them know the prices at the Whare houses of the Royal Manufacture of the several things you have indulged them with the sight & use of. They are sensible that the extent & success of their manufacture will depend upon the price, yet, as they have been at an immense expence to bring it to this point of perfection, they would have such a price for their ware as to re-imburse them & leave some advantage. They are without any light to guide them in a matter of this

Fig. 6.7 Bust of the Duke of Cumberland. Height (with stand) 19 cm (7²⁄₅ in). *c.*1750–52. The British Museum

moment, & w^d therefore be extremely thankful for the assistance they might receive, from the knowledge how those at Dresden govern. They met with good encouragement last spring, tho' they had little but separate Pieces to sell, except Tea and Coffee Services. They propose opening a Whare house in town by the King's birthday,[7] when there will be a large quantity of dishes, plates, etc. for table and desert services.

Your great civility upon the first trouble I gave you must be my apology for this, to w^h I shall only add the profession of the sentiments of acknowledgement & respect with w^h I shall be always, Sir,

Y^r. most ob^t humble Servt

Everard Fawkener

Fig. 6.8 Portrait of Sir Charles Hanbury-Williams by John Giles Eccardt, 1746. National Portrait Gallery, London

One or two points in the letter call for particular comment. Sir Everard refers to 'the Porcelain Manufactory at Chelsea' as 'this new manufacture'. This really confirms the establishment of the Lawrence Street site, and the whole business under Sprimont's management, from the beginning of 1750 as we have supposed. He also remarks that Meissen has 'all the support of a Royal expence' with the implication that Chelsea has not. This in itself is one of the strongest reasons for thinking that the Duke of Cumberland did not finance the factory, although he was certainly interested in it, since Sir Charles Hanbury-Williams remarked in his letter to Henry Fox 'that the Duke is a great encourager of the Chelsea China and has bespoke a set for his own Table'. Another strong reason for dissociating the Duke from any financial involvement with the Chelsea Porcelain factory is a notice published much later on, on 2 January 1764, when owing to Sprimont's illness, rumours of the sale of the factory were rife.

… The paragraph in the *Gazetteer* of Saturday, Dec. 24, 1763, that his Royal Highness the Duke of Cumberland has been lately at the manufactory, in order to purchase the Secret is without Foundation.

There would have been no possibility of such a rumour if the Duke had been one of the backers of the undertaking all along.[8]

Alexander Lind of Gorgie, near Edinburgh, an early porcelain-maker who seems to have kept a very close eye on events in London, through the good offices of the

3rd Duke of Argyll, was able in 1750 to visit the factories at both Bow and Chelsea.

> ... I had the opportunity of examining everything pretty minutely, I mean the structure of their Furnaces, and the other parts of their manual operations, which were what I chiefly wanted to see, as to the materials they use, Those they keep secret, as far as they can, but as I think I know them, and that my own are prefferable, I am the less curious to be informed about them ...
>
> At Chelsea I luckiely met with Sir Everard Falconer, Lord Hyndford who was alongst with his Grace introduced me to him.[9]

The years 1750–56 were probably the most successful of Nicholas Sprimont's entire career. He had become 'Chief Manager' of the Chelsea factory, he had a wealthy and aristocratic patron in Sir Everard Fawkener; and he had an enterprising local businessman and his nephew to secure the factory sites. Also the expanded factory was very well situated in relation to the metropolis with regard both to the production and the dispersal of Sprimont's beautiful porcelain.

From Midsummer 1749 until the early months of 1759 the Rate Books show that Andrew Lagrave was the tenant of the house at the south-east corner of the Lawrence Street factory site, and that from 1750/51 onwards either he or the 'Occupier' Nicholas Sprimont was responsible for the payment of the rates. Since it is now proved beyond doubt by the Middlesex Deeds Registers and by the Hand-in-Hand fire insurances for the house that it was part and parcel of Sprimont's Lawrence Street factory site, F.S. Mackenna's suggestion that Andrew Lagrave might be regarded as some sort of manager or foreman seems a sensible one.[10] This can be supported by the subsequent association of 'Mr Mead's' name with the house and with Sprimont in the Rate Books from March 1759, and also by Henry Porter's will made on 3 September 1766 and proved on the 24th of the same month.[11] In it, special reference is made to the Lawrence Street factory site and the corner house which Porter bequeathed to his second wife Elizabeth. The corner house is particularly described as 'that freehold Messuage or Tenement with the Appurtenances in the occupation of Mr Mead', together with 'all that part or parcel of Ground and the Erections [kilns] Buildings and Premises with the Appurtenances situate lying and being in the parish of Chelsea ... now in the Tenure or Occupation of Mr Nicholas Sprimont as Lessee or Tenant thereof'.

There can be little doubt that Mead succeeded Lagrave in the position that went with the tenancy of the corner house, even though references are so scanty. The only other we have for Lagrave, apart from mention in the Rate Books, is the baptismal record of his son, 'Andrew, son of Andrew Lagrave and Mary', recorded at Chelsea on 27 May 1750. The surname Lagrave suggests a Huguenot family.

Fig. 6.9 Detail showing Pall Mall, looking eastwards, from the print published by John Bowles in 1753. London Metropolitan Archives

It is certain that Henry Porter was closely involved with the Chelsea Porcelain undertaking. Not only did he own much of the ground on which the factory stood, but he plainly had much to do with the marketing of the porcelain. On 10 June 1751 his name was entered in the Watch Rate Collectors' Book for Pall Mall North[12] as ratepayer for the London warehouse of the Chelsea Porcelain factory; Sir Everard Fawkener said in August that it was to be opened 'by the King's birthday', i.e. 10 November. Pall Mall [fig. 6.9] was the most prestigious thoroughfare of eighteenth-century shopping, the Regent Street of its time; the new 'Whare house' had previously been occupied by Sandys Jones, a celebrated perfumier, and two doors along was the shop of Robert Dodsley, the famous playwright and bookseller. The rateable value of the Pall Mall warehouse was £75, nearly double that of the factory warehouse in Monmouth House, which was never rated at more than £40 while it was in Sprimont's possession. In 1751 Henry Porter seems to have gone to live in the Pall Mall warehouse, and he later conducted a business in carpets there on his own account also.[13]

CHAPTER 7

Raised Anchor Wares and Figures

Fig. 7.1 Lobed beaker, decorated with tiger, prunus, bamboo and rocks; also with chrysanthemum sprig inside. Height 7 cm (2¾ in). No mark. 1750–52. Private collection

Fig. 7.2 Octagonal soup dish with 'Hob in the Well' polychrome decoration. Width 20.8 cm (8⅕ in). No mark. *c.* 1752–5. The British Museum

It is high time to examine more closely the porcelain wares and figures which were probably the first productions of the works on the Lawrence Street site, that is, the Raised Anchor porcelains which were made from *c.* 1750 to *c.* 1752. The Raised Anchor body is one of the most beautiful ever formulated, either of true hard paste, or of artificial type. It is thickly potted and sturdy, and, except for a few early pieces, of a different chemical composition from the Triangle production, containing far less lead and much more lime.[1] It proved a more plastic body than the Triangle one, and though wares and figures are heavier than previously, firing faults and sagging in the kiln were much less likely to occur. The glaze was whitened by the addition of tin oxide, and so made more or less opaque, though there are cases where it is glassy, and has sometimes pooled with a tinge of blue-green. At its best, and most characteristic, Raised Anchor porcelain looks extremely rich, with the smoothness and whiteness of whipped cream. The potting is usually thicker than in the Triangle period, and it is with the Raised Anchor that the famous Chelsea 'moons' – lighter spots of transparency in the greenish yellow tone of the body, which are shown up by transmitted light – first occur. Their cause was not recognized for many years, but it is now known as a certainty that the 'moons' are air-bubbles trapped in the paste at the time when it was mixed, and before being shaped and fired. They are not, as was once thought, patches of glass. Moons continued to appear in the porcelain body in the earlier part of the Red Anchor period *c.* 1753–6, but when bone-ash became an ingredient in the stronger and heavier Gold Anchor paste after 1758, they were no longer a feature of Chelsea porcelain.

Sprimont's advertisement published on 9 January 1750 (NS) spoke of 'Variety of services of different forms and patterns, and of a great variety of Pieces for Ornament in a Taste entirely new', possibly the figures of various birds supported on tree stumps inspired by Meissen, though, as previously mentioned, many were copied from plates in George Edwards' *Natural History of Uncommon Birds*.

That the 'new shapes' of the useful wares were primarily those of oriental and particularly of Japanese inspiration seems both plausible and likely. It was at this

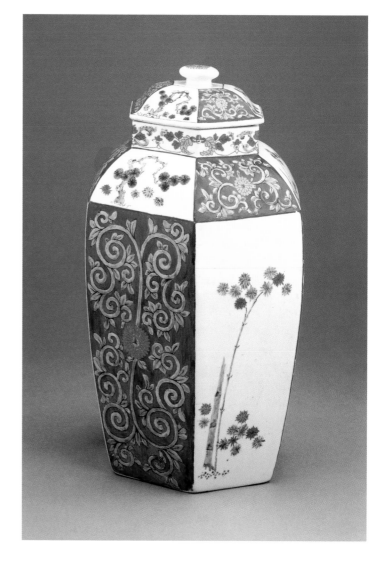

Fig. 7.3 top Rectangular fluted dish, painted with quay scene, with monogram ascribed to William Duvivier and dated 1751. 20.4 x 19.7 cm (8 x 7¾ in). Mark: a Raised Anchor. Museum of Fine Arts, Boston

Fig. 7.4 above Octagonal tea bowl and saucer with Flaming Tortoise pattern. Width of saucer 12.1 cm; height of bowl 4.6 cm. 1750–52. The British Museum

Fig. 7.5 above right Hexagonal lidded jar, with alternate red and oriental flower panels. Height 26.5 cm (10⅖ in). No mark. *c.*1752–4. The British Museum

time that such characteristic productions as the 'octagon teabowls' first appeared, together with the hexagonal teapots, finely fluted tablewares [see fig. 7.3], and dishes in the form of double leaves. All these were originally Japanese shapes of *c.* 1700, though it is uncertain whether the Chelsea copies were made from Japanese pieces, or from continental copies of the Japanese made at Meissen in Saxony or at Chantilly in France. The probability is that pieces of continental origin provided Chelsea's models. Lobed beakers in the style of Vincennes continued to be produced in the Raised Anchor period, as formerly in Triangle porcelain. A pair enamelled with flowering plants after the Chinese and marked with a raised anchor which has 'dropped' are in a private collection in Melbourne, Victoria.[2]

Some octagonal beakers may have been intended for use without saucers in the oriental manner; it is possible that fewer saucers than beakers were made, as certainly fewer have survived.[3] Raised Anchor cups, beakers and saucers of whatever shape are decorated with little in the way of moulded ornament except in the case of the scolopendrium leaf moulding mentioned below, and that of a single known saucer with integral surface moulding of three leafy sprigs [see fig. 7.7]. Intrinsic acanthus leaf moulding *underneath* [see fig. 7.6] was a form which continued in production into the Red Anchor period. In other cases, the raised decoration is sprigged on before glazing. A rare saucer with lightly scalloped rim, and a wreath of leaves in relief surrounding the well, which has the Raised Anchor mark on the back, can be seen at Williamsburg [fig. 7.8]. When first recorded in the nineteenth century, it was with two others and three strawberry leaf teabowls; these other pieces were of the Triangle period. Some saucers have a raised ring in the centre as a simple form of *trembleuse*. Six or eight-sided slop basins have a flanged rim, like their oriental originals.

Some wares of the Raised Anchor period are plain except for a shaped edge of ogee outlines. The double-leaf form of dish has already been mentioned; other leaf forms appear as small single ivy-leaf dishes, and in sauceboats. Scolopendrium leaves moulded in low relief occur on some lobed wares [see fig. 7.9]; and bowls, dishes and cream jugs [see fig. 7.10] of peach-shaped section exist, their form also deriving from Japan. The raised prunus design from China, so popular at many European factories, and in England particularly at Bow, is also seen in Chelsea Raised Anchor porcelain [see fig. 7.11]. It is found not only on beakers, plates and cutlery handles, but is noteworthy on a pair of hexagonal vases of Chinese form now at Colonial Williamsburg. Another example of these rare vases is in The British Museum, one with sparse polychrome decoration also was shown in the English Ceramic Circle Exhibition of 1948.

Fig. 7.6 Lobed saucer, with swirling acanthus leaf moulding underneath. Diameter 12.3 cm (4¹³⁄₁₆ in). *c.*1750–52. Salisbury & South Wiltshire Museum

Fig. 7.7 White saucer moulded in high relief with three foliate sprays. This saucer is unique; nothing else of this design is known. Diameter 12.7 cm (5 in). Mark: a Raised Anchor. *c.*1750. Private collection

Fig. 7.8 Saucer with a wreath of leaves moulded round the well, one of only three of this design recorded. Diameter 11.8 cm (4⁵⁄₈ in). Mark: a Raised Anchor on a pad applied to the base. *c.*1750–52. Colonial Williamsburg Foundation, Virginia

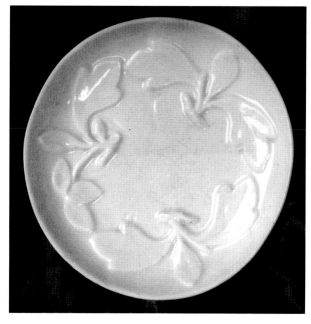

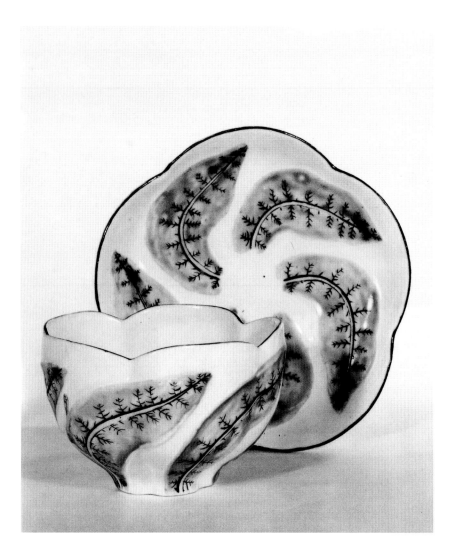

A few designs taken from silver are known in Raised Anchor porcelain, but the wares show nothing so elaborate as the moulded crayfish salts and 'chinaman' teapots made before 1749. Simple shapes which could be produced in quantity seem to have been the first requirement of the newly-founded Lawrence Street factory, and what we know of the initial demand for its production seems to bear this out.

The obvious silver forms of Raised Anchor date are two. In the first there are simple dishes of oblong octagonal shape with an elaborate moulded border of diapers and shield-shaped reserves, which have octagonal plates to match. The second silver shape introduced at this period is that of the shell-design dishes and plates copied after the silver sauceboat stands probably made by Sprimont himself and hallmarked for 1746/7, now in the Katz Collection.[4] This highly popular design [see figs 6.2 and 7.13] continued in production throughout the life of the Chelsea factory.

Some sauceboats were made with a lip at either end and with double handles. The spouts of octagonal-shape sauceboats, whether double or single, closely follow the oriental originals, which are of the narrow, sparrow beak type.[5] Teapot spouts also closely follow the oriental, being short, straight, and tapering towards the outer end. They can be round or square in section. The bases of the

Fig. 7.9 *opposite, top* Scolopendrium-moulded teabowl and saucer. Width of saucer 13.1 cm (5⅛ in). *c.* 1750–52. Private collection

Fig. 7.10 *opposite, below left* Peach-shaped cream jug, landscape decoration. Height 7 cm (2¾ in). Mark: a Raised Anchor on a pad applied to the base. *c.* 1750–52. Salisbury & South Wiltshire Museum

Fig. 7.11 *opposite, below right* Pair of beakers with moulded prunus decoration. Height 7.9 cm (3⅛ in). Mark: a Raised Anchor on a pad applied to the base. *c.* 1750–52. Salisbury & South Wiltshire Museum

Fig. 7.12 *above left* Teapot of fluted form painted in the Kakiemon style with a celestial dragon twined round a bamboo. The reverse side shows a tiger observing an insect. Height 12.1 cm (4¾ in), width 17.8 cm (7 in). *c.* 1750–53. Private collection

Fig. 7.13 *left* Silver-shape dish with wooded river landscape and distant buildings, the border with scattered flower sprays. Shell thumb-pieces and border edged with brown. Length 24.5 cm (9⅝ in). No mark. *c.* 1752. Private collection

Fig. 7.14 Octagonal cup with two flat scroll handles painted in the Meissen style with two figures standing on rockwork in an estuary with two sailing boats. The reverse side is painted with a bouquet of flowers. Height 7 cm (2.75 in). No mark. *c.* 1750–52. Private collection

octagonal and hexagonal teapots are usually perfectly flat and unglazed; but fluted or plain round teapots have their sides elongated into an inward-curving footrim, so that the base seems to be recessed [see fig. 7.12]. Footrims on all wares are often ground level, but some dishes were made entirely without them.

The handles on teapots can be of plain loop form, or sometimes, on octagonal teapots, a loop of square section. On cups and cream jugs, a simple stemlike handle with a long attachment piece at the lower terminal is often found, though scolpendrium moulded cream boats (of which an example is in an Australian private collection) have an ornately moulded handle with rococo scrolling overhanging the rim at the upper end. The handle itself is formed as a pendent swag of husks. A similar handle is shown on a scolopendrium-moulded teapot illustrated by William King,[6] who suggests it was derived from silver. The spout has a moulded acanthus leaf superimposed. However, the most typical handles on cups and cream jugs of Raised Anchor Chelsea porcelain are those of a flattened scroll type, narrow in section and

Fig. 7.15 Hexagonal teapot and lid, painted with the Fable of 'The Leopard and the Fox' after Barlow, Fable 58. The reverse side is decorated with a spray of flowers. Height 12.7 cm (5 in), width 19.1 cm (7½ in). No mark. *c.* 1752. Private collection

angular in outline. They have a hooked excrescence at the upper outer angle, and a scrolled knob where the lower end of the handle joins the side of the cup [figs 7.14, 7.16]. Such handles are not found on English porcelain of any other type or date.

A number of pieces which are neither wares nor figures were made in the Raised Anchor period. Such are the small pedestals, presumably intended as supports for porcelain figures, of which there are two well-known types. One is rectangular with concave panels on the sides which are pierced with panels of rococo design; the other is of lobed quatrefoil plan and resembles a small column. The pierced pedestals are always left undecorated; the columnar ones sometimes have a few flowers and insects enamelled on the front. Both types carry the Raised Anchor mark, but on the columns it is often picked out in red.

Vases are not common. Besides those in a Chinese shape decorated with applied prunus blossom which have already been mentioned, a pair is known of downward-tapering form with small lion-masks below the shoulders.[7] A pair of baluster-shape vases decorated in Kakiemon style with birds and shrubs which are over 30.6 cm (12 inches) high has been recorded.[8] Another pair of jars of hexagonal form, also decorated

Fig. 7.16 Octagonal cup with scroll handle and saucer, both decorated with floral sprays in Kakiemon style. Height of cup 6.9 cm (2¹¹/₁₆ in). Diameter of saucer 13.2 cm (5³/₁₆ in). Mark: a Raised Anchor on saucer only. c. 1750–52. Japanese beaker, eight-sided. Height 5.6 cm (2³/₁₆ in). c. 1700. Private collection

in a Kakiemon style with panels of flowering plants and exotic birds, was noted by Dr Geoffrey Godden.[9] This last type of hexagonal vase or lidded jar continued to be produced throughout the Red Anchor period 1753–8. All the vases here described are marked with the Raised Anchor.

Besides vases, a few pot-pourri jars of fluted oviform shape, with perforated shoulders and covers, have survived. They are usually no more than 17.8 cm (7 inches) in height.

F.S. Mackenna mentions a rare scent-bottle of the Raised Anchor period which was in Dr Bellamy Gardner's collection. It had a landscape decoration, and is probably the earliest Chelsea scent-bottle to be recorded. He also illustrates a pair of bottles, square in plan, which swell out at the base of a long four-sided neck and are beautifully decorated with flowering plants and ornate panels in the Kakiemon manner. These are undoubtedly inspired by Japanese saké bottles, though probably by way of the copies made at Meissen [fig. 7.17].[10]

Much of the decoration on useful wares in the Raised Anchor period derives, like many of the shapes employed, from the orient, and particularly from Japan. Kakiemon-type patterns were the most frequently used; the Kakiemon floral patterns include an especially striking one of panels of tall poppies and orange lilies. Other direct derivations were the 'quail and banded-hedge' pattern (also much used at Bow); the tiger and banded hedge; ho-ho birds (sometimes called phoenixes), both flying over banded hedges and flowering prunus and also sitting on a rock (the Sir Joshua Reynolds pattern); 'twisted dragons'; and the rat (or squirrel) and vine. Patterns of this type including human figures are comparatively rare; the most common (which also occurs on Bow porcelain) is the Lady in a Pavilion pattern [see fig. 7.20]. At Bow it was known apparently as the 'Lady pattern'.[11] Bow, as well as Chelsea, also produced wares decorated with the Japanese 'Red pannel'd' pattern. Oriental figures in a garden appear on a small peach-shaped jug now at Colonial Williamsburg and on another with a replacement handle which was sold at Sotheby's in 1982 [fig. 7.21];[12] while F.S. Mackenna notes two unmarked kidney-shaped dishes likewise decorated with a polychrome scene of oriental figures in a garden.[13] The colours used are clear and brilliant. They include iron-red, yellow, and a fine blue, as well as turquoise and dark green. Underglaze blue was never

Fig. 7.17 opposite, top left Pair of 'Japanese' bottles. Height 18.8 cm (7²⁄₅ in). *c.* 1750–52. Mark: a Raised Anchor on one. The British Museum

Fig. 7.18 opposite, top right Pair of bottle-vases (or guglets) of onion shape with slender knopped necks, painted in vivid colours with Vincennes-type bouquets and flower sprigs. Height 16.6 cm (6½ in). No mark. 1750–52. Private collections

Fig. 7.19 opposite, below Six-lobed dish decorated with flying pheasant, banded hedge, pine and prunus in Kakiemon style. Diameter 19.1 cm (7½ in). Mark: a Raised Anchor. 1750–52. Private collection

Fig. 7.20 Hexagonal teapot with Kakiemon decoration known as the Lady in a Pavilion pattern. The lady is seated beside a birdcage in an elegant pavilion; the reverse side shows a songbird and scattered flowers. The palette is a rare one, employing dark green instead of the usual turquoise. Height 12.7 cm (5 in), width 18.4 cm (7¼ in). No mark. *c.* 1750–52. Private collection.

employed in the Kakiemon-type patterns, but gilding was sometimes sparingly used to give emphasis. The quality of painting is much superior to that on the Triangle wares, and in some cases is of extreme delicacy and fineness.

The European styles of decoration were also exquisitely executed, particularly in the case of realistically treated flowers, almost botanical in their exactitude but rendered with a dash of verve and with great feeling for simple beauty. A circular lobed dish decorated in this manner with a pink rose and yellow anemone is illustrated by F.S. Mackenna,[14] who also illustrates an octagonal dish with similar decoration of a rose and hyacinth. Both are illustrated here [figs 7.23–4].

Fig. 7.21 top Peach-shaped jug (with replacement metal handle), painted with an oriental figure leaning towards a boy holding an umbrella, flanked by flowers; the reverse with a butterfly near a flowering prunus trailing above a leafy plant. Height 6 cm (2.4 in), *c.* 1750–52. Private collection

Fig. 7.22 above Large 'Japonaiserie' plate with polychrome butterflies. Diameter 28.4 cm (11⅕ in). No mark. *c.* 1752. The British Museum

Fig. 7.23 opposite Ten-lobed plate decorated with a rose and anemone and scattered flower sprays. Width 17.8 cm (7 in). No mark. *c.* 1750–53. Private collection

Fig. 7.24 A unique, large rectangular octagonal dish, painted in the centre with a spray of flowers including a hyacinth and a rose, the border with moulded rosettes in trellis and reserves of flowerheads. Length 32 cm (12.5 in). Mark: Raised Anchor missing; this was noted by Mackenna. *c.* 1750–53. Private collection

Fig. 7.25 above Peach-shaped cream jug with a Fable scene, the Fox and the Crane. Height 6.4 cm (2½ in). *c.* 1752. Museum of London

Fig. 7.26 above right Octagonal tea bowl and saucer with Fable decoration: the Lion and the Frog (saucer); and the Wolf, Goat and Sheep (tea bowl). Width of saucer 13.6 cm (5⅖ in), height of bowl 5.5 cm (2⅕ in). *c.* 1752–3. The British Museum

Simpler and more conventional types of floral decoration – bouquets of mixed flowers and scattered small blossoms – were also produced; and sometimes a single bloom, perhaps an anemone, a rose or a turk's cap lily, was used on its own as the main decorative feature. Insects, as well as small flowers, continued to be used to cover blemishes, and to give emphasis to the main decoration.

Gilding was very seldom employed, and never used as an edge finish in the Raised Anchor period. The usual edging colour is chocolate-brown, and some edges were left plain. Small star-shaped blossoms often decorate the bottoms of cups with Kakiemon decoration outside. Those decorated with natural flowers have a flower or small spray.

The pieces moulded with scolopendrium leaves in low relief have these sometimes coloured green with yellow mid-ribs and black veins, but sometimes with only a pink mid-rib. They often have varied painted insects added to the decoration, though apparently only one example of a real butterfly on Raised Anchor porcelain is recorded. This is a Small Tortoiseshell, which occurs on a large dish painted with numerous flower sprays in the Schreiber Collection at the Victoria and Albert Museum. Dr Paul Riley believes it to have been a pattern dish, painted by a Chelsea master painter for other workers to copy.[15]

The 'Fable painting', one of the most characteristic and justly famous of all the forms of decoration employed at Chelsea, first appears in quantity during the short

Fig. 7.27 Octagonal saucer, over-printed in black with a landscape with figures, the transfer then washed over with colours. This is the only known example of transfer printing on Chelsea porcelain. Diameter 14.1 cm (5½ in). Mark: a Raised Anchor applied beneath. *c.* 1750–52. The British Museum

Fig. 7.28 Octagonal bowl, flanged rim, decorated in underglaze blue with panels of Chinese lotus, alternating with Chinese immortals. Diameter 11.1 cm (4⅜ in). Raised or early Red Anchor period. *c.* 1750–55. Colonial Williamsburg Foundation, Virginia

Raised Anchor period [see figs 7.25–6].[16] The work has been variously attributed between three named decorators, though none of it is incontrovertibly signed. The painters suggested are Jean Lefebre, William Duvivier, and Jefferyes Hamett O'Neale. However, this decoration will be considered more closely in the following chapter.

Wares decorated in underglaze blue only are now as scarce from the Raised Anchor period as from that of the Triangle. An octagonal bowl with flanged rim decorated with panels of Chinese immortals alternating with panels of lotus plants, formerly in the Dominey Collection, is now at Colonial Williamsburg [fig. 7.28]; and a lobed, unmarked beaker at the Victoria and Albert Museum has a delicate design of oriental figures in a garden. A pierced plate and a basket with underglaze blue decoration of pagodas and islands were attributed to Chelsea by William King[17] but seem to relate rather to Derby. Otherwise only two more Chelsea blue and white designs remain, and these will be mentioned in the chapter referring to wares of the Red Anchor period.

The only example known of printing, either over or underglaze, on Chelsea porcelain of any period, occurs on an octagonal saucer with a Raised Anchor mark, given by A.W. Franks to The British Museum [fig. 7.27]. The landscape scene of a lady and gentleman seated in a garden with buildings behind is printed in black overglaze, and washed over with colours. The print occurs nowhere else and its source has not been traced: it may have been printed experimentally *c.* 1751 at a works near

Chelsea mentioned by Rouquet, where he witnessed transfer-printing in the early 1750s; or slightly later, 1753–6, across the river at the Battersea enamel works in York House.

The statement of Ann Chetwood (formerly Sprimont) in the Chancery suit, *Chetwood v. Burnsall*, of 1766 was probably misreported, when she apparently referred to a set of Chelsea dessert porcelain decorated in mazarine blue and gold 'which had sustained some damage ... in the *printing*, burning or burnishing thereof'.[18]

It seems probable that before Sprimont opened his works on the Lawrence Street site in the middle of 1749, he engaged the services of a man who was to prove of the greatest importance in the development of a 'house' style in Chelsea figure-making. The modeller Joseph Willems was a fellow countryman of Sprimont's, who perhaps heard of him through his own personal contacts in the Low Countries. Willems, born at Brussels in 1715, was very slightly older than Sprimont. By the age of twenty-four he was at Tournai, where he married Marie-Josephe Lahaize on 16 November 1739. He may have continued to work at Tournai in the faience factory of François Joseph Carpentier for the next few years, leaving it to go to England, where he is recorded in the rate books for Chelsea from 1748. In 1750 François Joseph Peterinck converted the faience factory into one for the manufacture of soft-paste porcelain; by that time, however, Joseph Willems was demonstrably already in England.

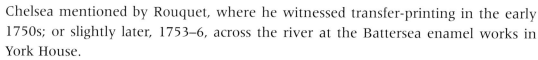

Fig. 7.29 Pair of painted terracotta figures of a man and woman dancing, each incised with the name 'Willems' and the date '1749' on the base. Height 30.5 cm (12 in). Ashmolean Museum, Oxford

A pair of terracotta models of a man and a woman dancing, each incised with the name 'Willems' and the date '1749', are now in the Ashmolean Museum at Oxford [fig. 7.29]. So dated, they must have been made in England, and are considered as works of art in their own right, of a kind exhibited by Willems before he returned at length to Tournai. These original terracotta figures have a strong affinity with Willems' known style in figures of later Chelsea manufacture. They are heavily built, with long trunks and disproportionately short legs. Although they are of dancers, no sense of movement is conveyed since there is no curvature in the spine, or tilt in shoulders or hips, such as would compensate for the weight being carried on one leg. They stand straight up and down, with the heads tilted slightly sideways. The foreheads are broad, with eyes set wide apart, the brows arched, and full cheeks curve downwards to a pointed chin. Brow and chin recede slightly in profile. Each figure has a slight smile, and the lady a suggestion of a double chin. Her dress has thick folds which serve as a support; the man has his legs backed and strengthened by a low wall. Both are on plain square bases with chamfered corners. Willems' signature in each case is incised on one side of the base.

The stocky peasant type of figure suggested by these dancers was often represented in Willems' work in porcelain, and their broad, slightly smiling faces recur in Chelsea figures of all dates. A porcelain cane handle formed as a female head [fig. 7.30] has features very similar to those of the terracotta figures, and as it is made in a Triangle porcelain body, it tends to confirm that Willems was already working at Chelsea from 1748.

The influence of Meissen on Chelsea was not particularly strong between 1749 and 1751. It was not till June 1751 that Sir Everard Fawkener first borrowed on behalf of the factory from Sir Charles Hanbury-Williams' collection of Meissen porcelain at Holland House. Broadly speaking, in the Raised Anchor period, most of the figure models at Chelsea derived from sources other than the Saxon porcelain works.

There were fifty or so of these models produced between 1749 and 1752. As in Triangle days, they included copies of Chinese *blanc-de-chine*, the models of Kuan Yin [fig. 7.33] and of a little Chinese boy with a gourd over his shoulder [fig. 7.32]. It was at this time that the figure group of the wet-nurse and baby [fig. 7.31], adapted from a French pottery model made at Avon by Berthélémy de Blénod (a copy perhaps suggested by Willems?), was first introduced. It proved so popular that it

Fig. 7.30 Porcelain cane handle, female head. Height 7.7 cm (3 in). *c.* 1750. The Victoria and Albert Museum, London

Fig. 7.31 Group of a nurse and child. Height 18.4 cm (7¼ in). *c.* 1752. Private collection

Fig. 7.32 Figure of a Chinese boy with a double gourd on his back. Height 15 cm (5⅞ in). Mark: a Raised Anchor on a pad applied to his back. *c.* 1750–52. Fitzwilliam Museum, Cambridge

Fig. 7.33 Figure of Kuan Yin in imitation of *blanc-de-chine* porcelain. Height 11.4 cm (4½ in). Mark: a Raised Anchor on back of figure. *c.* 1750–52. The British Museum

Fig. 7.34 Britannia lamenting the death of the Prince of Wales. Height of figure 26.3 cm (10²⁄₅ in). *c.* 1751. The British Museum

continued in production throughout the Raised and Red Anchor periods, that is up to *c.* 1760.

It has been suggested that the first model made at Chelsea by Joseph Willems was that of Ceres in the Triangle paste[19] [fig 3.15]. She may have been copied directly from a garden statue, as she stands so stiffly, with a wreath of ears of corn and holding a sheaf and a reaping hook. In a similar stance and on a similar plain square base, is the figure of a 'Femme du Levant' decorated in enamels and taken from an engraving by Ravenet after Boucher, the eighth print in a set of twelve entitled *Receuil de diverses figures étrangères*. Another of a 'Dame de Constantinople' comes from the fifth print in the same source. The example of the 'Femme du Levant' in the Lady Ludlow Collection at Luton Hoo had the Raised Anchor mark unusually outlined in violet.

A number of the early Raised Anchor models appear to have been copied from three-dimensional originals of pottery, stone, bronze or oriental porcelain. The head of the Duke of Cumberland [see fig. 6.7] is treated very much in the manner of a bronze casting, and the well-known and charming head of a young child [fig. 7.35] was probably copied from a plaster model of a cherub figure carved in 1629 by Francois Duquesnoy (Il Fiammingo) for the monument to Adrien Vryburch in the church of Santa Maria dell'Anima in Rome.[20, 21] Arthur Lane suggested that the Chelsea version of 'Britannia mourning the death of the Prince of Wales' [see fig. 7.34] could have been adapted from a sculptor's model for a monument. He also thought that the portrait of the Prince would have appeared on Britannia's shield, painted in unfired 'cold' colours, which would explain why it has now disappeared.[22]

The series of birds perched on tree-trunk bases, which were adapted from the plates in the first two of the four volumes of George Edwards' *Natural History of Uncommon Birds* published between 1743 and 1751, are probably among the earliest models which were adapted from engravings rather than from a three-dimensional source [see figs 6.3–4]. There are about twenty different models of these Raised Anchor birds. Some now 'in the white' were perhaps originally decorated in oil-colours in the workshop of William Duesbury, the account-books for whose decorating workshop in London, dating between 1751 and 1753, have survived. Duesbury also decorated in fully fired enamels however; though the colours used often bore little resemblance to the natural colouring of the birds. Among the avian models recorded as passing through his workshop are 'Drooping birds', 'Goldfinches', 'Flapwing Birds', and 'Houls'; other Chelsea models included 'Doggs', Hares, 'Gotes' [fig. 7.36],[23] and Sheep; as well as figures of the Doctor (from the Italian Comedy), the Nurse already mentioned, Jupiter, Juno, 'Dominoes' (Harlequins), monks and 'Sphinks'. Since Duesbury is thought to have left London in 1754, his decorating cannot be associated with any later models. There is no proof that he was

Fig. 7.35 Head of a young girl, formerly known as 'Sophie Roubiliac'. Height 19 cm (7 7/16 in). *c.* 1752. Ashmolean Museum, Oxford

employed directly by Chelsea, but he did decorate white porcelain from various manufactories which was brought to him by some of the London 'Chinamen'.

Thirty-two of the sixty-four Raised Anchor figures listed by Peter Bradshaw[24] are models of birds, and of these twenty-two were taken from George Edwards' designs. Ten birds therefore derive from other sources. A marked Raised Anchor Barn Owl unrecorded by Bradshaw has since come to light. There are five characters from the Italian Comedy (including two versions of 'Dottore Baloardo', one after Reinicke, the other taken from Watteau). The other Italian Comedy characters are Pantalone, shown bearded in skull-cap and gown and holding a purse, Scapino and Scaramuzzi, both after Reinicke, and Isabella [fig. 7.37]. The last is a statuesque lady

Fig. 7.36 Group of two goats, perhaps decorated in the workshop of William Duesbury. No other example of this model is known. Width 16.5 cm (6½ in). Mark: a Raised Red Anchor. *c.*1751. Private collection

Fig. 7.37 Isabella, modelled by Joseph Willems, and derived from a woodcut in Vecellio's *History of Costume*, published 1590, 'Nobile Matrona Francese di Orliens'. Height 24.2 cm (9½ in). Mark: a Raised Red Anchor. *c.*1750. The Victoria and Albert Museum, London

Fig. 7.38 Group of two recumbent kids, coloured (left). Four similar examples of this group are known. Another, white, is at Colonial Williamsburg. Height 6.7 cm (2⅝ in), width 11.9 cm (4¹¹⁄₁₆ in). Mark: a Raised Red Anchor applied to the side. *c.* 1752. Private collection. Group of two recumbent lambs, coloured (right). Only one other example is known. Width 10.8 cm (4¼ in). Mark: a Raised Red Anchor. *c.* 1752. Private collection

Fig. 7.39 Pair of sphinxes. These models occur in both Triangle and early Raised Anchor paste and some bear the respective marks. Height 11.6 cm (4⁹⁄₁₆ in), length of base 14.9 cm (5¹³⁄₁₆ in). *c.* 1749–52. Colonial Williamsburg Foundation, Virginia

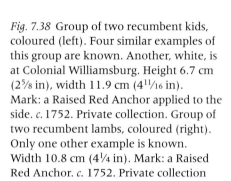

of noble appearance, her hair drawn back in a snood and long cap, and wearing a long, full skirt, laced bodice and ruffed collar. She, like the 'Dame de Constantinople' and the 'Femme de Levant' already mentioned, is copied from one of the set of twelve prints *Receuil de diverses figures étrangères*, of which ten were engraved by Simon-François Ravenet and the other two by Gabriel Huquier, after Boucher. These prints derive from woodcuts in an illustrated treatise on dress by Cesare Vecellio, published in Venice in 1590,[25] and Isabella represents in reality a 'Nobile Matrona Francese di Orliens'. This porcelain figure has the characteristics of stance and modelling which suggest immediately that it was the work of Joseph Willems.

Several of the Raised Anchor oriental groups have been mentioned already. Besides these there is a 'Lady with a Child and a Cat playing with a string toy' copied from Pierre Aveline's engraving *La Mérite de tout Pays* after Boucher; a lady pouring chocolate from a jug into a cup held by a boy; with another separate crouching boy en suite from the engraving *Les Délices de l'Enfance* by Baléchon after Boucher; and a boy in a leaf-shaped hat with a cloak and puffed cheeks, after Watteau. The figures of the Chinese boy and gourd, Kuan-yin and the two Levantine ladies have already been discussed.

Peter Bradshaw lists five allegorical and commemorative

groups: Europa and the Bull; Britannia mourning the Prince of Wales; a bust of the Duke of Cumberland; a pair of sphinxes [fig. 7.39]; and the head of a smiling girl [fig. 7.35]. This last is in the Ashmolean Museum at Oxford, and was at one time thought to represent Sophie Roubiliac, Sprimont's god-daughter, at the age of about six. Far from being a portrait, it has now been suggested by Malcolm Baker that the head is probably derived from one of a pair of busts representing the philosophers Heraclitus and Democritus as children.[26] These have been produced in materials other than porcelain, bronze, plaster and marble, with the laughing child accompanied by a crying one. Baker suggests that Roubiliac should not be ruled out as the author of the original pair.

Of the other fifteen or sixteen listed figures of the period 1750–52, one of the most beautiful is the Rose-seller [fig. 7.40], also derived from a print by Huquier in the same series as Isabella, after the woodcut 'Donzelle contadine di Parma'[27] in Vecellio's history of costume. The fact that both Isabella and the Rose-seller have poses which correspond to the prints, but are transposed in the woodcuts, suggests that the prints are indeed the source used by Willems. The so-called 'Gardener's Companion' in a brimmed hat was adapted from the same series of engravings, and was originally a 'Girl from the Island of Patmos in the Greek Archipelago'; Willems has made her a robust young Englishwoman leaning forward, with a flower basket supported on a hummock under her right hand.

As has been mentioned, various groups of pastoral animals, goats, kids, and sheep occur; also a lion, a seated hound, a pug dog on a tasselled cushion, and in Triangle paste the recumbent models of Hogarth's dog, Trump.

At this date very few of the Chelsea models are drawn from Meissen. One that was is a 'Standing Peasant with a Hurdy-Gurdy', another, a peasant sitting on the ground to play a similar instrument. A male dwarf in a tall hat derived from a etching by Giacomo Calotto may have been copied directly from a Meissen prototype, but also possibly from a figure produced at Mennecy; the companion female dwarf was not made at Chelsea before the Red Anchor period. Finally, a standing figure of a 'Peasant Toper' may also have derived from Meissen. The lively bare-headed boy twists his body as he pours wine into his mouth from a jug, in a pose quite different from the solid stance of Willems' earlier models. An example of this figure has only comparatively recently been recorded.[28]

Fig. 7.40 Rose-seller, after a woodcut by Vecellio, 'Donzelle contadine di Parma'. Height 24.2 cm (9½ in). Mark: a Raised Anchor. *c.* 1750–52. Museum of Fine Arts, Boston

CHAPTER 8

Red Anchor Wares

The wares and figures produced by the Chelsea undertaking during the period when a small painted red anchor with each fluke double-barbed was the usual form of the factory mark (*c.* 1752–8) are thought by general consensus to be the finest body of pieces that it ever produced. Although some beautiful items were made earlier, and the gilding and painting of some later things are of supreme quality, it is the general high standard of both taste and execution throughout, which enable us to say with complete confidence that the Red Anchor productions are the apogee of Sprimont's manufacture.

Although the change in the form of the mark from an applied Raised Anchor pad to a small simple symbol executed with a few strokes of the 'pencil' seems now almost to denote a new start in the effort and emphasis of the factory, it was probably intended to do no more than help to speed the work, and did not indicate a conscious change in style, or even a changed formula for the porcelain body.

The anchor mark was usually placed just inside the footrim on useful wares, and somewhere towards the back and upper part of the base on figures. It is never more than 0.7 cm (¼ inch) in size. There are a few variations in the colour of the mark. A blue anchor occurs on various useful wares bearing one of four particular patterns, all of which were produced only during the Red Anchor period. Two of these are executed entirely in underglaze blue. The third, a splendid copy of a Japanese brocaded Imari design in underglaze blue, overglaze red, green and gilding, also has underglaze blue branches under the rim in the oriental manner, as well as the oriental double circle mark at the centre back, and in the middle of this, sometimes but not always, the Chelsea blue anchor. Incidentally, the Blue Anchor is sometimes drawn with a wide flat bow, and not the close U-shaped one of the Red Anchor. The fourth pattern known to be marked with the Blue Anchor is a design of oriental flowering branches, in underglaze blue and overglaze enamels of bluish-green, clear pale yellow, and orange/red. It is in the style of Japanese Nabeshima ware, and the plate on which it appears is the first piece of English porcelain to be discovered with this decoration.[1] F.S. Mackenna said it was the only example known to him.

Fig. 8.1 Pair of dishes decorated with bouquets of flowers and various insects, the one below including a monarch butterfly and a privet hawk moth. Length 44.5 cm (17½ in), width 35.6 cm (14 in). Mark: both dishes marked with a Red Anchor. *c.* 1753. Private collection

The two designs which occur in underglaze blue only are both derived from the oriental. One is a simple painted pseudo-Chinese pattern of islands, with willow and pine trees, a pagoda-type house or two, and a man in a boat in the foreground [fig. 8.2]. The other pattern shows a central painted design of ho-ho birds on a rock to the right, balanced by a leafy tree and shrubs to the left. There is a wide border of diaper work with five kidney-shaped reserves each filled with a conventional flowering shrub, though an alternative border of groups of plants and grasses is sometimes used instead. This pattern comes from Japanese Kakiemon inspiration, and has been made familiar to many who have no idea of its origin or history by commercial copies printed on white earthenware which were made in the first half of the twentieth century. The island pattern is known on only six surviving octagonal Chelsea saucers, and on an unglazed octagonal teabowl which was discovered in 1906 on what is now known to be the Chelsea factory site. It is in the Katz Collection at the Museum of Fine Arts, Boston, and no other similar piece is known.

After 1758 the anchor mark was also sometimes painted in brown, but this seems to have no special significance, and was probably due simply to the decorator's convenience, though it is sometimes associated with decoration possibly executed in the workshop of James Giles. As in the case of the Blue or Red Anchor forms, the painter probably used what colour came most nearly to hand, though it can be presumed that from 1753 to 1757 the management preferred that the mark should be done in red. The brown anchor commonly appears on later Red Anchor pieces as well as on some of those of the Gold Anchor period.

Generally speaking, however, wares decorated in underglaze blue only were primarily utilitarian, intended for ordinary everyday use; and by Sprimont's own showing in *The Case of the Undertaker of the Manufacture of Chelsea Ware c.* 1752, such wares were neither the main interest nor the staple of Chelsea. 'The more ordinary sort of wares for common uses' Sprimont firmly assigned to Bow, which had been set up specifically to imitate and undercut the porcelains being imported in such vast amounts, and so cheaply, from the Far East. Chelsea's chosen market was the aristocratic one of luxury and quality, though the factory did produce an amount of blue and white porcelain for ordinary use of which a good deal must have been broken (see Chapter 3).

The body used for the porcelain at this time at first differed very little from that of the Raised Anchor period. As in the Raised Anchor pieces, the paste is often irregularly spotted with 'moons' when seen by transmitted light. The surface colour ranges from cool white to a warmer

Fig. 8.2 Octagonal saucer, decorated solely in underglaze blue with an island pattern after the Chinese. Width 12.1 cm (4¾ in). Mark: an anchor painted in underglaze blue. *c.* 1752–8. Colonial Williamsburg Foundation, Virginia

greyish-cream, and a blue tinge sometimes shows in the glaze. On the finest pieces, both wares and figures, the warm white glaze, like that of the Raised Anchor, owes its quality to the inclusion of tin oxide. About 1756 a more transparent glaze came into use, and in the best examples is absolutely perfect, though in other cases under-firing seems sometimes to have resulted in a crazed surface. Refinement in Red Anchor wares increased as time went on; useful wares were made with great neatness. The narrow footrims are often found ground down to remove surplus glaze and make the pieces stand level, though occasionally completely unglazed bases can be found, as on the late bucket-shaped teacups where there is no footrim. The paste then shows grey brown and stains easily, while the marks of clay pads used to support the cups in the saggar during firing show up clearly.

The later Red Anchor paste can be broadly regarded as a transitional one between those used in the Raised and Gold Anchor periods. A table published by F.S. Mackenna[2] shows that Red Anchor porcelain on the whole contains more silica than the Raised Anchor, but a lot less than the Gold. In both Raised and Red Anchor porcelain the alumina (hydrated silicate of aluminium), which comes from the clay and gives plasticity to the paste, is only about half that found in the Gold Anchor porcelain body. Lime, included to stiffen the paste and prevent collapse during firing, was added at Chelsea in large amounts during the Raised and Red Anchor periods, possibly in the form of calcined sea-shells, but in the Gold Anchor recipe lime was provided in even greater quantities by bone ash, the proportion being similar to that employed at Bow. Lead oxide, derived from cullet (crushed glass), an important constituent of the Triangle paste, shows only a very small amount in Raised Anchor porcelain and none at all in the later Red and Gold Anchor porcelains. The varying bodies produced at Chelsea were all frit porcelains, artificial porcelains used as substitutes for the true oriental-type hard paste, but having a composition which in fact is more akin to that of glass than to oriental porcelain. The recipes included the soluble and fusible alkaline salts of soda and potash. To overcome the drawback of the carbonate of potash effervescing when brought into contact with the silica in a porcelain mixture, it was heated with a certain amount of silica and some other substances in advance, so that the effervescence took place in controlled circumstances and alkaline silicates were formed. These were then ground finely, and used as a component of the porcelain mixture. The preliminary process was known as 'fritting', hence the term 'frit' porcelain.

A number of shapes for teawares and dishes already in production in the Raised Anchor period continued to be made under the Red Anchor. Certain forms of decoration continued as before, notable among these being the 'Fable' painting, suggesting that it was already a success and that demand for it continued [see figs 8.3–4].

The shapes in question were the Japanese-inspired octagonal teabowls [fig. 8.4], saucers and beakers, the sugar bowls with a flanged rim, the hexagonal teapots, and

Fig. 8.3 Pair of small vases, with Fable decoration. Height 14.9 cm (5¹³/₁₆ in). *c.* 1753–5. Fitzwilliam Museum, Cambridge

Fig. 8.4 Octagonal teabowl and saucer, with Fable decoration. Height of teabowl 5 cm (1¹⁵/₁₆ in), width of saucer 10.9 cm (4 1/4 in). Mark: a Red Anchor mark on base of teabowl. *c.* 1755. Private collection.

Fig. 8.5 opposite, above Soup plate, border divided into eight alternately larger and smaller panels, the size of the edging lobes to match. 'Gotzkowsky' floral moulding in the larger panels, and as a wreath round centre of dish. Smaller panels painted with floral sprigs, centre with a rose and a few sprigs and small flowers with a ladybird. Diameter 24.2 cm (9 ½ in). No mark. *c.* 1752–8. Private collection

Fig. 8.6 opposite, below Miniature lemon tureen. Height with lid 8.1 cm (3⅕ in). Mark: a Red Anchor. *c.* 1754–5. The British Museum

plates with a reeded or moulded edge. Pieces with closely placed fluting also continued to be made, as did the plates and dishes with shell moulding directly copied from Sprimont's marked silver. There seems to have been some continued production of the crayfish shell salts, since some were mentioned in the 1756 Catalogue, though these could have been Triangle pieces, with decoration perhaps added by William Duesbury's outside decorating establishment, which was probably working in London until 1754.

Some new forms and borders in dinner wares were brought into production, particularly as regards the designs of moulded rims for plates and dishes. Undulating rims and mouldings with alternate shallow and deeper hollows are found, and Meissen was the inspiration for distinctive patterns which include various surface mouldings. Among these are the 'damask'd' flowers, usually a wreath in the centre of a plate, with groups of flowers separated by plain panels on the rim. This is the Gotzkowsky pattern [see fig. 8.5], called after a Meissen service made for a Berlin merchant of that name. In another design the centre is left plain, but the rim is divided by moulded diapers and scrolls into panels, edged by moulded foliage, which are then decorated with painted flowers, birds or figures, or with Fable scenes [see fig. 8.21]. A later edging consists of moulded feather scrolls picked out in colour, and a few services were produced of extreme rococo form, both in outline and in the convoluted moulding of the wide borders of the plates. These were probably inspired by silver forms.

Among the Red Anchor holloware shapes are leaf-moulded bowls (also made at Longton Hall), finger bowls (water cups) and stands, all sorts of open-work baskets for sweets and cakes, ice-pails, jugs of various shapes, bell-shaped mugs, and many leaf-shaped dishes. These were made in varying sizes, and artichoke, cabbage, fig, lettuce, mulberry and vine leaves can all be found among them. The smaller ones were intended specifically to go with the various miniature tureens in natural forms [see fig. 8.6] in which were served 'a Desart of fruit or cream and the like', as Benjamin Franklin explained in a letter home to his wife in 1755.[3]

The small tureens were a feature of the Chelsea sale of 1755, conducted by Richard Ford in his 'Great Room in the Haymarket'. This is the earliest sale for which a copy of the catalogue has survived, and it was discovered by Mrs Radford, a well-known collector, in 1915. A copy of the 1756 catalogue had been found thirty-eight years earlier, in 1877, by Mr Raphael W. Read of Salisbury, bound up in a volume of tracts entitled *An Enquiry concerning the Virtues of Tar Water* by Bishop Berkeley; but the catalogue for the earliest Chelsea sale in 1754 is as yet undiscovered.[4]

Apart from the Chelsea figures of the Red Anchor period, the tureens of all sizes in various vegetable, animal, and avian shapes, coloured 'according to nature', are today considered among the most desirable (and so the most expensive) items which a collector of Chelsea porcelain can acquire. The catalogues give a clue to the contemporary popularity of the various models by the numbers of each which were offered for sale to the public. Then as now among the most sought after for individual servings must have been the apples, 'four fine apples and four leaves for desart', the roses, the 'artichoaks' with their bird knops, and the melons [fig. 8.8]. Larger melons and pineapples, the former often offered in pairs with cabbage leaf stands, were presumably the dishes out of which a fruit fool or some similar pudding could be

Fig. 8.7 Sunflower dish. Width across leaves 22.5 cm (8¹³⁄₁₆ in). Mark: a Red Anchor. *c.*1755. Private collection

Fig. 8.8 Small melon tureen with snail knop. Height (including snail shell) 8 cm (3⅛ in). Mark: tureen and lid each marked with painted Red Anchor and numeral. *c.*1755. Private collection

served. Small tureens in the form of partridges (some with stands ornamented with ears of corn [fig. 8.9]), and others modelled as young rabbits, were listed too, the partridges being especially numerous, no fewer than thirty-eight pairs in 1755.

The most splendid tureens, and the largest, however, were those made in the form of full grown animals, birds and fish. In the 1755 catalogue eleven shaped as a hen and chickens 'big as the life, in a curious dish adorn'd with sunflowers' were offered. On the Continent tureens in zoomorphic form were being produced in faience between 1748 and 1754 by Paul Hannong of Strasbourg, and also at some German factories, as well as in Hungary and Portugal. The design of the hen and chickens soup tureen made in porcelain at Chelsea was apparently taken from a print by Francis Barlow published nearly a hundred years earlier, which was also copied for the decoration inside a Bristol delftware punchbowl dated 1759. Examples of the 'Hen and Chickens' and 'Rabbit' tureens can be seen at the Victoria and Albert Museum, and at the Fitzwilliam Museum, Cambridge [figs 8.10 and 14.3].

Each type of tureen had its proper dish; the carp lay on one moulded with various water plants and weeds; the rabbits' dishes were usually described simply as 'oval'. Most elaborate of all was one of the variants made to accompany a boar's head tureen [fig. 8.11]. It appeared to be made of pink quilted satin (perhaps the hunter's protective coat), overlaid with an oak branch, a partly obscured quiver of arrows, and the hunting knife with which the head had presumably been severed; all moulded in high relief as part of the design. The other dish made to go with a boar's head tureen was more conventional, being circular with a lobed edge and with reserves painted with flowers on the rim. In the centre was painted a stag-hunting scene derived from a print by Johann Elias Ridinger of Augsberg (1698–1767).[5] These particular tureens are exceedingly rare, only two being listed in the 1755 catalogue, and three in 1756. A tureen with the circular painted version of the dish was sold by Christie's from Queen Charlotte's collection in 1819 and bought by Lord Weymss for £15 10s. Known as the Gosford tureen, it has remained in the family ever since and was last exhibited at Washington,[6] in 1985.

The tureens in the form of carp and of coiled eels are perhaps less immediately appealing to modern taste, though the eel tureens, sold in pairs, occurred fifteen times in the catalogue of 1755. Plaice sauceboats are not mentioned until 1756, but those which have survived show this to have been one of the most successful of Chelsea's 'memorable fancies'. The 1756 catalogue describes them (Fifth day, 3 April, lot 79), as 'A beautiful pair of plaice sauceboats, with spoons and plates' [fig. 8.12].

Fig. 8.9 Stand for a pair of partridge tureens. Length 29.9 cm (11¾ in). Mark: a Red Anchor. *c.* 1754. Private collection

Fig. 8.10 Hen and chickens tureen and stand. Height of tureen 24.8 cm (9¾ in), length of stand 48.9 cm (19¼ in). Red Anchor marks. *c.* 1755–6. Fitzwilliam Museum, Cambridge

Fig. 8.11 Boar's head tureen and stand. Height 24.8 cm (9¾ in), length 36.9 cm (14½ in). *c.* 1755. Winterthur Museum, Delaware

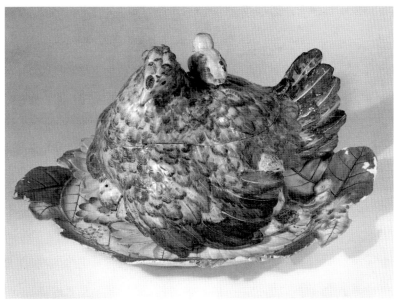

They are delightful small tureens, with each fish set on a stand with a moulded border of striped cockleshells and seaweed. The fish's tail, attached to the lower part of the tureen, is curled up to form a handle. The lid, the plaice's spotted back, is lifted by means of a frond of green seaweed curled across it. The open mouth forms the aperture for the spoon, and the spoon completes the fantasy. Each is made with a fish-tail handle, so it seems as if the plaice were greedily gulping in the smaller creature. Wales is rich in plaice tureens. There is a pair at the Yorke's great house at Erddig,[7] perhaps mistakenly referred to as 'Carp sauce boats' in the inventory made in 1789, but these have lost their spoons. However, in the National Museum of Wales at Cardiff can be found, on loan, the only pair now known which still possesses them.

Besides the hen and chickens and partridges already mentioned, there is a series of bird tureens ranging from small pigeons to the great and rare swan. In the catalogue of 1755 'a beautiful tureen in the shape of a double pigeon with a fine basket workt dish' is mentioned eleven times, a design which was plainly popular, and was even copied at Worcester.

In the catalogue of 1756 were offered drake and duck tureens each 'as large as life, with a dish to ditto'. Duck tureens are known in various forms [fig. 8.13]. Two swans were offered without stands in 1755; in 1756 the swan tureen was offered with a dish. Although described as 'large as life' a swan tureen is in reality something like 36.9 cm (14½ inches) high and 50.8 cm (20 inches) long. The curved neck must have made it a very difficult object to fire, and silver bands which seem to be contemporary on the necks of the examples in the Cecil Higgins Museum [fig. 8.14] and in the Victoria and Albert Museum suggest that the tureens may have been made in several pieces.

The rarest of all tureens are a pair made in the form of fighting cocks, modelled and painted to appear plucked and spurred as in reality, objects of extraordinary virtuosity and yet exceedingly unattractive. The only known examples are now in the Fitzwilliam Museum, Cambridge.

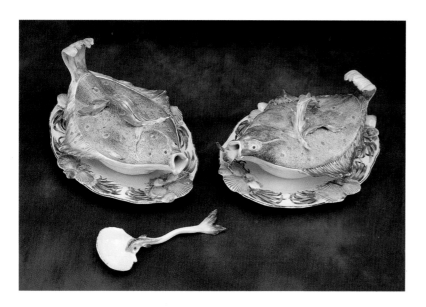

Fig. 8.12 Pair of plaice tureens, with stands and fish-tailed ladles. Height of tureens 15.8 cm (6¼ in). *c.* 1756. National Museum of Wales, Cardiff

It remains to say something more of the enamelled decoration on Red Anchor wares, and what little has been discovered about the artists who applied it.

Of those who produced the exquisite copies of the Kakiemon designs we know little or nothing. These patterns follow the originals pretty exactly, both in detail and in colouring, but are more associated with Chelsea Raised Anchor production than with that of the Red Anchor, though the Kakiemon style of decoration continued to be employed during the earlier part of the Red Anchor period. Meissen was proba-

Fig. 8.13 Duck tureen. Height *c.* 8.6 cm (3³⁄₈ in). Length *c.* 16.5 cm (6¹⁄₂ in). *c.* 1756. Ashmolean Museum, Oxford.

Fig. 8.14 Swan tureen. Height *c.* 36.9 cm (14¹⁄₂ in). *c.* 1756. Cecil Higgins Art Gallery, Bedford

Fig. 8.15 Circular dish with scene including a statue of Hercules and Antaeus, painted by J.H. O'Neale. Width 31.1 cm (12¼ in). Mark: a Red Anchor. *c.* 1753. Museum of Fine Arts, Boston

bly the main source of these designs, so Chelsea may have received many of them at second hand. Those used on Red Anchor pieces included most of the patterns already produced *c.* 1750 to 1752, described in Chapter 7, as well as the 'flaming tortoise' [fig. 7.4], and the comparatively rare Kakiemon scene with the nickname 'Hob-in-the-Well' [fig. 7.2]. It illustrates an eleventh-century Chinese story in which a boy was rescued from drowning by the quick action of his friend Sze-ma Kwang[8] (later a great statesman), who broke the porcelain cistern into which he had fallen. The English name for the pattern was probably appropriated from the popular farce of *Flora, or Hob in the Well*, adapted in 1711 from a one-act play by Thomas Doggett, originally published in 1698. Though the design occurs on Meissen porcelain, it is possible that in this case the Chelsea factory copied direct from a Japanese original. Chelsea also produced one or two original 'Kakiemon' designs of Japanese inspiration.

Occasionally an enamelled central motif and edge panels of Japanese derivation were added to plates with the purely European moulded designs of the Gotzkowsky pattern [fig. 8.5]. This curious mixture, though it could be very effective, was not always entirely happy. Enamelled European flowers, the *deutsche blumen*, combine better with this particular moulded decoration.

As in the earlier period, a few pieces decorated after the style and palette of Chinese *famille rose* occur. One such is the kidney-shaped dessert dish, with a central design of flowering branches in a hanging basket, which is now in the Cecil Higgins Museum at Bedford.[9]

About 1752 a type of decoration including 'landskip' scenes, in some cases with figures in classical dress, began to be produced. They are known both in purple monochrome and in polychrome, and occur on pieces of fluted as well as angled form [figs 8.17–19]. A famous hexagonal teapot painted in purple monochrome with a classical scene was illustrated by Frank Tilley.[10] Part of the importance of this pot lies in the fact that it is inscribed, on a box which occurs in the painted scene, with letters which have been taken to read 'ON.S.C.', though it cannot be denied that in photographic reproduction at any rate, they look like 'M.S.C.'. The reading 'ON.S.C.' (O'Neale sculpsit) has suggested that the decoration, evidently inspired by the engravings of Stefano della Bella (1610–46), was executed by Jefferyes Hamett O'Neale, the gifted Chelsea artist whose name is so closely associated with some of the Fable decorated wares. An octagonal teacup with an ornate handle, now at

Colonial Williamsburg [fig.8.16],[11] which also has purple monochrome landscape decoration, can perhaps be attributed to the same hand, and may indeed have been part of the same service as the teapot, as there are details in the designs which link them together.

Both contain ruins of classical type, with vegetation growing from them, and pendent from the top of columns. Both include a prancing horse with a martial rider, and the teapot has a group of figures in classical dress, one of whom is pointing towards the architecture. This detail further corresponds with a similar figure on a Red Anchor marked plate in the Katz Collection, one of a group (again in classical dress) who are admiring a statue of Hercules and Antaeus raised on a plinth, in a landscape which also contains ruins with pendent foliage [fig. 8.15]. Among the flowers randomly scattered round this central scene is a bunch with two of the stems crossed to form a distinctive wishbone shape. The same peculiar arrangement occurs also in a similar bunch of flowers on the reverse side of the inscribed teapot, this coincidence of detail seeming to offer another clue to work which can be attributed to O'Neale.

A fluted teabowl and saucer, again painted with a scene containing classical ruins, but this time executed in polychrome, is at Colonial Williamsburg.[12] A Chinese saucer decorated in England in green monochrome with a like scene, attributed to the same hand, now in the Victoria and Albert Museum, actually has the name 'Owen Rowe O'Neale' concealed in a mock inscription on an obelisk in the design. Pieces of Chelsea porcelain painted in a similar manner occur sometimes marked with the Red Anchor and sometimes with the Gold. Examples with the latter are thought by some authorities to have been decorated at the workshop of James Giles Jr, the well-known independent decorator, whose workshop was situated first in Kentish Town until he moved it to Berwick Street in 1763, in place of his father, also James Giles, who had been there at least from December 1747. From 1767 to 1776 he had showrooms in Cockspur Street, Charing Cross.[13]

Two dishes dating from *c.* 1753 which seem to show an actual signature by O'Neale are recorded. One was published by Major Tapp in his monograph *Jefferyes Hamett O'Neale* (1938), where in plates 28 and 29 he reproduced the dish on which it occurs written in full, though concealed in a nonsensical inscription on an obelisk in the painted scene. The other signature, from a dish in the Katz Collection, is also included in a make-believe inscription, and in cursive writing simply reads 'oneall'.

Major Tapp was responsible for the attribution to Jean Lefebre of other small decorative landscapes painted in the manner of the Meissen artist J.G. Herold. Two were discovered with the initials J.L. on a rock in the foreground, and another with J.L.P. concealed amongst foliage (the 'P' standing for 'pinxit'). Lefebre is said to have come to Chelsea *c.* 1750, at the time when Sprimont was establishing the Lawrence Street factory, and may have stayed until 1756 or even later. A child supposed to be

Fig. 8.16 Teacup with decoration in purple monochrome, probably by J.H. O'Neale, after an engraving by Stefano della Bella (1610–46). Height 4.9 cm (1^{15}/$_{16}$ in). Mark: a Red Anchor painted beneath. *c.* 1752–5. Colonial Williamsburg Foundation, Virginia

his son was baptised at St Luke's (Old Church), Chelsea, in 1761; the burial of the same child was recorded eighteen months later. It has been suggested that Lefebre may also have painted some of the pieces with Fable decoration.

More positive is the suggestion that a good deal of the Fable decoration and some of the landscape painting was the work of William Duvivier. There is a noticeable difference between the style of painting on the earlier Fable wares (both of Raised Anchor and early Red Anchor dating) and those of the later Red Anchor period. There is no proof as such that William Duvivier was indeed responsible for the earlier pieces, but it is known that he came from Tournai to London in 1742 or 1743, and that he died in 1755. His burial is recorded in the register of St Anne's, Soho, '1755, March 9, William Du Vivier of Chelsea'. A fortnight later, on 22 March, the *Public Advertiser* carried a notice of the sale of some of William Duvivier's property.

To be sold by Auction by Mr Darress. By Order of the Executors at his House in Coventry Street near the Hay Market, on Monday next, and the six following Evenings, the Entire Collection of Prints, Drawings and Books of Prints, of M. Du-Vivier, late of Chelsea, Painter, and of another Gentleman.

The Fable paintings on the earlier Chelsea wares in general have no cloud effects, and the palette as a whole is more subdued than that on later pieces. F.S.

Figs 8.17 & 18 Teapot moulded in form called 'Old Strawberry Pattern'. Decoration by J.H. O'Neale shows, on one side, cows, goats and sheep grazing beneath trees; on the reverse, two travellers are in discussion by the wayside, with a lake and blue-topped mountains in the distance. Height 14 cm (5½ in), width 19.1 cm (7½ in). Mark: a Red Anchor on the base. *c.* 1752–4. Private collection

Mackenna points out that animals with lumpy-looking 'arthritic' joints are often found on earlier wares, but seldom seen among those on the later.

The sources from which the designs were taken include *Aesop's Fables*, with engravings by Francis Barlow, first published in 1666 and again in 1687 – perhaps the best known; the *Fables* of La Fontaine, first published in 1746, and one or two others, both Continental and English. The illustrations were adapted rather than copied, the backgrounds being frequently simplified, while the poses of the animals were sometimes modified to suit the design, or the shape of ware on which they were to be rendered. Nevertheless their origins can usually be discovered without too much difficulty.

Besides being executed in a soft palette of colours, the earlier Fable-decorated wares have certain points of technique in common. These include diagonal hatching, usually on rocks, but sometimes on mountains; trees washed with yellow-green, and with the shading in a mauve-grey tint; mauve-blue background mountains and flocks of birds in formation, firmly painted in. The animals very often have spotted coats or hides. The same sort of details can be found in other Chelsea decoration of the time, which include animals, both real and imaginary. Some of the latter are evidently related to the strange creatures painted by Löwenfinck on Meissen porcelain *c.* 1730.

Mackenna states that the engravings by Gillot which illustrate the version of *Aesop's Fables* by de la Motte were particularly influential in forming the painting style of J.H. O'Neale. His landscape work, as already mentioned, is pretty well known from pieces with designs which include a hidden signature; and also from the *Ladies' Amusement*, published by Robert Sayer, of which a complete copy of only the second edition of 1762 survives.[14] This includes a number of prints of various subjects which are signed by O'Neale. Seventy years ago his work was known only in its later form, from signed pieces of Worcester porcelain.

In many cases the Chelsea Fable and animal decoration occupies the centre of plates and dishes. On saucers the scenes are surrounded with a double ring painted in black, red, or in black and red. On dishes and plates the scenes fade away into the porcelain at their edges, while on hollowares the design follows the circumference of cup or teapot in a natural way without any suggestion of limit.

Apart from their much stronger colouring, the later Red Anchor Fable decorations generally show clouds in the skies, and are without diagonal hatchings. The animals are sometimes depicted with red tongues. Some of the quirks of the

Fig. 8.19 Hexagonal teapot decorated in purple monochrome with Hercules slaying the Nemean lion watched by two other figures. This scene is attributed to J.H. O'Neale. The reverse is decorated with a central bouquet and scattered flowers. Height 14 cm (5½ in), width 19.1 cm (7½ in). Mark: Red Anchor inside upon base of pot. *c.* 1752–5. Private collection

earlier type can also appear, such as occasional lumpy joints in animals' legs, but since the artist in all probability was trained by his predecessor, this is not altogether surprising. The chief point to be re-emphasized is the much heavier colouring found on the later examples.

Small vignettes of fables or of animal subjects, as mentioned earlier, were sometimes used as decoration in the reserves of moulded border patterns, in conjunction with painted sprays and bunches of flowers scattered in the centre area of plates and dishes [see fig. 8.21]. This sort of decoration is a feature of the 'Warren Hastings' pattern, called after a very large service once belonging to the politician, which was sold among his effects in 1818.[15] George Savage had little doubt that the numerous vignettes with which it was decorated (including three on the border of every plate) were the work of Jefferyes Hamett O'Neale. Said to have been born in 1734, the young Irishman would have been about twenty when this work was performed, and, if Savage is right, he is thus shown to be one of the most able and prolific artists ever to paint on china.

The Red Anchor mark is not common on fable-decorated pieces of Red Anchor date, but there seems no good reason to suppose that they were decorated anywhere other than at the factory itself, though Major Tapp believed that O'Neale was working for the decorating establishment of Thomas Hughes in Clerkenwell from 1754 to 1756. With Fable decoration so closely identified with the Chelsea factory and unknown anywhere else in similar form, it is extremely difficult to believe that it can have been added to Sprimont's porcelain by anybody who was not working exclusively for him.

Speaking of a famous set of six plates that have a wavy outline and are decorated with central scenes illustrating children's games after Gravelot, W.B. Honey said that they showed 'the Red Anchor style of painting at its most gracious'.[16] Each scene is painted in colours and has a different half-frame of scrollwork. The borders of the plates have scattered flower sprays, and the rims, as so often on Red Anchor plates and dishes, are outlined in brown. Of the five plates of this set illustrated by F.S. Mackenna,[17] two are now in the Victoria and Albert Museum, two were sold in 1986,[18] and one, showing boys flying a kite, from a private collection, was exhibited in the English Ceramic Circle 50th Anniversary Exhibition, 1977, and at the Victoria and Albert Museum in 1984.[19] The sixth plate, illustrated by Honey,[20] formerly in the Hutton Collection, is in the Museum of Fine Arts, Boston. The decorator of this set is anonymous, but has a recognizable manner of indicating foliage by inverted U-strokes, and of

Fig. 8.20 opposite Large octagonal bowl with the Fable of 'The Lion and the Four Bulls' painted by J.H. O'Neale. Width 15.5 cm (6½ in). Mark: a Red Anchor. *c.* 1753–4. Private collection

Fig. 8.21 Small size 'Warren Hastings' dish with fable subjects in reserves on border, the centre painted with a bouquet and scattered sprigs of flowers. Length 29.3 cm (11½ in). Mark: a Red Anchor. *c.* 1753. Private collection

Fig. 8.22 Plate with a painting of 'l'Arbaleste' after a design by H.F. Gravelot which appeared in England in 1740. Width 21.6 cm (8½ in). Mark: a Red Anchor. *c.* 1755. Museum of London

Fig. 8.23 Moulded dish with 'Hans Sloane' decoration of a sprig of puce 'Turk's Cap' lilies, plums and insects. The insects are shadowed in the manner of Johann Gottfried Klinger at Meissen. The border is moulded with cartouches and trelliswork. Width 24 cm (9½ in). Mark: a Red Anchor and numeral three. *c.* 1755. Private collection

stippling flesh in red. He has sometimes been confused with J.H. O'Neale; his work at Chelsea seems to date between 1753 and 1756. Another similar plate, a seventh, in the collection of the Museum of London, is illustrated here [fig. 8.22].

Flower decoration of several kinds is plentiful on Red Anchor porcelain, but one type in particular is especially associated with Chelsea, and the wares on which it was executed are another of the peculiar glories of the Chelsea manufactory. This decoration consists of specimens of plants, flowers, leaves, vegetables and fruit, displayed on plates and dishes and sometimes on holloware shapes in the same manner, and sometimes identically, with those coloured engravings used to illustrate certain contemporary botanical works. Dr Bellamy Gardner in the 1930s was the first person to connect these designs with the advertisement which had appeared in *Faulkner's Dublin Journal* for 1 July 1758. (This refers to the second of the three sales of Chelsea porcelain held in Dublin that year, in which the contents of the former Piccadilly warehouse, and possibly other remaining Red Anchor marked porcelain from the factory warehouse, were dispersed as far from London as possible, probably because it was essential for Sprimont to sell them, and they were no longer very fashionable in town.) The July advertisement mentions a tureen '… in curious Plants with Table Plates, Soup Plates, and Desart Plates, enamelled from Sir Hans Sloan's

Fig. 8.24 Dish with 'Hans Sloane' botanical decoration. Width 23.7 cm (9¼ in). Mark: a Red Anchor. *c.* 1755. The British Museum

Fig. 8.25 Small silver-shape dish/stand with 'Hans Sloane' botanical decoration of lilies, with butterflies and a fly. Width 21.2 cm. Mark: a Red Anchor. *c.* 1755. The British Museum

Plants …'. In 1752 Philip Miller, FRS, Curator of the Chelsea Physic Garden, had published *The Gardener's Dictionary*, and followed it with two volumes of *Figures of the most Beautiful, Useful and Uncommon Plants described in the Gardener's Dictionary*.

Patrick Synge Hutchinson[21] realised that three of Miller's illustrations which Dr Bellamy Gardner had matched with botanical decoration on Chelsea wares, and three other designs which he had himself discovered, were all taken from the first volume of Philip Miller's *Figures of Plants*. Further, since the contributions of all Miller's illustrators fell into separate sets, he saw that for chronological reasons (as the plates were published individually between 25 March 1755 and 20 December 1756) all the subjects which he and Dr Bellamy Gardner had matched, and which all had names beginning with the letter A,[22] were illustrated by the same artist, Georg Dionysius Ehret. Ehret, an immigrant German, was married in 1738 to Miller's sister-in-law, Susanna Kennett. He was an internationally celebrated botanical artist and produced a large number of exquisite paintings and drawings, encouraged particularly by Dr Christopher James Trew of Nuremberg and Dr Mead, the English Royal Physician. Many of his paintings were published by Dr Trew in a work entitled *Plantae Selectae*, being issued in groups of ten between 1750 and 1773. Ehret himself published the fifteen plates making up *Plantae et Papiliones Rariories* between

1748 and 1750. At least four plant designs have been translated from this work on to Chelsea porcelain, and some of the butterflies which appear on the 'Hans Sloane' pieces can be credited to him. He became a Fellow of the Royal Society in 1757 and died in September 1770.

As Philip Miller,[23] Ehret's brother-in-law by marriage, was Curator of the Chelsea Physic Garden with which Sir Hans Sloane, Lord of the Manor of Chelsea, had been long and intimately connected until he died in January 1752 at the age of ninety-three, the attachment of the label 'Sir Hans Sloan's [sic] plants' to the botanical decoration on Chelsea porcelain can be easily appreciated. Sir Hans Sloane, however, died too soon ever to have been able to see or own any of the Chelsea botanically decorated china.

The 'Hans Sloane' decoration has been criticised as not being of a quality comparable with that of other kinds on Chelsea Red Anchor porcelain, but the panache with which the painted flowers, vegetation and insects are laid out upon the wares to create a really splendid and original effect is undeniable [see figs 8.23–5].

Pieces with similar decoration were produced for a time at Bow, *c.* 1757, perhaps by a painter who had migrated from Chelsea during the lean period at about this date, when production there fell off owing to Sprimont's first illness. They are comparatively rare, but are not so much sought after as Chelsea 'Sir Hans Sloane' decorated porcelain.

Other floral decoration on Chelsea porcelain derives mainly from either the *indianische blumen* of Meissen, which were called 'India plants' at Chelsea and had originally an oriental inspiration; or from the *deutsche blumen* also employed at Meissen and consisting of scattered sprays and loose bunches of semi-realistic flowers. It is not difficult to learn to recognize the characteristic mannerisms of several Chelsea floral painters, but it is impossible to say who they were. When one considers the quality of painting in the Red Anchor years [see fig. 8.26], the realization that most of it must remain for ever anonymous never ceases to astonish. There are three names known, however, which belong to people who must have been trained in the early Raised and Red Anchor periods, though we cannot attribute to any of them a particular type of painting or a single example of their work.

The apprenticeship indenture of 'Richard Dyer Son of John Dyer of St Margarets Westminster in the County of Middlesex' still exists, dated 7 February

Fig. 8.26 Teabowl and saucer painted with scenes of playing putti. Height of teabowl 4.2 cm (1⅝ in). *c.* 1755. Birmingham City Museum and Art Gallery

1750/51, when Nicholas Sprimont undertook to teach him the art of 'painting in enamel'.[24] The apprenticeship was, as was usual, for seven years.

Robert Boyer, who attended Sprimont on his deathbed, and is known to have worked at Chelsea under Duesbury's ownership, recorded that he had first become acquainted with Sprimont at the age of about eleven years. This suggests that he was perhaps one of the children trained in Sprimont's 'nursery of painters' in the early 1750s.

By chance also has been preserved the name of William Brown. He wrote to the Earl of Charlemont on 28 September 1772, seeking financial support for a proposal to open a porcelain manufactory in Dublin.[25] Brown said that he had 'served an apprenticeship to Mr Sprimont of Chelsea whom I believe I need hardly inform your lordship, was the first person who brought English china to the perfection it has now arrived at. Under him I was made master of the various branches of this art, and though painting was my particular department in his manufactory, yet with attention I have obtained a thorough practical knowledge of the whole process.'

After leaving Sprimont, Brown said he had 'turned to the enamel painting branch', but on 14/17 September 1765 the *St James's Chronicle* reported a fire 'in the Furnace of Mr Brown, China Painter and Enameller, near Cold Bath Fields'.[26] Notices in the *Daily Advertiser* of 15 and 18 September 1773 show that William Brown opened his proposed porcelain manufactory in London rather than Dublin, and in 1774 moved from Cold Bath Fields to the premises of John Crowther's

Fig. 8.27 Circular teapot stand en suite with teapot on the right. This is the only stand discovered. Diameter 16.5 cm (6½ in). Mark: a Red Anchor. *c.*1755. Private collection

Fig. 8.28 Teapot of truncated pear shape with bifurcated twig handle and flower terminals. Painted with large butterflies and moths in the manner of J.G. Klinger of Meissen (active 1726–45). Height 12.5 cm (4⅞ in). Mark: a Red Anchor on base. *c.*1755. Private collection

defunct porcelain manufactory at Bow, apparently in partnership with one William Hay. The Poor Law Overseer's Account Book records that he paid the rates at Bow until 1776, though the partnership with Hay was dissolved in May 1775. What happened to him after this is uncertain, but a sale of 'genuine household goods belonging to Mr William Brown near the Coach and Horses at Stratford in Essex' was announced on 6 October 1778. It is perhaps unlikely, however, that this was the same William Brown known to have been employed as a clerk at the Bow factory in 1753, since in all probability at that date William Brown the enameller would have been still in his apprenticeship at Chelsea.

The earliest coloured ground used at Chelsea seems to have been yellow, mentioned five times in the 1755 catalogue as applied to two shapes of compotier, 'half round' (possibly kidney-shaped) and 'deep'; and to double-leaf dishes. A yellow ground is also recorded on Red Anchor two-handled cups and saucers, a teapot, a saucer dish and a sauceboat.[27] It has been suggested that yellow as a ground colour may have been used as early as the Raised Anchor period; it certainly precedes blue, the only other ground used with the Red Anchor, by several years. The earliest blue ground was added overglaze, and was not the famous mazarine blue underglaze which followed later in the 1750s.

The 1755 catalogue, 16th day's sale, has three consecutive lots, of a tureen, cover and dish; twelve soup plates; and twelve table plates respectively, all of which pieces are 'of an exceeding rich BLUE ENAMEL, with gold flowers etc', that is to say with a ground of *overglaze* blue.

Most of the vases made in the Red Anchor period are of simple form, though the use of rococo detail increased with time. A plump baluster vase with a high domed cover is one of the typical forms, which was given interest by the fine quality of the painted decoration. Jars and beakers were sometimes issued in sets or 'garnitures', for mantelpiece decoration, as, for instance, lot 90, sold on Thursday, 20 March 1755: 'A set for a chimney piece or cabinet, consisting of 7 JARS and BEAKERS, beautifully enamelled with flowers, and the beakers filled with flowers, after nature.'

The biggest of all Chelsea vases are the 'High Jarrs', approximately 61 cm (24 inches) high, four of which were sold, as separate lots, in the sale of 1755. Three were described as white, embossed with flowers and 'richly gilt'. The fourth was not only 'richly gilt' but also enamelled with flowers. The only two recorded surviving examples with such enamel decoration are now in the collection at Colonial Williamsburg.[28]

A charming form of more elaborate vase which first appeared at Chelsea in the Red Anchor period was that made as an eel trap, with figures of ducks amidst rushes and water weeds set round the bottom [fig. 8.29]. Five varieties of elaborate

Fig. 8.29 Pair of eel-trap vases. Height approx. 22.9 cm (9 in). *c.*1758. Museum of London

pot-pourri jars are mentioned in the 1755 catalogue, but as they are as much ornamental as useful are discussed in the chapter on Red Anchor figures.

Decoration on Red Anchor vases was of many kinds, and included everything from simple flower sprays to complex figure subjects. The execution was usually superb, and flower painting on vases was of a particularly high standard. Gilding was used with restraint, often only as an edging line at the foot of a vase, or at the junction of body and neck, and on the rim of the cover.

Bird decoration was also of splendid quality, and groups of graceful, long-tailed exotic birds perch on branches in elegant attitudes. Flying birds were not always so successfully painted, and have been described as having been 'mangled flat'. Figure subjects, however, are much less common, and though well done are usually not of a like quality to those on the later Gold Anchor vases.

Other more unusual items made in the Red Anchor years are flat-backed bough-pots, tied round the middle with a simulated ribbon, and with a wavy edge [fig. 8.30]; flower-pot holders, or cachepots, which are usually urn-shaped; and ice-pails of a very similar form, with moulded as well as painted decoration. Clock-cases, sometimes mis-called 'watch-stands' were also made. These are of the same ornate ornamental type as the pot-pourri vases, one being disguised as a hen-house, complete with figures of chickens, a wolf and a dog [fig. 8.31]; another as a pagoda with Chinese figure, balustrade and steps. One elaborate case represents 'Dawn', and shows two putti, one asleep, one awake, on a balustrade above a 'setting dog', while a drake emerges from rushes beneath a waterfall and a small sphinx also rouses itself.[29] Even more elaborate clock-cases were produced in the Gold Anchor decade of the 1760s.

Pairs of toilet candlesticks made as adjuncts to the dressing table, were likewise embellished with pretty conceits of modelled birds and flowers. Although all the expensive and luxurious 'toys' of Chelsea were available only to the rich, they had about them nevertheless a feeling of delight and wonder at life, stimulated by the widening scientific interests and curiosity of the time, which still finds an echo amongst us, even today.

Fig. 8.30 Wavy-edged bough-pot, or wall jardinière, decorated with coloured ribbon in relief and sprays of painted flowers. Height 9.9 cm (3⅞ in). *c.* 1753–5. Tullie House Museum and Art Gallery, Carlisle

Fig. 8.31 Clock-case in the form of a hen-house cum pigsty. Height 21.5 cm (8⁷⁄₁₆ in). Mark: a Red Anchor. *c.* 1756. The British Museum

CHAPTER 9

Red Anchor Figures

I t was apparently not until quite recent times, about the beginning of the twentieth century, that the porcelain figures made during the Red Anchor period at Chelsea began to be perceived as the finest of all the factory's creations, and to be given the value and high rating which they now command. For some reason few were included in famous collections made in the nineteenth century, either because the Red Anchor pieces were eclipsed by the prodigious admiration accorded to Gold Anchor productions, or because they were confused with pieces made by other factories, or else simply because they did not appear on the market.

The high prices for which they are sold today reflect the perfection they are now seen to possess, a perfection created by a combination of brilliant modelling, a wonderfully suitable porcelain body, and the exercise of restrained but absolute taste in the presentation and decoration.

As we have already seen, the Red Anchor paste was closer grained than earlier compositions, with no trace of lead oxide; it was whiter, more plastic and perhaps most important where the production of figures is concerned, stable in the kiln. The improved paste allowed sharper detail in modelling, more ambitious groups and poses, and the manufacture of some figures on a larger scale than formerly.

The earlier Red Anchor glaze was whitened with tin oxide, but *c.* 1756 a fine glaze, transparent and with a hint of straw-colour, was introduced. At its best it gave a perfect finish without any kind of flaw, but if underfired it had a tendency to craze, which became even more troublesome on the transition to the Gold Anchor porcelain body.

The most active, most splendid years of the Chelsea porcelain factory are reflected in the comparison of the numbers of figure models for each Chelsea period which have been correlated and listed by Peter Bradshaw.[1] Nineteen figure models were made in Chelsea Triangle porcelain; with the Raised Anchor, 1750–52, sixty-three were produced. The output of figures more than doubles in the Red Anchor years 1753–8, with 139; then falls back slightly to 119 in the Gold Anchor period, 1759–69. The

Fig. 9.1 Pair of Chinese boy musicians seated on tree stumps. Height of figure on right 15.9 cm (6¼ in). Mark: a Red Anchor on back of base. *c.* 1755–7. The British Museum

creativity of the Raised and Red Anchor years is, moreover, underlined when one considers how much variety was introduced in such comparatively short periods of time. The Gold Anchor years were in these terms less productive than the seven of the Red.

The Red Anchor figure production can be broken down into a number of subject groups, though some items can be entered under more than one heading. The major groups are perhaps the Commedia dell'Arte; mythological and allegorical subjects; the Cries of Paris; beggars and itinerants; pastoral and peasant groups; the Seasons; the Senses; the Elements; the Quarters of the Globe; religious subjects, and the Arts and Sciences. Besides these, there are Chinoiserie and foreign figures, musicians, dancers, sportsmen, grotesques, animals, birds, and legions of 'Cupids in Disguise', as well as a number of family groups of various kinds.

The main purpose of many of these pieces at the time they were made was, according to the sale catalogues of 1755 and 1756, to be 'ornaments for a desart', though as early as January 1750 the famous bluestocking Mrs Elizabeth Montagu had written to her sister of 'ornaments of Chelsea China or the manufacture of Bow, which makes a room look neat and furnished'.[2] Some then were evidently also intended for cabinet or mantelpiece display.

The custom of decorating a dessert table with elaborate displays of porcelain figures was a natural progression from the earlier form of extravagant table decorations in wax or sugar. In an essay published in the magazine *The World* on 7 February 1752, Horace Walpole under the pseudonym of 'Julio' lightly mocked the passion for nature (that is to say, the passion for asymmetrical style) which was then apparent in all forms of applied art.

In gardening the same love of nature prevails. Clipped hedges, avenues, regular platforms, straight canals, have for some time been very properly exploded. There is not a citizen who does not take more pains to torture his acre and half into irregularities, than he formerly would have employed to make it formal as his cravat …

The last branch of our fashions into which the close observation of nature has been introduced, is our desserts; a subject I have not room now to treat at large, but which yet demands a few words …

Jellies, biscuits, sugar-plumbs, and creams have long given way to harlequins, gondoliers, Turks, Chinese, and shepherdesses of Saxon China. But these, unconnected, and only seeming to wander among groves of curled paper and silk flowers, were soon discovered to be too insipid and unmeaning. By degrees whole meadows of cattle, of the same brittle materials, spread themselves over the whole table; cottages rose in sugar, and temples in barley-sugar; pigmy Neptunes in cars of cockle-shells triumphed over

Fig. 9.2 An extremely rare figure of Flora, probably modelled by Joseph Willems. She stands beside a vase that may originally have had a pot-pourri cover. Height 23 cm (9¼ in). No mark. *c.*1756–7. Private collection

oceans of looking-glass, or seas of silver tissue; and at length the whole system of Ovid's metamorphoses succeeded to all the transformations which Chloe and other great professors had introduced into the science of hieroglyphic eating. Confectioners found their trade moulder away, while toymen and china-shops were the only fashionable purveyors of the last stage of fashionable entertainments; Women of the first quality came home from Chenevix's[3] laden with dolls and babies, not for their children, but their housekeeper.

Walpole's mention of 'Saxon China' in this essay points to the source from which in the Red Anchor years the Chelsea factory drew so much of its inspiration. Whether by direct copying of figures and decoration or the issuing of original pieces in a similar style, the productions of the Royal Porcelain Factory at Meissen were at this period plainly the model for almost everything made at Chelsea.

This is seen especially clearly in the figure production. We have already mentioned in Chapter 6 the borrowings made by Sprimont in 1751 from the collection of Meissen porcelain owned by Sir Charles Hanbury-Williams and kept at Holland House. This collection included a dinner service for thirty people which incorporated a dessert service, and T.H. Clarke has shown that a splendid Meissen table service with decoration of specimen animals surrounded by wreaths of realistic flowers, now at Alnwick Castle, was certainly copied to some extent at Chelsea and is probably the actual service which once formed part of Sir Charles' Meissen property.[4] The list of his porcelain also included 166 'Figures to adorn the middle of the Desert'. Some of these must have been among the figures which Chelsea imitated, though the low mound bases scattered with applied flowers and leaves on which a number of Red Anchor figures and groups are set are simple by comparison with the Meissen rococo scrolled bases of 1748 or 1749. Other bases given to Red Anchor groups are low flat circles or squares about 1.3 cm (½ inch) thick, which firmly support the figures but do nothing to distract the eye from their dramatic impact.

Chelsea figures illustrating the Commedia dell' Arte, the Seasons, the Continents, beggars and peasants, Arts and Sciences and the extraordinary Monkey Band, almost all find their originals at Meissen, many of them after the work of the great modeller Johann Joachim Kändler. While the hard paste and sharp modelling give the satirical exaggeration of the German originals a peculiar tenseness, the English paste and workmanship translate the same models into softer feeling and more gentle movement.

The Tyrolean (sometimes called 'Dutch') dancers first produced at Meissen in the 1730s, modelled by Eberlein, were probably amongst the most popular figures of the period, since they were copied not only in England at Chelsea and Bow, but also in China for the western market. Four Chinese examples were indeed among the

Fig. 9.3 Group of Tyrolean dancers, based on a Meissen model of *c.*1740. Height 18.2 cm (7⅕ in). Mark: a Red Anchor. *c.*1755–7. The British Museum

vast quantity of wares salvaged in 1985 by Captain Hatcher from the wreck of the Dutch East Indiaman, the *Geldermalsen*, which had sunk in the East Indies in 1752. The group was first issued at Meissen in 1735; a later Meissen version showed the man wearing a face mask, and this, with its delicately rococo base, is the one copied at Chelsea [fig. 9.3].

The Chelsea models from the Commedia dell' Arte include 'Dottore Balloardo' in a histrionic pose, 'Pedrolino' and Harlequin, as well as Scaramouche, a Lawyer, Pantaloon and the Captain. Both Columbine and Isabella also appear. Columbine is depicted dancing and wearing a hat, Isabella shown as a crinolined figure holding both a mask and a fan. All the Chelsea Commedia figures relate fairly closely to those from Meissen.

The origins of the Commedia dell' Arte can be traced right back to ancient Rome, and its lively and bawdy characters were familiar throughout civilized Europe. Only in England, to which country the mountebank actors did not travel, and where religion was more restrained and puritan, was the Commedia less familiar. Sprimont's porcelain figures are probably the chief form in which it was known in these islands, made for an aristocratic clientele, many of whom would have become acquainted with its drama while in their youth, on the Grand Tour [see fig. 9.4].

Figs 9.4 & 9.5 Figures of Pierrot and Columbine as Musicians. Height of Pierrot 15.2 cm (5¹⁵⁄₁₆ in). No mark. Height of Columbine 15.3 cm (6 in). Mark: a Red Anchor behind on tree stump. Both figures play restored instruments, he a pipe and she a flute. Note the U-shaped opening behind each base, perhaps to secure the figures to a dessert-table centrepiece. *c.* 1755–7. Private collection

Fig. 9.6 opposite, far left Seated figure, the Sense of Touch, one of the Five Senses, modelled by Joseph Willems. Height 30.6 cm (12 in). *c.* 1755. Museum of London

Fig. 9.7 opposite, left Figures of two little girls emblematic of Astronomy and Painting. Height 13.7 cm (5 3/8 in) and 13.4 cm (5¼ in) respectively. *c.* 1755. Victoria and Albert Museum, London

Fig. 9.8 opposite, below left Leda and the Swan, adapted from a painting by François Boucher. Height 17.5 cm (6⅞ in), width 17.2 cm (6¾ in). Mark: a Red Anchor. *c.* 1755. Victoria and Albert Museum, London

Fig. 9.9 left A Hippocampus, or seahorse, one of a pair. Length 26.7 cm (10½ in). *c.* 1755–8. Cecil Higgins Art Gallery, Bedford

Fig. 9.10 above Marine figure groups. Boy riding on a Seal. Height 10.8 cm (4¼ in), length 18.4 cm (7¼ in). No mark. *c.* 1755–8. Leda on a Dolphin's back. Height 11.5 cm (4½ in), length of base 17.2 cm (6¾ in). Mark: a Red Anchor. *c.* 1755–8. Private collection

Fig. 9.11 left River God and Goddess. Height 12.7 cm (5 in) and 12.6 cm (5 in) respectively. No marks. *c.* 1755. The British Museum

The five large figures, each about 4.8 cm (12 inches) high, representing the Senses, show the modeller Joseph Willems employing the Baroque style in statuesque and twisted poses, with the draperies falling in heavy diagonal folds [fig. 9.6]. The catalogue of 1756 makes plain that these figures were sold as individual lots, and they are each there described as 'fine' and 'large'. They have more recently been ranked among the most impressive of all European porcelain sculptures.[5]

There are as many as five sets of Chelsea 'Seasons'. One set, which has two groups of paired putti on low rocky bases, derives from Meissen,[6] as does a group in which all four infant seasons are arranged on a low base round a central tree.[7] Two later sets which can be adapted as candlesticks have low bases with mild rococo scrolling. In one, each season is represented by a single adult figure; in the other, by two peasant children.[8] The most original of the sets of Chelsea seasons is in the form of four individual adult peasant figures, each about 16.5 cm (6½ inches) high.[9]

A set of Red Anchor Continents again are taken from Meissen and are in the form of pairs of children mounted on candlestick bases with elaborate rococo scrolls. A series of Arts and Sciences copy Meissen closely and are represented by individual children with appropriate attributes who are perched on pedestals.[10] Examples from a different series (the Liberal Arts) are illustrated here [fig. 9.7].

The mythological figures produced at Chelsea are many, but generally have no direct Meissen prototype, and some are apparently original designs by Joseph Willems. One of the most beautiful in its early form is the group of Leda and the Swan with Cupid, adapted from Boucher, a lovely example of which is in the Victoria and Albert Museum [fig. 9.8]. In the Gold Anchor period the model was smothered in flowers and a bocage which obliterated its sculptural simplicity.

Other fine models are the reclining pair of a river god and goddess [fig. 9.11], probably derived from marble figures representing the Seine and the Marne by Edme Bouchardon (1698–1762) on the fountain of Grenelle in Paris.[11] In the same vein is the figure of Leda on a dolphin [fig. 9.10], and those of children riding on a seahorse and on a seal [fig. 9.10]. Dr Watney suggested that the figure of the boy riding a seahorse may stem from a sketch by François Girardon for the fountain known as La Pyramide at Versailles.[12] These three last models were table ornaments made to be displayed triumphing over 'seas of silver tissue'. Two similar children struggling with a large fish, perhaps a flower holder, were possibly intended as a decoration for a table centre, though the origin of the group was probably a bronze fountain.

A complex group of Perseus and Andromeda, and a simple Rape of the Sabines, are mentioned in the 1755 catalogue, as are a considerable number of cupids (or Love) 'in disguise for a desart'. Many of these derive from Meissen. The cupids' disguises are legion; they appear as beggars, actors, doctors and so on, but perhaps one of the most appealing impersonates a magic lantern man, with his equipment carried on his back. The earlier Red Anchor cupids stand between 10.2 to 12.1 cm tall (4 and 4¾ inches) on mound bases with slight rococo scrolling but without applied flowers. Their production continued in the Gold Anchor years, when many new models were added.

Also in the classical vein are the large pot-pourri vases, with a seated figure of Atalanta and her hound, or Meleager with the boar's head [fig. 9.12], both on rococo bases. 'Perfume vases' are a feature of the 1755 catalogue, which includes no fewer than fifteen. Atalanta and Meleager each appear twice. The other pot-pourris are in

Fig. 9.12 Pot-pourri vases, with the figures of Meleager, holding the head of the Calydonian boar (left), and Atalanta (right). Height 40.2 cm (15¾ in), 39.5 cm (15½ in) respectively. 1755. The British Museum

the form of a pigeon-house 'with pigeons, a fox etc'; a scene with hunting dogs and rabbits; arranged as a group with a woman with a vase, or with three cupids picking flowers round the jar; in all, five different designs offered that year.

The 'perfume pots', which are allied to porcelain figures, also have something in common with such complex pieces as the epergne 'ornamented with flowers, figures etc. on a glass stand', lot 77 of the fifteenth day of sale in March 1755; and lot 66 on the sixteenth: 'A large and magnificent LUSTRE beautifully ornamented with FIGURES and CURIOUS FLOWERS in a superb Taste'. The distinction between use and ornament is blurred here.

To return to the classical theme: a set of figures of gods and goddesses is mentioned in the 1755 catalogue; examples of only seven of these can now be located, as Juno and Minerva have apparently not been discovered or published. The hand of Joseph Willems is immediately recognizable in this set, and his source may have been a series of as yet unidentified engravings. There is also a set of small busts of gods and goddesses on pedestal bases. Similar models were made at Bow, and all derive from Meissen.

But it is perhaps amongst the figures in contemporary dress that the most memorable of the Chelsea Red Anchor models are to be found. Their immediate inspiration came from the figures modelled at Meissen by J.J. Kändler and Peter Reinicke in two series derived from Bouchardon's contemporary prints the *Cries of Paris*. The first Meissen series was issued in 1745–7 and the second in 1752. Willems took only two models from the earlier set, a map-seller [fig. 9.14], and a standing peasant wearing a tricorn hat and playing a hurdy-gurdy. The map-seller was originally made in the white in Triangle porcelain, but was reissued as a Red Anchor model decorated in enamels.[13] He steps forward with his back on his back, a rolled map in his left hand and an open one in his right, which sometimes, but not in all cases, portrays America.

The *Cries of Paris* of the second Meissen series were based on a watercolour by Christoph Huet. From these Chelsea copied a rat-catcher with his ferret and trap [fig. 9.13]; a Jewish pedlar who has a fur-lined cap and a tray of goods suspended by a strap round his neck, and the pedlar's female companion, the trinket-seller. A Savoyard drummer holds a flute to his lips and his drum hangs from his belt, while a female ballad-singer sits with songsheets in her hand

Fig. 9.13 below Rat-catcher. Height 14.7 cm (5¾ in). Mark: a Red Anchor. *c.*1755. Fitwilliam Museum, Cambridge

Fig. 9.14 below right Map-seller. Height 18.5 cm (7¼ in). Mark: a Red Anchor. *c.*1755. Fitwilliam Museum, Cambridge

and a child by her side. An itinerant musician with his bagpipes walks alongside a child and a dog. Two bird-catchers, male and female, with huge cages, were also copied; the woman from this pair was adapted at Chelsea to serve as well as a flower-seller, with a basket of flowers instead of a cage. A pair of cooks, male and female, carrying dishes of food, were copied both at Chelsea and at Bow.

All these derive directly from Meissen, but Joseph Willems added his own creations to the series made at Chelsea. His carpenter is justly famous, and stands with his tricorn on his head and a bag of tools over his left shoulder [fig. 9.15]. The names of some of the eighteenth-century inhabitants of Chelsea have been preserved to us, and it is pleasant to think that this might be a portrait in his younger days of Robert Ranson, who in September 1770 tendered a bill totalling £1 0s. 3d. for various bits of carpentry work he had done on the Chelsea factory premises.[14] Other figures once supposed to be original models made by Willems are two standing beggars, 'the 'Blind Beggar' wearing a scarf round his head and extending his hat for alms, and the 'Italian Beggar', who wears his hat but gathers a blanket round him while holding out a pouch in which there is already a coin. The 'Blind Beggar' is sometimes paired with a 'Beggar Woman' who could be a peasant rather than a beggar, since she carries a basket of vegetables.

The Red Anchor models of fishermen derive mostly from Kändler's work. There are four of them, but only one known model of a fishwife. A dramatic pose is that of the 'Drunken Fisherman'[15] who stands grinning on a squarish rocky base, astride an eel trap, with his bulging shirt and breeches full of fish, and another in each hand. A second fisherman,[16] in a peaked cap with open shirt and rolled up breeches, is removing fish from a quantity in a long handled net between his knees [fig. 9.16]. A third in similar garments but with a brimmed hat holds up a fish in his left hand, with his right ready to catch if it need be.[17] The fourth Chelsea fisherman model has a pose adapted from the 'Borghese Warrior',[18] a favourite Academic model of the time, examples of which occur in terracotta, marble and lead. He leans backwards with his weight upon his right leg, holding the pole of an enormous net in his left hand so that it lies almost level across the back of his neck, and grasps a fish in his right hand.

In contrast the fishwife, of whom only three examples are recorded, stands simply, wearing a linen cap and with her dress looped up to show her petticoat, leaning back slightly from the weight of a large dish loaded with fish which she holds before her. She may have been inspired by Meissen; 'a fisherwoman with a basket' was paired with a carpenter in the sale catalogue of 1755. Two examples of a fishwife were correctly paired with fishermen in the sale of 1756. John C. Austin, formerly Assistant Director, Department of Collections at Colonial Williamsburg believes, as did Arthur Lane,[19] that the fisherwoman with the dish was, like the carpenter, an original model by Joseph Willems.

Fig. 9.15 Figure of a carpenter. Height 19.1 cm (7¼ in). *c.*1755. Private collection

Fig. 9.16 Two figures of fishermen. Height 18.5 cm (7 ¼ in). One marked with a small Red Anchor on the back. *c*.1755. National Trust, Saltram House, Devon

Peasant figures may have in some cases been inspired by those depicted by David Teniers and other Flemish artists. Their work, as Peter Bradshaw points out, was probably familiar to Joseph Willems, who was himself from the Low Countries, and it is interesting to learn that the notice for the abortive sale of Nicholas Sprimont's picture collection in January 1759 (see Chapter 10) listed nineteen painters, of whom at least six were Flemings, six Dutch, and the others French or German. Some may have provided models for rustic Chelsea figures.[20]

Among such possible models we find a cooper, an ostler and a carter, the latter holding a mug of beer. The cooper, who sits on a barrel, with barrel hoops over his shoulder, echoes a figure by Kändler, but a drunken peasant and a dancing peasant could well have been taken from a Flemish painting. A centrepiece known as the 'Maypole Dancers' consists of six figures, four peasants, a lady and a gentleman, dancing round a flowery mound with a tree trunk on top of it. Against the trunk stands a lad with a small leather barrel, and near him a fiddler. The peasant figures have their clothing simply coloured in yellow, brown or black, or just left white. The gentleman, however, has a turquoise coat, and his lady's dress is decorated with floral sprays. The Cheyne Book states that three of the peasants derive from a painting by David Teniers called the 'Rural Fête', dated 1645. It has been suggested that this group, an example of which is in the Fitzwilliam Museum, Cambridge, was built up piecemeal from individual figures. If so, the result is a successful one. The group stands 35.6 cm (14 in) high.[21]

Two seated figures 22.9 cm (9 in) high, of a young fruit seller and his companion who have baskets of interlaced osiers mounted beside them on an extension of each rocky base, are also reminiscent of Tenier's peasants. The vital poses, as each flings out an arm to offer the ware, and heavy folds of the apron and skirt show yet again the hand of Joseph Willems. Other seated figures which bear a resemblance to them are the fisherman and his wife, he with a large basket between his knees and she with her apron pierced, both intended as flower holders. These, however, are

Fig. 9.17 Figure of a Spanish sportsman. Height 21.6 cm (8½ in). Mark: a Red Anchor. *c.* 1755–8. Fitzwilliam Museum, Cambridge

Fig. 9.18 Figure of the sportsman's companion. Height 21 cm (8¼ in). *c.* 1755–8. Fitzwilliam Museum, Cambridge

static figures compared with the seated Spanish sportsman and companion [figs 9.17–18] whose vigorous attitudes and alert air are reminiscent of those of the fruit sellers.

The Spanish couple, however, by their dress and appearance, are gentle folk; so also is the 'Polish Lady' in a crinoline, who wears a headscarf and jacket and lifts her skirt with her right hand to show off her petticoat. She has only recently been recognized as a copy of a Meissen figure modelled by Kändler in 1743 to be the companion of a moustachioed Pole designed by Friedrich Eberlein.[22] One of the finest examples of the figure of a Polish lady is in the Cecil Higgins Museum in Bedford [fig. 9.19].

A set of a hundred engravings made by various artists and published by La Hay of Paris in 1714 were originally drawn by order of the French Ambassador to Constantinople, Comte Charles de Ferriol.[23] They showed examples of the many nationalities then to be seen in the streets of that Islamic city, including Armenians, Bulgarians, Hungarians, Levantines, Persians and Turks. Many of these figures were copied in porcelain at Meissen; Chelsea reproduced the Meissen 'Seated Turk in a Plumed Turban' and the 'Levantine Lady' his companion, who sit beside shell containers and were first modelled by Kändler and Reinicke *c.* 1748 [fig. 9.20]. Meissen also copied the figures in plate 5 of another production of de Ferriol, *Le Capi Aga ou Chef des Eunuques blancs*, a Turk in a tall hat and a Levantine lady adjusting her headdress. These again were copied at Chelsea, and also at Bow. Chelsea issued a negro in a turban, clad in loose robes and holding a longbow, paired with a negress in crown and cloak. The sale catalogue of 1755 calls them 'an Indian Prince and a Queen'. Both follow the Meissen versions, though the Prince is unusual in being a mirror image of the Meissen example.

Two standing Chinoiserie figures of a Chinaman with a large moustache and a man in a Chinese mask, are amongst the most prized of Chelsea Red Anchor productions. Both of swashbuckling appearance and clad in loose cloaks, they are 17.8 and 18.4 cm (7 and 7¼ inches) high respectively.

There are smaller Chinoiserie models, a Chinaman in a conical hat with his hands hidden in his huge sleeves, and a delightful pair of a Chinese boy with a fife and girl with a drum. A group of a Chinaman sitting by a large urn with Chinese heads as handles, beneath which a boy is stoking a fire, illustrated by J.L. Dixon (*English Porcelain of the 18th Century*, pl.25), although lacking a lid, seems to be another example of the marriage of art and utility in the form of a pot-pourri jar. It is in the Cecil Higgins Art Gallery, Bedford.

Most splendid, however, is the large decorative group of Chinese musicians. They were designed as a centrepiece and described in the Chelsea sale catalogue of 1756, tenth day, as 'A most magnificent LUSTRE in the Chinese taste, beautifully ornamented with flowers and a large groupe of Chinese figures playing on music'.

The four figures are seated in a ring on a mound decorated with many vari-coloured applied flowers, facing outwards, and consist of a young man holding a bell in his left hand, while with his right he holds that of a little boy who likewise holds up a bell in *his* right hand. Next comes a girl in oriental, patterned robes with a tambourine in her left hand and a bell in her right, her head bowed in concentration on the rhythm. Beside her another girl with her hair dressed à la Japonais, pauses, holding her flute in both hands and waiting for her moment to recommence playing. The whole group is so expressive of concentration and the absorption of the players, that one can only call it a masterpiece of ceramic sculpture. An example is in the Untermyer Collection in New York, and another, happily, at the Victoria and Albert Museum.

Strangely perhaps in a Protestant country, and at a factory presumably managed by a Protestant Frenchman, a number of figures and groups on a religious theme were nevertheless made at Chelsea. One of the finest of these is the Virgin with the Holy Child, who is standing on a terrestrial globe placed beside his mother [fig. 9.21]. In some versions he holds a cross, and the group seems to be the one described in the 1755 catalogue, lot 14 on the sixth day's sale, as 'A very fine figure of a madonna with a child and a cross'. The globe is depicted with a band of Roman numerals round the equator which correspond with the lines of longitude, and the Continents are pencilled in and named, as are also certain countries and oceans, i.e. 'Mar di India'. The arrangement of the words 'Mar di' has perhaps been misinterpreted by one writer as the name of the month March, and thus, coupled with the supposed numerals of the hours, gave rise to the suggestion that the group was derived from an ornamental clock. This is not really likely; the symbolism as it stands means simply that Christ is the ruler of time and of the world. The Serpent with the forbidden fruit in his mouth lurks beneath the globe.[24]

Another religious group modelled by Joseph Willems which is justly famous is the Pietà, probably from a print of the marble by Nicholas Coustou (1653–1733)[25] in the choir of Notre Dame in Paris. The Virgin, her eyes lifted to heaven, sits with the body of the dead Christ laid across her knees, while a kneeling angel lifts the lifeless left hand. Only two examples of this Chelsea group are known, one decorated in colours produced in the Red Anchor years, which is now in the Victoria and Albert Museum; the other re-issued in the white with an added mazarine blue and gold plinth in the Gold Anchor period. This example is now in Australia. Willems' Pietà is also known in the biscuit from Tournai. After Joseph Willems died at Tournai in 1766, the inventory of his effects included prints and drawings by various hands, plaster models, and a number of terracotta figures and groups. Among these was one '… représentant la Vierge et le Sauveur descendu de la croix, avec un adorateur'.[26]

Perhaps more to be associated with the fashion for 'Gothick' architecture and decoration which occurred in the middle of the eighteenth century, than with a truly

Fig. 9.19 opposite, above Figure of a Polish lady. Height 15.3 cm (6 in). Mark: a Red Anchor on top of base at back. *c.* 1755–6. Cecil Higgins Art Gallery, Bedford

Fig. 9.20 opposite, below Pair of seated Turks, with shells. Height of male figure 15.4 cm (6¹/₁₆ in). Height of female figure 14.4 cm (5⁵/₈ in). Female marked with a Red Anchor. *c.* 1753–5. Tullie House Museum & Art Gallery, Carlisle

Fig. 9.21 below Group of the Virgin and Child with a globe. Height 21.6 cm (8¹/₂ in). Mark: a Red Anchor. *c.* 1755. Fitwilliam Museum, Cambridge

Fig. 9.22 The Mater Dolorosa, St James's Factory. Height 19.4 cm (7 3/5 in). No mark. *c.* 1752–4. The British Museum

religious feeling, are the porcelain figures of monks and nuns. They are unlikely to have been thought suitable for table decoration, and are not representations of saints, such as might have been used for devotional purposes. They were made in England at Chelsea, Bow, Longton Hall and Liverpool, in various postures and decorated in various ways. A seated Chelsea nun reading a book, an example of which is in the Pettit Collection at Wallington Hall, Northumberland [fig. 9.23], is a direct copy of a nun modelled at Meissen by Kändler in the 1740s for the Abbess of Herfordt.[27] This nun was perhaps a pair to a monk, similarly reading.[28] A standing nun, wearing a ruff, is in the Cecil Higgins Art Gallery at Bedford.[29] Arthur Lane traced the source of this figure to Plate XIV in *Kurze and grundriche Historie*, a book published by Daniel Steudner in Augsburg in 1693. She is there called 'a noble Canoness of Cologne, St Maria im Capitol'. A similar figure occurs in a *Catalogue of Religious Orders in the Church Militant* published in Rome (1706–10) by Filippo Bonanni, and the nun with a ruff is probably intended as a pair to the Chelsea figure of an abbot (sometimes described as a lawyer), also deriving from one of Bonanni's plates [fig. 9.24]. An example of the abbot figure is to be seen at Wallington. A standing nun with a breviary and rosary and a monk with a breviary only are also recorded.[30]

The models of monkey musicians copied at Chelsea from Kändler's Meissen *Affenkapelle*, like their originals, are not to everyone's taste, though some may appeal more than others. A set of twelve is in the collection at Colonial Williamsburg. The conductor, as in the Meissen monkey orchestra, is proportionately higher than the other members of the band, being 20.3 cm (8 inches) tall, while they are all in the region of 15.2 cm (6 inches). The source of two of these monkey figures seems to be a series of undated prints by J. Guelard after designs by Christoph Huet published in France in the earlier part of the eighteenth century. The monkeys in question are the ones playing the pipe and tabor, and a group in which a monkey is playing an organ mounted on the back of another. The fashion for 'singeries' in which monkeys 'ape' the pursuits of the human race, and which are really a version of the craze for Chinoiseries, arose first in France, so Kändler may have received his inspiration from there. Not many members of the Chelsea monkey band have survived, and it may never have greatly suited English taste.

A female dwarf, made as partner to the male in a tall hat which first appeared in Raised Anchor paste, was produced in the Red Anchor period, and also two odd figures taken from the illustrations to *Aesop's Fables* by Francis Barlow, published in 1687. These are one of Aesop himself, a hunch-backed negro wearing the gold chain of a freeman,[31] and a fox dressed as a poacher, of which an example is in the Untermyer Collection. The fox has the same droll, sinister quality as the 'foxy-whiskered gentleman' in Beatrix Potter's illustrations to *The Tale of Jemima Puddle-Duck*; it is a vein of humour which runs through from the English Middle Ages to modern times.

In the later part of the Red Anchor years a number of 'family groups' were issued at Chelsea in a style which to some extent foreshadows the coming Gold Anchor period. They are on bases with more pronounced arabesques and scrolls picked out with gilding, and the surfaces beneath are both concave and glazed. Sometimes the scrolls develop naturally into short curved legs. The subjects represented include outdoor meals, musical entertainments, fruit gathering, and the selling of fish.

Bird models continued to be made, though derived from sources other than George Edwards' *Natural History of Uncommon Birds*. A pair of 'Bantom Cock and Hen' may have been made for table decoration; many models of sheep, cows, calves and so on were used for this purpose, with their attendant keepers, 'whole meadows of cattle' as Horace Walpole described the Meissen originals.

A standing lion 25.4 cm (10 inches) long, with his left paw resting on a ball, and modelled after one of the late sixteenth-century Florentine marble pair by Flamminio Vacca which stand at the entrance of the Loggia dei Lanzi, is a larger, rare survival from the early Red Anchor years. He was left in the white and has an experimental look as the whitened glaze has failed to take in some parts and has 'crawled', leaving bare patches. A figure of a squirrel eating a nut, 11.4 cm (4 ½ inches) high, probably after a Meissen model, and similar to one issued in the Triangle period, appears *c*. 1755 with enamelled decoration, and a pair of pugs, seated with roses in their collars, also date from about this time.[32]

Fig. 9.23 Figure of a seated nun. Height 14.4 cm (5⅛ in). *c.* 1755. National Trust, Wallington Hall, Northumberland

One really cannot conclude a chapter on Red Anchor figures without some mention of the miniature objects, the scent-bottles, seals, bonbonnières (or cachou-boxes), thimble cases, bodkin cases and snuff boxes, aptly described as 'the soul of porcelain wit'[33] which were produced throughout the Red and Gold Anchor periods 1753–69.

The sale of Chelsea miniature pieces which took place in December 1754 had not been foreseen earlier in the year, judging by a notice which Sprimont had published in March. It stated that after the spring sale he would 'positively not open his Warehouses, not exhibit any Article to Sale, after this, till next Year'. Notices of a second sale at the latter end of 1754 which were published in the *Public Advertiser* between 23 November and 21 December appear to be in flat contradiction to this statement; and a failure to realize a slight difference in the wording of the advertisement from 16 December onwards helped to give rise to the theory that Gouyn's second (St James's) factory failed in 1754, the remaining stock of its figures and 'toys' being bought up and dispersed by Sprimont in his 1754 Christmas auction sale. This theory, which received such credence in the last half century that it almost turned into accepted fact, is quite altered by Mrs Valpy's discovery of the changed wording in the second version of the December advertisement[34] of 1754, which removed one of the cornerstones of the argument. The advertisement did not at first specify that the 'Porcelain Toys' to be sold were of a named manufacture; Mrs Valpy discovered that from 16 December onwards they were properly described as 'Chelsea Porcelain Toys', brought from the Proprietors' Warehouse in Pall Mall'. Apart from the additional word 'Chelsea' and the alteration to emphasize that the Proprietors of the Chelsea factory were also the owners of the Warehouse, the earlier and later versions of the advertisement are identical.

In 1977 Dr and Mrs Alwyn Cox provided evidence that Nicholas Sprimont was selling porcelain scent-bottles at least as early as January 1754 (and these *must* have been made in the previous year) when they published an invoice of goods supplied to the Marquess of Rockingham.[35] On 16 January 1754, bought directly from Sprimont, and not from a retailer was a 'double squirrel scent bottle, mounted in gold' of which he was certainly the manufacturer.

The details of Sprimont's insurance policies show that the value of the goods in his Pall Mall Warehouse nearly doubled between May and October 1754, from £3000 to £5000.[36] I suggest that in 1754 the manufacture of miniature items in Sprimont's factory got into full production, enabling him to offer a full and attractive range at Christmas time that year.

Many natural forms of animals, birds, fruit and flowers are to be found among the Red Anchor scent-bottles. Among the animals are a cat (with a mouse), pugs both male and female, squirrels with young (as a double or triple scent-bottle), and several versions of monkeys. A monkey with her young in a basket slung on her back is a double scent-bottle, both mother and baby's heads being the stoppers of the separate containers. Another double monkey bottle is formed of two animals, one in the neck, the other in the spout of a porcelain jar.[37] A triple squirrel scent-bottle was known to be in a private collection in Melbourne, Victoria.

Three bottles are made up into a group of a hen and two chickens,[38] and single bottles as a peacock and as a swan are illustrated by Kate Foster.[39] A duck and ducklings are also known, as well as examples of double and single bottles as Aesop's Fable of the Fox and the Crow.[40] There are bottles in the form of vases and bouquets of flowers, or as a single tulip; in the form of a pineapple, an apple, a pear, three figs, or plums, or mixed fruit and flowers. Dolphins and fish in a net represent the watery world. Among human subjects is the series of monk and nun bottles, as well as the humorous one in which a monk carries a woman on his back disguised as a wheatsheaf, entitled 'Provender for the Monastery'. Red Anchor bottles are decorated in a manner similar to the decorations of Red Anchor figures. The bases usually have gilt dentil rims and large sprays of flowers painted on the undersides.

Besides the scent-bottles there are also the 'precious trifles' of étuis (or bodkin cases), seals [see fig. 9.25], bonbonnières, snuffboxes, thimble cases, and combinations of étui and scent-bottle, or étui and bonbonnière. All these are made in wonderful detail and all sorts of designs, the boxes, for instance, ranging from human

Fig. 9.24 Figure of an abbot (or lawyer) Height 15.3 cm (6 in). *c.* 1753–6. National Trust, Wallington Hall, Northumberland

heads through nestfuls of birds to trophies and complicated groups containing both human figures and animals.

The progression from Red Anchor 'trifles' to those of the Gold Anchor period is a natural and unbroken one. Some of the earlier models were used after 1760, though new ones were of course brought in. Among these appear a number of bottles in which Cupid engages in various activities, riding on a lion or on a donkey, fighting the devil, or working as a sculptor or painter. Others show little boys, not unlike cupids themselves, who are hunters, gardeners, goat-herds, flute players and so on.

The most noticeable difference between Gold Anchor and the earlier models is the more elaborate and colourful decoration, and the much increased use of gilding on the Gold Anchor pieces. Sometimes their bases are washed over with green enamel, and they are usually decorated with a gilt spray on the underside. Some of the Gold Anchor toys have mottoes on ribbons incorporated as an integral part of the design.

Fig. 9.25 Three seals. Bagpiper with motto 'Berger Fidele', possibly St James's factory, unmounted, *c.*1754. Mother and baby, Chelsea seal with motto 'Resultas d'Amour', mounted with bloodstone seal with an intaglio of Cupid and the inscription 'Fixe le Jour'. Height 2.6 cm (1 in). Mandolin player, Chelsea seal, bloodstone mount, with intaglio of two circling flying birds facing each other. Private collection.

Fig. 9.26 Chelsea scent-bottle, cat and mice, after a Meissen model, mounted in gold. Height 7.7 cm (3 in), width 3.9 cm (1½ in). *c.*1755. Private collection

CHAPTER 10

A Difficult Time

Tradition says that the Chelsea factory was closed for a period owing to Sprimont's illness which, as indicated in Chapter 2, was probably chronic kidney trouble aggravated by dropsy. Annual sales by public auction of Chelsea porcelain were held in 1754, 1755, 1756 and 1758 and were conducted by Richard Ford, 'at his Great Room, the Upper End of St James's Haymarket'. Each lasted about a fortnight and enabled both dealers and private buyers ample opportunity to purchase individual items or to lay in stock. However, no sale occurred in 1757. Instead, a notice appeared in the *Public Advertiser* on 15 February and on several occasions after.

> The Public is hereby acquainted that the Chelsea Porcelaine Manufactory has been very much retarded by the Sickness of Mr Sprimont; Nevertheless several curious Things have been finished, which will be exposed to Sale at the Warehouse in Piccadilly, some time the Beginning of March, of which more particular Notice will be given.

A warehouse near to the fashionable quarters of Westminster had been first opened by Sprimont in Pall Mall in the summer of 1751. As mentioned in Chapter 6, it may be deduced from newspaper advertisements that during the early period of the factory's life, *c.* 1744–9, there had been some particular sales arrangement with the dealer Richard Stables in St James's Street, but this apparently came to an end at the time of Charles Gouyn's presumed withdrawal of interest in the Chelsea undertaking, *c.* 1749.

Sprimont's Pall Mall warehouse was situated on the north side of the street and was rated at £75, nearly double the rate of the factory warehouse in Chelsea. Pall Mall was one of the most fashionable shopping streets of the time. However, at mid-summer 1755 the warehouse was removed to Piccadilly, to a site 'over against the White Bear', that is, occupying a position just west of the Haymarket, on the south side of what is now Piccadilly Circus. This building was rated at only £30, obviously

Fig. 10.1 Pair of dishes with basket-weave border and moulded vine leaf and twig handles. The centre of one is decorated with a dark green fritillary butterfly and a few scattered flowers; that of the other with a snail. Length 26.7 cm (10½ in). No mark. *c.* 1754. Private collection

Fig. 10.2 Pair of pierced bowls and stands. Diameter of bowl 15.3 cm (6 in), width of stand 22.9 cm (9 in). Both items marked with a Red Anchor. *c.* 1755. Private collection

a less expensive showroom than that in Pall Mall, but even so Sprimont occupied it only until April 1758, when he vacated it, perhaps as a result of Sir Everard Fawkener's withdrawal from the business in 1757.

At one time it had been thought that the only auction sales of Chelsea porcelain which took place in 1758 were those in Dublin in April, July and December that year. However, Mrs Valpy's discoveries of notices from the *Daily Advertiser* show that there *was* a London sale in 1758, lasting twelve days and running from 9 to 22 March. Twelve days afterwards, on 3 April, stock covered by the Sun Company policy 148790[1] for £2000 was taken from the Piccadilly warehouse to Mr Ford, the auctioneer in the Haymarket. Twelve days later again, on 15 April, the first of the three Chelsea sales held in Dublin in 1758 began.

In Dublin a notice appeared in the *Universal Advertiser* on 15 April 1758.

Dublin Sales. At Young's great Auction Rooms on Cork Hill opposite Lucas' Coffee House will continue to be sold by Auction all remaining part of the ornamental and useful china; a magnificent Epargne, some Branches and Flower-Pots etc. belonging to the Proprietors in London and must all be sold without reserve.

Mrs Valpy noted[2] that in the Custom House records for 1757/8 is the item 'Chinaware British £1932. To Ireland from Outports'. This could refer to the quantity of Chelsea Porcelain worth about £2000 which was removed from the Piccadilly warehouse in April 1758. We know for certain that the porcelain mentioned in the

Universal Advertiser's notice of 15 April was Chelsea, because another announcement a few days later remarks that 'The Kerry amethysts will be offered for sale by Mr Young at the Auction Rooms on Cork Hill where the Chelsea China was sold'.

The porcelain sold in Dublin in April, July and December 1758 therefore could conceivably have been the stock removed from the defunct Piccadilly warehouse, Red Anchor porcelain now perhaps becoming a little unfashionable, and perhaps too easily recognised as old stock in London, and so removed to Ireland for sale. The Watch Rate Book for St James's parish (Piccadilly South) gives Nicholas Sprimont 'Gone' from the Piccadilly warehouse before Midsummer 1758.[3]

William Chaffers[4] quotes a statement by a workman named 'Mr Mason' (to whom F.S. Mackenna gives the Christian name Alfred without giving reference or documentation) who said that he went to work for Nicholas Sprimont at Chelsea in about 1751.

> I think the Chelsea China Manufactory began about the year 1748 or 1749 … It was first carried on by the Duke of Cumberland and Sir Everard Fawkener, and the sole management was intrusted to a foreigner by the name of Sprimont, report says at a salary of a guinea per day, with certain allowances for apprentices and other emoluments. I think Sir Everard died about 1755, [actually, 1758] much reduced in circumstances, when Mr Sprimont became sole proprietor; and having amassed a fortune, he travelled about England, and the manufactory was shut up about two years; for he neither would let it or carry it on himself …

This last sentence of Mason's has always been supposed to be true, but does not seem to be borne out by the facts. After Fawkener's death in November 1758, Sprimont was nearly forced to raise funds to keep the factory going until the following March by auctioning his own collection of fine pictures, but the sale appears to have been cancelled, and the pictures were eventually sold in 1771. In late March and early April another in the series of annual sales of Chelsea porcelain was held, conducted 'by the Desire of several Persons of Distinction' by David Burnsall 'at his Great Auction-Room in Charles-Street, Berkley-Square'. Sixteen years later, in a Chancery suit, *Chetwood v. Burnsall*, brought by Sprimont's widow and concerned with the misappropriation of porcelain, David Burnsall, the defendant, stated that in 1759 Francis Thomas, the factory manager, had had to lend Sprimont, 'the proprietor', 'about £700, in order to enable him to bring on the public sale of the china of the manufactory, conducted by Burnsall himself.'

The departure from the London warehouse was a symptom of Sprimont's increasing problems, and further signs of the need for retrenchment and realignment

Fig. 10.3 A rare leaf-shaped bowl, or sauceboat, with small stalk handle and four leaf-moulded feet, modelled with applied strawberries, and painted with insects and sprays of flowers. Length 19.7 cm (7¾ in). No mark. *c.* 1753–4. Private collection

of the Chelsea factory business were the decisions of Henry Porter and his nephew Isaac to sell off their properties in Church Lane East, Mr Supply's house and Mrs Phillips' house, until now occupied by Sprimont as part of the factory complex. Both properties were bought by Charles Ross, a speculative builder from St James's, Westminster, who acquired Mrs Phillips' house in March 1759[5] and Mr Supply's house, four months later, in July.[6] Charles Ross almost immediately demolished Mrs Phillips' house, and built five new houses on the site, all of which were in occupation by 1762. Mr Supply's house was occupied by a Mr Crosland, who continued there for quite a number of years.

On 26 September 1759, the factory having been concentrated on the Lawrence Street site by the sale of both Mr Supply's and Mrs Phillips' houses and premises in Church Lane East, Sprimont gave notice in the 'London' column of the *Daily Advertiser* that he was in need of more hands, apparently with some urgency:

> Altho' many Painters have left other Manufactories to come to me I still want more Hands; and any good ones in the Porcelaine Way that will apply to me, shall be immediately employed; I give the best Wages, and always keep as usual to my Agreement with them. All Apprentices that I have discharged from my Service that will return and behave well, shall be received as Journeymen, and all Faults forgot. Any excellent hands in the History Way are likewise much wanted. None but what are ready in Composing, and Masters of Drawing need apply. N. Sprimont.[7]

This does not sound like a man intent on shutting up his factory. On 20 February 1760 Sprimont followed it up in the 'London' column of the *Daily Advertiser* with an even more forthright notice.[8]

> Chelsea Porcelaine Manufactory, Feb. 19. Hearing that some enemies to our Home Manufactory have industriously reported that there would be no Sale of the Chelsea Porcelaine this Year, I take the Liberty to assure the Nobility, Gentry and others, that I am fully resolved to have one some Time in April next; and as I have spared no Expence nor Study to make perfect Pieces of exquisite Beauty and Richness in the Mazarine Blue, Pea-Green, and Gold etc. I am in Hopes that what I shall offer to the Publick will merit the Continuance of the National Protection, and the farther encouragement of the Nobility, etc.

Fig. 10.4 Bucket-shape cup with saucer, each decorated with a bouquet of mixed flowers and scattered sprays. Rims edged with brown. Height of cup 6.2 cm (2⁷⁄₁₆ in), diameter of saucer 13.2 cm (5³⁄₁₆ in). Marks: on cup base, a Brown Anchor and painter's no. 17 below; on saucer, a Brown Anchor and no. 7 below Anchor and 8 above it. *c.* 1758–60. Private collection

The sale duly took place 'at Mr Burnsall's Auction-Room in Charles Street, Berkeley-Square' and ran from Monday, 28 April to Friday, 2 May inclusive. It was only half the length of the great annual sales of 1754, 1755, 1756 and 1758, which suggests that production was less than in those years, but of course the factory premises had been contracted into the Lawrence Street site only since 1759, which would go some way to account for this apparently smaller output. The advertisement of the sale in the *Public Advertiser* as well as giving a comprehensive list of the articles available underlines Sprimont's close involvement with the factory processes, and his insistence on the Chelsea factory as a British undertaking.

> … There will likewise be in this national Sale … a few pieces of some new Colours which have been found this year by Mr Sprimont, the Proprietor, at a very large Expence, incredible Labour, and close Application, all highly finished, and heightened with the Gold peculiar to that fine and distinguish'd Manufactory, which makes this Porcelain the most beautiful and magnificent ever seen, and cannot be made at any Foreign Manufactory.

On 27 June 1760 Nicholas Sprimont took out a fire insurance for the factory with the Sun Company in his own name.[9] According to the evidence of David Burnsall in the Exchequer suit, *Chetwood v. Burnsall*, in 1776, Sprimont had become actual owner of the factory buildings in 1757.

> This defendant says he has been informed and believes that Sir Everard Fawkener, Knight of the Bath, deceased, was several years before the year 1757, owner and proprietor of the houses, warehouses, kilns and other buildings used for the manufacturing of porcelain and in that year did decline such business in favour of Nicholas Sprimont, to whom he assigned by sale or gift the whole business.

This is supported by the fact that before 1760 Sprimont insured in his own name only the goods in the two West End warehouses. From 1760 he insured the factory itself. The policy included his household goods in his dwellinghouse (by then in fact part of the factory warehouse in Monmouth House) and also the 'China and Glass therein' valued at £1000. A year later the value of the stock was £2000, but right through to the policy of 1765 the factory buildings themselves remained at a valuation of only £500. This was about one fifth of the value of the Bow factory in 1755.

Fig. 10.5 Plate with twelve-lobed border, which consists of panels of engine-turning alternating with plain panels decorated with various single multicoloured birds, the outer rim of the lobes being traced in maroon. The centre of the plate is charmingly painted with scattered single sprays of semi-realistic flowers, and a loose bunch including an iris and a mauve poppy. Plates of this design and a few very rare teawares are the only examples of Chelsea porcelain on which engine-turning can be seen. Width of plate 21.6 cm (8½ in). No mark. *c.* 1758. Private collection

CHAPTER 11

Gold Anchor Wares and Figures

1759–69

Fig. 11.1 below Saucer with green landscape decoration of a church in wooded countryside. Gilt dentil rim. Diameter 12.1 cm (4¾ in). No mark. *c.* 1760–65. Private collection

Fig. 11.2 opposite Pair of mazarine blue and gold trumpet vases with applied lizards. Height 24.5 cm (9⅗ in). Marks: Gold Anchors on both. *c.* 1758–68. The British Museum

In May 1756 the Seven Years' War began, and this had a considerable effect on European porcelain manufacture. Exports from the Meissen factory were largely cut off; the town was occupied by the Prussians, and many of the factory staff fled to look for work elsewhere. The Meissen factory lost its pre-eminence, never to regain it, and thus the influence of France on European porcelain making became more important than that of Saxony.

The French royal factory, founded at Vincennes in 1738, was moved to Sèvres in 1756, and quickly took over the position that Meissen had formerly enjoyed. Within three years, just as Nicholas Sprimont had succeeded in weathering the difficult period after Sir Everard Fawkener's death in 1758, the influence of Sèvres had spread to England, bringing the rich ground colours and elaborate rococo gilding that were to distinguish Chelsea productions for the rest of Sprimont's life.

In spite of all the difficulties of both health and finance against which he had to struggle in the decade between 1759 and 1769, the quality and finish of the porcelain produced at the Chelsea factory under Nicholas Sprimont's proprietorship never declined in any way. The style of the later Chelsea productions may not now appeal as it once did to contemporaries and to collectors of the later nineteenth century, but the execution of the painted decoration and of the gilding is faultless.

The knowledge of the properties of calcined bones as an ingredient to strengthen and whiten a porcelain body must have percolated to Chelsea from Bow by the middle 1750s, in the same way as it reached other British factories, through the agency of inquisitive principals and migrant potters. It was impossible, as makers everywhere in Europe found, to keep a 'porcelain secret'. Alexander Lind writing to Lord Milton from Gorgie, near Edinburgh, as long ago as December 1749 said he thought he already knew the materials employed both at Chelsea and at Bow,[1] and he had, through the good offices of the Duke of Argyll, had 'an opportunity of examining everything pretty minutely, I mean the structure of their Furnaces, and the other parts of their manual operations, which were what I chiefly wanted to see.'

It has been suggested that Chelsea did not change to the use of bone-ash until

Fig. 11.3 Teapot with botanical and insect decoration. Height 14.4 cm (5⅗ in). No mark. *c.*1762–4. The British Museum

Fig. 11.4 Broth bowl and lid. Rabbit and pheasant decoration on lid, pigeons and greenfinches with sunflower on sides. Height with lid 10.2 cm (4 in). No mark. *c.*1762. The British Museum

a decision to produce larger objects and figures made it necessary. Bone-ash as an ingredient of porcelain was first publicly mentioned in Robert Dossie's book *The Handmaid of the Arts* in 1758.

Gold Anchor porcelain is fine and white, with a thick glassy glaze which can easily be seen lying over the body on a broken piece. The glaze often crazed badly during firing owing to inconsistencies between its expansion and that of the porcelain, and it gathered heavily in hollows, showing a greenish-yellow, or sometimes bluish, tinge. It is a soft glaze, easily scratched or rubbed, and the gobbets which ran down in the heat of the kiln often had to be ground away from footrims to make the articles stand evenly.

The translucency of Gold Anchor porcelain varies, and there may be none in large, thick pieces of ware. In thinly potted items such as teacups, however, it is good, and the paste shows creamy-green. Potting generally is more substantial than it was in the Red Anchor days, except in the finest of teawares. Nevertheless, large pieces such as vases are often very light in weight considering their size.

The Gold Anchor mark varies from the Red in that the anchor bow is V-shaped, with only a single, down-pointing fluke at either end. Also the ring above the cross bar is quite frequently left out. Occasionally, at this period, the Gold Anchor form of the mark occurs painted in red or brown. Generally speaking, the marks were made larger than previously, between 6 and 9 millimetres high. A double anchor mark on certain classes of figures is discussed later in this chapter, and letters such as A, G, R, and T which were sometimes enamelled or incised on figures, probably relate to their assemblers or 'repairers'.

As previously explained, the change in colour of the anchors probably happened in the course of events and was not intended to signify a change in paste or style. This is exemplified in the bucket-shaped teacups and saucers, which have flat under-glazed bases, and which were first produced *c.* 1757–8. At that time they were decorated with conventional bouquets and flowers and marked with the Red or Brown Anchor. Although cups and saucers of the same shape continued to be made *c.* 1759–65, they were decorated not with flowers but with black-outlined green-washed landscapes, and given gilt dentil edges and sometimes a Gold Anchor mark [see fig. 11.1]. These green landscapes are by some associated with the workshop of James Giles, as similar English decoration is found on Chinese porcelain, but it seems a little unlikely that Giles would add the factory mark if the decoration was his.

Other Gold Anchor teawares are less stark in outline than the plain bucket-shaped pieces. Those with scalloped edges and shallow fluting recall the Japanese influence of Raised and early Red Anchor days. Others, more elaborate, have a little moulding on the body and shaped edges with small and larger concave curves. The saucers made to match have a shallow *trembleuse* gallery round the well.

Pine-cone moulding occurs on both teawares and the covered bowls with stands (écuelles) in which soup or broth could be served [see figs 11.5, 11.6, 11.18]. This form of moulding was used at Bow and at Bristol as well. At Chelsea it was sometimes enhanced by the addition of glorious shades of green, blue and purple, with added gilding, the whole giving an impression of peacock feather brilliance.

In dessert wares the variations in moulding are generally confined to the borders of plates. Even so, there are probably no more than a dozen basic forms, though they range from the simple feather edge, so familiar in cream-coloured earthenware, to the most extreme rococo shell-like convolutions.

Tureens were no longer made in the elaborate natural forms favoured in the early 1750s, but became comparatively plain, of round or oval plan, with added rococo moulding and strongly rococo feet, handles and knops.

Dishes were sometimes made in earlier forms, with leaf-moulded or diaper-moulded borders, and with edges echoing the old silver-shapes; some may even have been earlier-made stock, brought up to date by the addition of magnificent painted

Fig. 11.5 Pine-cone moulded sugar bowl and lid, carmine, tagged border outlined with gilt vine tendrils, and the body scattered with small flowers. Exquisite many-petalled dahlia flower knop on lid. Height 12.3 cm (4⅘ in). Mark: a Gold Anchor. *c.* 1759–60. The British Museum

Fig. 11.6 Small pine-cone moulded jug (cover missing); rococo shell spout and handle, picked out in gilt; exotic bird decoration. Height 10.5 cm (4⅕ in). *c.* 1759–60. Mark: a Gold Anchor. The British Museum

decoration. Some pistol-butt dessert knife handles are known, and there are others moulded with fruit and leaves.

An innovation in the Gold Anchor period were the large handleless beakers, magnificently decorated in various ways, but especially by the use of coloured grounds, over which birds, flowers and figures were laid in chiselled gold. These may have been a variety of 'cabinet cup' made for display rather than use, such as are mentioned in the catalogue of 1761. Others advertised in 1759 were described as 'large Cabinet two handled cups and covers', apparently similar to the écuelles.

All-in-all, although the basic shapes of wares are not many in the Gold Anchor years, their decoration is of unmatched variety and magnificence. The main components inspired by Sèvres are the splendid ground colours, yellow, mazarine blue, pea-green, crimson and gold, to which were added chased and chiselled gilding in multitudinous designs and of a quality unmatched anywhere else in England.

Yellow, the earliest ground colour, generally thought to have been introduced during the Red Anchor period about 1755 (though a double leaf dish is recorded marked with the Raised Anchor, which has a yellow ground on the reverse),[2] was the least used at Chelsea, but it does also occur at Worcester. The 'inimitable Mazarine blue' as Sprimont himself described it in an advertisement of 1761, was first mentioned in the sale catalogue of 1756, and its production continued thereafter throughout the Gold Anchor period [see figs 11.2, 11.9–11]. Although called 'inimitable' it was itself an imitation, inspired by the 'gros bleu' of Sèvres, as much a copy as were the varying shades of rose and crimson introduced in imitation of the celebrated Sèvres 'rose-pompadour'.

In an advertisement in the *Daily Advertiser* of 12 March 1759 Sprimont 'begs leave to acquaint the Nobility, Gentry and others, that he intends, the beginning of April next, to sell by Auction, all his entire new Productions of the Chelsea Porcelaine factory… 'Among them were 'some Perfume Pots of the Pea-green and Gold, never exposed to Sale before…'[3] Green, if not pea-green, had been advertised in 1758: '… the much admir'd Purple, Green and Mazarine Blue heighten'd with Gold.'

Fig. 11.7 opposite, above Two vases in the form of carp. Height 17.1 cm (6¹¹⁄₁₆ in). No mark. *c.* 1760. The British Museum

Fig. 11.8 opposite, below Jug and basin, silver form (helmet jug) painted with flowers in gilt, gilt moulded-decoration reserves. Width of basin 34.8 cm (13¾ in), height of jug 20.9 cm (8¼ in). Mark: a Gold Anchor on basin. *c.* 1759–60. The British Museum

Fig. 11.9 left Oval dish, painted with birds in four reserves set against a mazarine blue border, with gilt flowering shrubs, and trellis work. Centre painted with a leafy spray, a scattered leaf and various insects. Length 31.8 cm (12½ in). Mark: a Gold Anchor. *c.* 1758–60. Private collection

Fig. 11.10 below left Teapot, narrow, angled shape, mazarine blue ground, floral gilding, delicate bird painting in reserves. Height 12.5 cm (5½ in). No mark. *c.* 1760–65. The British Museum

Fig. 11.11 above Cabinet beaker, mazarine blue ground and gilt, decorated with a scene of a couple with tambourine and parasol. Height 9 cm (3½ in). Mark: a Gold Anchor. *c.* 1765. The British Museum

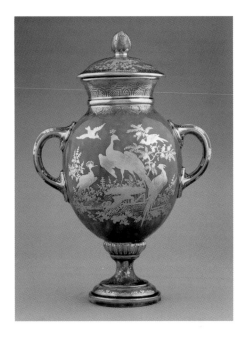

Fig. 11.12 Vase and cover, apparently unique turquoise ground colour. Gilt chinoiseries on one side, gilt birds on the other. Height 29.2 cm (11½ in). Mark: a Gold Anchor. *c.* 1759–60. The British Museum

Fig. 11.13 Pieces from the famous Thomson tea service decorated with a claret ground and polychrome figures playing musical instruments in reserves. Height of teapot 13.6 cm (5⅜ in). Gold Anchor marks. *c.* 1760–65. Victoria and Albert Museum London

Fig. 11.14 opposite, above Teacup and saucer, claret ground enriched with gilding; the swags of flowers in polychrome. Height of cup 5.1 cm (2 in), diameter of saucer 13.5 cm (5⁵⁄₁₆ in). No marks. *c.* 1760–65. Private collection

Fig. 11.15 opposite, below Plate with extremely rococo moulded border picked out in gilding, with pairs of vari-coloured dove-like birds in its three sections. Diameter 21 cm (8¼ in). *c.* 1760–65. Private collection

In the spring advertisement of 1760 colours mentioned are '… Mazarine Blue, Pea-green and Gold'; also '… a few pieces of some new Colours which have been found this year by Mr Sprimont, the Proprietor, at a very large Expence, incredible Labour, and close Application, all highly finished, and heightened with the Gold peculiar to that fine and distinguish'd Manufactory …'.

The new colours referred to were probably crimson and turquoise blue [see fig. 11.12]. Sky-blue (bleu céleste) was not introduced until 1771, after William Duesbury had taken control of the factory. One of the most justly famous examples of the use of crimson as a ground colour is the complete tea service with its original case which was bequeathed to the Victoria and Albert Museum by Miss Emily Thomson of Dover [fig. 11.13]. The teapot is of a shape that may be called 'the angled-barrel'; the lid is quite flat and flush with the top of the pot. Relief from this severity of form is, however, provided by the pierced rococo handles of both pot and lid and the rococo curves and scrollwork which support and decorate the spout. Spouts of teapot and milk jug and handles or knops throughout the service are white (but picked out in gilding), in contrast to the crimson ground colour of the pieces. Also contrasting are the white reserves which are surrounded with the most magnificent but wonderfully delicate gold trellis work, leaves and flowers done over the crimson ground. In the reserves are seated various Chinoiserie figures amidst flowers and foliage, while each figure plays a different musical instrument. These scenes are executed in polychrome enamels, with exquisite delicacy and skill.

The rich gilding on Gold Anchor Chelsea porcelain is thought to have been applied as an amalgam of gold ground finely and mixed with honey. It could be applied in varying thicknesses as required, and fired sufficiently to amalgamate the

mixture with the glaze on the surface of the porcelain. As Hugh Tait points out, gold was an expensive item,[4] and on the luxurious objects made at Chelsea in the Gold Anchor period Sprimont made lavish use of it, embellishing it even more with the most delicate tooling.

Shaped borders of coloured grounds with waved or cornucopia-like inner edges appear on Gold Anchor tea, coffee and dinner wares, and the gilding is superimposed in infinite variety – as scrolls, foliage, flowers, birds, or trellis work. Where the decoration includes panels of a coloured ground, gilt chased insets are added over the colour [see fig. 11.14]. Even the plainest articles have at least a gilt dentil edge, and where there is a moulded border, however intricate its rococo complexity, the details of the varied curves are all followed and sometimes hatched in gold [see fig. 11.15].

The Mecklenburg-Strelitz service [fig. 11.16], 'the very triumph of rococo art', is even today the best known of all Chelsea services, and has attracted attention from the time it was made. It was ordered by George III and Queen Charlotte in 1762 as a present for her brother, Duke Adolphus Frederick IV of Mecklenburg-Strelitz. Horace Walpole saw it on 3 March 1763, and strangely, did not like it. He wrote to Horace Mann the following day.

> ... There are dishes and plates without number, an épergne, candlesticks, salt-cellars, sauce-boats, tea and coffee equipages – in short, it is complete – and cost twelve hundred pounds! I cannot boast of our taste; the forms are neither new, beautiful nor various. Yet Sprimont, the manufacturer, is a Frenchman: it seems their taste will not bear transplanting – But I have done; my letter has tumbled from the King of Prussia to a set of china – *encore passe*, if I had begun with the King of Poland, *ce roi de faïence*, as the other called him. Adieu!

The service remained at Strelitz until the 1920s, though a few pieces 'escaped'. For instance, branches from the candelabra were secured by Lady Charlotte Schreiber in 1867, and are now in the Victoria and Albert Museum, and a dish from the service is in the Katz Collection. In 1948 the service was

Fig. 11.16 Dish from the Mecklenburg-Strelitz service. Length 27.4 cm (10¾ in). No mark. *c.* 1762–3. The British Museum

generously returned to the British Royal Collection by Mr James Oakes. Pieces from it were most recently exhibited in the Rococo Exhibition at the Victoria and Albert Museum in 1984.

The service is sumptuously decorated. Areas of white porcelain, which include the wells of plates and the centre area of dishes, are enamelled in colours with exotic birds and insects or with swags of flowers. On holloware, panels of mazarine blue alternate with the decorated white porcelain; on the borders of plates and dishes the coloured ground appears in shield-shaped reserves. In both cases the mazarine blue is decorated at random with gilt butterflies and moths. Everywhere raised scrollwork moulding is picked out in gilding.

In March 1764 a second service rather similar to the Mecklenberg-Strelitz was advertised as 'the same as the Royal Pattern which sold for £1150 Pounds', and as 'the last that will be made of the Pottery'. The difference between the design of the two lay chiefly in the fact that in the shaped moulding of the rims of flatware, the Mecklenburg-Stelitz service had a convex outer edge to the blue reserves, and in the second service these were concave. The second service was put on display by the 'Chinaman' Thomas Williams of St James's, before it was 'sent abroad'.

Plates and dishes with the Mecklenburg-Strelitz type of moulding are found with other kinds of enamelled decoration, but hollowares, tureens and sauceboats, as well as cruets and oil and vinegar stands, seem to have been made only for the original service.

On the whole, human figures were not much used as components of Gold Anchor decoration, and mostly appear on dessert services (though occasionally on tea wares), and in scenes on vases. Animals still occur as the protagonists of Fable decoration, often on such items as butter-dishes and stands, or large covered bowls. Landscape decoration is uncommon, apart from that executed in green, though late, plain punch-bowls are known with continuous polychrome landscape round them.

Although used much less often than flower painting, fruit painting of very fine quality is found on Gold Anchor porcelain. Cut fruit was often included in the arrangements; and the peeled fruit sometimes depicted in punchbowls seems as if it were ready for the concoction of the punch. Piled-up moulded fruit topped with knops in the shape of birds, form the lids of two little pots in the collection at Wallington Hall.

A service with Mecklenburg-Strelitz moulding, apart from the convex head to the panels of mazarine blue, and known as the Duke of Cambridge service after its most celebrated owner, is enamelled with fruit and insects. Vegetables were, however, not much esteemed or used as decoration on Gold Anchor pieces.[5] Birds, especially the exotic ones apparently related to pheasants or peacocks, appear in splendour on all kinds of Gold Anchor porcelain, and are usually painted with very great skill [fig. 11.17].

It seems convenient to include here mention of the decorating technique of engine-lathe or rose-engine turning, which appears to have had its earliest application to English ceramics at Chelsea. Knowledge of its use there was forgotten or largely overlooked until the publication in 1993 of Bernard Dragesco's monograph giving us new and important facts to do with Jacques Louis Brolliet, 'failed ceramic maker and industrial spy' and his observations about the manufacture at Chelsea.[6]

Brolliet's second visit to England, mentioned in Chapter 5, must have been an unwilling one, as he came back a prisoner of war, from Louisbourg in Canada, in the later months of 1758 and remained until 14 January 1759, when he managed to escape to France. However, it produced information of the greatest interest to Jean Hellot, the eminent French chemist.

Fig. 11.17 Pair of tall vases and covers, decorated with exotic birds. Height (including covers) 33.6 cm (13 3/16 in). Gold Anchor marks. *c.* 1768–9. Tullie House Museum & Art Gallery, Carlisle

Fig. 11.18 Pine-cone moulded beaker with a pair of rococo handles and matching *trembleuse* saucer, both painted with naturalistic fruit and mushrooms and a few sprays of insects. The beaker handles are picked out in turquoise; both rims are edged with brown. Height of beaker 8.4 cm (3⁵⁄₁₆ in), diameter of saucer 14.9 cm (5⁷⁄₈ in). Marks: a Brown Anchor with single down-pointed flukes on both pieces. *c.* 1760. Private collection

Fig. 11.19 Lobed plate with alternate engine-turned and floral-decorated panels on rim; exotic birds in centre. Gold-edged rim. Width 22.1 cm (8³⁄₄ in). *c.* 1760. Mark: a Gold Anchor. The British Museum

Hellot wrote to Jacques René Boileau, director of the Sèvres factory, on 3 February 1759 to recommend Brolliet as an employee, while Brolliet was actually staying in his house. Brolliet

> ... saw Chelsea porcelain being worked and can entice away from that factory the man Martin, a clever craftsman, who works on the wheel and the rose-engine, where he produces each day 1,000 to 1,100 cups which he later finishes. That workman is earning there one guinea a week.

This was nearly double the usual wage.

Rather than being 'enticed away' by Brolliet, Martin left Chelsea to work in Lambeth for a delftware maker named 'Jacson'. There was in fact a potter named Jackson there in 1759. John Mallet suggests, however, that Martin perhaps returned to Chelsea, or another turner was found, as Chelsea was still selling engine-turned wares in 1761.[7]

The engine-lathe or rose-engine enabled wavy, horizontal lines, or vertical patterning to be cut into wares with absolute regularity. Simple lathe turning was used only on unfired leather-hard wares, cutting away surplus clay with a tool to give a smooth finish. In work done with an engine-lathe the cutting tool did not move, but wavy, horizontal or vertical patterns were incised by reciprocating motion, bringing the object being decorated into and out of contact with the tool at regular intervals.

Wedgwood claimed in 1763 that he was the first to bring this process into use in the Staffordshire potteries,[8] but seems to have been quite unaware that it was in use at Chelsea from *c.* 1758.

John Mallet has identified two kinds of article on which engine-turning was used at Chelsea. The first consists of plates with a twelve-lobed border which carried alternate plain and engine-turned panels. The plain panels, smooth and hollowed by the engine-turner to be lower than the rose-engine turned ones, are painted with various individual multi-coloured birds; the others show delicate engine-turning beneath the clear glaze. Mallet noticed two examples of these plates (inv. C. 251 B & B – 1935) in the Victoria and Albert Museum in the late 1970s, and others have been recognized elsewhere since. He dated those in the Museum between 1756 and 1758. There is no trace of tin in the glaze; it is a pure glass, allowing the turned patterning to be clearly seen. Another similar plate in the Museum (inv. 2944–1901) must date from no earlier than 1759 as the rim is decorated with the 'Pea Green' enamel first mentioned that year in the sale announcement. It has the Brown Anchor mark used in Gold Anchor years on pieces without gilding. Two similar plates in the British Museum have both gilt rims and Gold Anchor marks.

Brolliet had also said that the Chelsea turner Martin could produce more than 1,000 cups a day with engine-turning, but very few are now known. One with a matching saucer, is in the Victoria and Albert Museum (inv. 2927 & A – 1901). 'Concentric engine-turning forms a band towards the rim of the saucer, and encircles the border of the cup's exterior, much like the basket-weave borders found on Meissen and that factory's European imitators.'

John Mallet concludes that Chelsea made a limited use of engine-turning between *c.* 1758 and about 1765, in other words, the earlier years of Sprimont's Gold Anchor porcelain-making.[9]

In an article published in the *Victoria and Albert Museum Bulletin*, vol. 1, no. 1, of January 1965, John Mallet pointed out that between *c.* 1750 and the mid-1760s the Chelsea factory chronologically produced vases in the various fashions and styles popular in the earlier half of the eighteenth century, from Kakiemon to the extremes of rococo, and culminating in 'the great showpieces of the 1760s, where Sèvres decor is applied to 'Chippendale' form.

A rococo influence can be seen in the ornate perfume pots of the Red Anchor

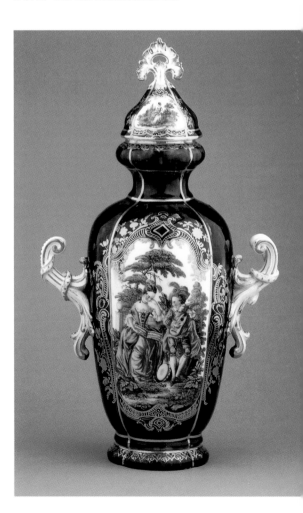

Fig. 11.20 Pair of beakers of Chinese form, with blue ground perhaps applied over the glaze. Height 17.7 cm (7 in). No mark. *c.* 1755. The British Museum

Fig. 11.21 Vase with Watteauesque gallant scenes. Underglaze blue and gilt. Height 34.2 cm (13½ in). Mark: a Gold Anchor. *c.* 1759–68. The British Museum

period, though it is confined chiefly to the ornamental curves on moulded bases, and to scrollwork on some of the pot-pourri containers and their covers. With Gold Anchor vases and lidded jars the basic holloware form is quite plain to be seen and makes a firm statement, but is amazingly embellished with extraordinarily flamboyant scrolling of feet and handles; on the pot-pourris with elaborate piercing of necks, shoulders, and covers; and of course always with brilliant gilding and sometimes with magnificent ground colours. To the basic fantasy is applied the finest painted decoration. The rococo scrolling, however lavish, is so contrived that panels on the sides of the jars are left clear for painted classical scenes, for simpler scenes of peasant life 'after Teniers', for pastoral figures in the style of Watteau, or for fantastic birds or massed realistic flowers. The last two forms of painted decoration are frequently set against a solid gilt background. The painted reserves are often bordered with exquisite gilt trellis work, shown to advantage on a brilliant ground colour.

Vases were issued in pairs, or in sets (known as garnitures) of three, five or seven, the sets being intended for display, usually on a mantelpiece or in some similar position. The central piece is always the largest, the others being of graduated size, and also of two different forms. In other words, a garniture could consist of two different-sized and differently shaped pairs, with a larger central vase. The subsidiary pairs are linked together by shape, the whole by ground colour and the decoration. It is usual for the decorative paintings to differ on the two sides of the vases, for instance on one side all may have classical scenes and on the other exotic birds on a gold ground. This was to enable the purchaser to vary his interior decoration as he wished, or if the vases stood against a looking-glass, to enjoy the decoration of both sides at once.

As a typical example of such a garniture of vases – if indeed such ornate pieces can be designated typical – one may cite the seven pot-pourri vases now named after one of their nineteenth-century owners, Lord Dudley. The garniture consists of a central ovoid vase flanked by two large pear-shaped vases, two vases of inverted pear-shape, and two smaller pear-shaped vases. Each has an elaborately pierced cover and neck, and scroll handles and feet. The painted decoration in the reserved panels on one side consists mostly of mythological scenes of a lightly amorous character, which are in several instances after Boucher; and on the other of peacocks and similar decorative fowl, rather than in the manner of Hondecoeter (1636–95).

This set of vases is one of the most elaborate known, magnificent in their crimson ground, stunning painted decoration and gold. They are traditionally said to have been a royal wedding present, ordered by George III for Lady Cope who was married in 1767.

Other magnificent pieces of Gold Anchor porcelain are listed in a Christie's catalogue for a sale which took place a few years later on Friday and Saturday, 10 and 11 February 1775, of pictures, china, etc. 'Late the Property of the Hon. Charles

Fig. 11.22 Chinoiserie pot-pourri vase (probably once had a cover), modelled as an urn over a furnace attended by three 'Chineses' and with Chinese-head handles. Height 21.3 cm (8²⁄₅ in). No mark. *c.* 1760. The British Museum

'Dillon'. Lots of 64–82 were a series of 'Select Pieces of Chelsea Porcelaine', interestingly described as 'designed by the late Mr Sprimont'. They included four pairs of vases, and several single ones. Lot 64 was 'An elegant vase of the *rich mazarine blue*, heightened with groups of *burnish'd and chas'd gold birds* and other decorations' and lot 71, 'a superb pot pourri vase of the beautiful crimson, painted in birds on a burnished gold ground'.

In his detailed paper on 'Chelsea Gold Anchor Vases'[10] delivered to the English Ceramic Circle in April 1998, John Mallet began by referring to the portrait group painted in oils by an unknown artist [see Frontispiece]. The picture has been given by him, and by others, a date of *c.* 1758–62, and identified as a portrayal of Nicholas Sprimont with his wife Ann and sister-in-law Susanna Protin, shown at about the time that he became sole proprietor of the Chelsea Porcelain factory. This suggestion is supported by the fact that Sprimont took out a fire insurance policy with the Sun Company for the factory, showing his own name alone, on 27 June 1760.[11] John Mallet also sees the picture as a vehicle for the display of various Gold Anchor vases of which Sprimont was particularly proud. In it he holds the jeweller's scales with which to measure the weight of gold to be applied to the vases, and the scene illustrates incidentally different stages in their manufacture and decoration. Mallet goes on to categorize the shapes in which such vases were made, and shows that several are in fact illustrated in the picture. The only completed vase shown is that held by Susanna – a fully gilded and decorated 'High square potpourrit'.[12]

Since only catalogues for the Chelsea sales of 1755 and 1756, and an incomplete one for 1761, have survived, and no Chelsea vase is actually dated, Mallet feels it is impossible to assign any vase to a specific date of manufacture. However, he lists the categories of basic design of the Gold Anchor vases as follows:

A   Chinese Forms and Forms Fairly Closely Derived From Them.
B   Other Non-Functional Vase Forms.
C   Pot-Pourri Vases ('Perfume Pots').

In the picture we see on the table top on the right a 'square jar' of pure Chinese shape, with its underglaze mazarine blue ground already applied. Beneath the table, and in reproduction difficult to see, between and behind the two other vases, is a tall, slender mazarine blue vase, with a cover very similar to the Chinese, though its knop and the vase handles are pure rococo. To the left, and a little nearer than the blue vase, is a lobed bottle with a pea-green ground and handles of mixed Chinese and rococo design. On a stool to the right of the picture is a large vase, still in the white, and either in biscuit or glazed, but not yet painted. There are hints of the Chinese in its form; one example at least is known which has panels with oriental figures painted in polychrome.

Fig. 11.23 Pot-pourri vase, cover and pedestal, with turquoise blue ground sumptuously decorated and gilded. Height with lid 42.8 cm (16⅘ in). No mark. *c.* 1765. The British Museum

Fig. 11.24 Rouleau vase with rococo handles. Six panels of alternate mazarine blue and white grounds, the latter painted with swags of flowers, the former decorated with flying gilt birds. Height 28.5 cm (11¼ in). No mark. *c.* 1758–68. The British Museum

Another basically Chinese Gold Anchor vase form, though not included in the picture, is that of the 'row-waggon', the tall rouleau vase of bottle shape, which sometimes has elegantly curved rococo handles added on either side. This form is often divided into sections by alternate upright panels of mazarine blue and white, the blue sometimes decorated geometrically in gold, the white in polychrome with designs often including flowers.

The table in the picture shows an openwork, lidded, four-footed pot-pourri jar near Sprimont's elbow, which is a form of considerable importance to the Chelsea factory, as John Mallet's article shows. He deduces from the 'weekly bills' of Chelsea between 1770 and 1773 (when the factory was run by William Duesbury in tandem with the Derby factory) that the pot-pourri jar is, in fact, what the bills refer to as a 'Vincent', i.e. Vincennes pot, being of the shape originally designed in silver by 'M. Duplessis', the French royal goldsmith Jean Claude Duplessis *père*, in the early 1750s for production at Vincennes, and after 1756 at Sèvres. Chelsea made several variations based on Duplessis' design.

The Seven Years' War began in 1756 and until it ended in 1763, as John Mallet points out, further French vases for copying at Chelsea (or anywhere else) would have been all but impossible to obtain. 'Ignorant of the neo-classical turn taken by much French design precisely during the War years, Chelsea continued to develop extreme tendencies in the rococo, no doubt under the delusion it was second-guessing the fashions of Paris.'

But amongst the stock sold off by Sprimont in 1770 (which could not have been made at Chelsea later than 1768) were at least three items that indicate that he was aware of rising neo-classical influence. These were 'one mazarine, blue and gold vase, with goats' heads', 'Satyr bottles', and 'small antique urns upon pedestals ... decorated with women's heads'. Examples of the first and second of these are in the Victoria and Albert Museum, and of the third at Colonial Williamsburg.

The copies of real paintings used as decoration on the Chelsea pieces were to some extent stock patterns, and the same scenes were reproduced on a number of vases. However, it should by no means be thought that because this was so the Chelsea decoration was therefore merely mechanical repetition. Artists of ability were engaged on the work; two whose names are celebrated for their ceramic painting, first at Chelsea and later elsewhere, are Zachariah Boreman and John Donaldson.

Zachariah Boreman is generally supposed to have been born in 1738, and would therefore have been about twenty-one when he married Sarah Burnett on 26 December 1759 at St James's, Westminster. They had at least eight children, all of whom were baptised at St Luke's, Chelsea, the eldest in 1760.[13]

The first indisputable evidence of his employment at the Chelsea porcelain factory, however, dates from a weekly wage bill, 1–8 December 1770, which lists him among the Chelsea workmen,[14] though Major Tapp[15] remarked that 'there are references to his employment at Chelsea in the Advertisers' Chronicle from 1767 to 1783.' (It has so far not been possible to trace this publication.)[16]

John Mallet thought that Boreman might not necessarily have 'been employed full time by Sprimont [since] Chelsea was becoming known as a place where artists could hope to pick up a living from other work, including teaching, and a few artists, including Richard Askew [later] worked only intermittently for Duesbury at Chelsea.'[17] From October 1770 Boreman at the Chelsea factory was paid a guinea and a half each week, the highest rate given, which increased to two guineas when *c.* 1784 he went on to Derby.

In 1794 Boreman returned to London, where he is said to have 'worked as an outside decorator at one of the London establishments. His work, executed in quiet tones, possesses a certain sober dignity. It was painted in the eighteenth century water-colour technique of glazing local colours over a monochrome foundation, possibly learned from Sandby.'[18]

A number of watercolours by Boreman are known, some dated between 1785 and 1787 which 'show that Boreman kept abreast of developments in landscape painting and drawing.' It is not clear whether they were painted as patterns for ceramic decoration, though some are of scenes which appear on Derby porcelain. However, none of Boreman's watercolours appear to have been formally exhibited, and he was not a member of any art society of the time. Only two documentary paintings of his on porcelain are known to exist.

Boreman died in 1810. Landscape painting was his forte, and on some of the more important Chelsea pieces he is thought to have been responsible for the background of scenes in which the figures were painted by John Donaldson.

Donaldson was a Scotsman, born in Edinburgh in the spring of 1739. He showed an early aptitude for painting, and produced some landscapes, but also figures and still-life subjects. From the age of fifteen he won several premiums offered by the Guild of St Luke, a society founded for the encouragement of the arts in Scotland. Franklin A. Barrett states that Donaldson was living and working as a miniaturist in London 'in 1760, having migrated there from his birthplace, ... at about that time. He was a well-known exhibitor of his work and lived at Princes Street, Leicester Fields.'[19]

James Boswell, the diarist, was acquainted with Donaldson, and records in his London Journal, 1762–3, on Friday, 4 March 1763, that 'Donaldson the painter drank tea with me. He reminded me of former days in Edinburgh ... Donaldson is a kind of speculative being, and must forsooth contravert established systems. He defended adultery, and he opposed revealed religion. I could not help being much diverted with his abusing Edinburgh and saying it was a place where there was no company ...'

Fig. 11.25 The 'Foundling' vase. Height 59.7 cm (23½ in). Mark: a Brown Anchor. *c.*1762. Victoria and Albert Museum, London

As an independent decorator Donaldson did some work for the Chelsea factory, and decorated some of Sprimont's most splendid vases with figure subjects. These were copied from several sources including works by Boucher, Watteau and Greuze. However, he apparently signed none of his work done for Chelsea, and only a few of the magnificent vases of Worcester porcelain decorated by him bear his monogram. It is now thought that he never actually went down to work at Worcester, but that the factory sent pieces to him to decorate in London.

Boreman and Donaldson, along with J.H. O'Neale, are thought to have been the best artists ever to work at Chelsea. Details of very few of the Chelsea artists or decorators have come down to us, but among this small number is the name of Richard Askew, associated with the scenes of cupids among clouds which are executed in *rose camaïeu* on certain Gold Anchor tewares, though he also apparently painted some other figures and birds.

A reference in a letter from Josiah Wedgwood to his brother John in London in 1765 refers to 'one Jenks who was a gilder in enamel at the Chelsea works … he wo^d perhaps tell you how (the gilding) is polished … for a little money. I believe it is neither a secret, or a very curious art, for women only are employ'd in it at Chelsea …'[20]

It has been suggested that Jenks, who like Boreman continued to work at Chelsea under the regime of William Duesbury, may have been the man responsible for much of the elaborate gilding on coloured grounds which was such a typical feature of the Gold Anchor period. As F.S. Mackenna commented, '… whether we are or are not correct in assigning it to Jenks (no other candidate for the honour can be suggested with equal conviction), its creator must rank as one of the most brilliantly clever ceramic artists of the eighteenth century.'[21]

Some of the vases of extravagantly rococo form had nevertheless restrained decoration, without any ground colour and with handles and scrolls picked out in colour and gilt instead. The Fable and figure painting ascribed to J.H. O'Neale usually occurs on such vases; and square-bodied, tapering vases after a Chinese form also frequently carry simpler decoration, which includes both bird and figure painting. Others are decorated with formal flowers; painting *en grisaille*, however, can be found not only on the plainest pieces but also on vases which are a riot of colour and gold.

Gilding was sometimes added in the form of a scale pattern over a ground colour, and sometimes used to give the impression of solid gold ornament by being painted over a moulded design, such as a satyr's head or vine leaves, against a coloured background. Figure painting in various sorts of gilt which was then chased and engraved in detail has already been touched on.

Other than the garniture of Dudley vases, the most celebrated examples made at Chelsea in the Gold Anchor years must be the two known as the 'Foundling' [fig. 11.25] and the 'Chesterfield' vases. The former was presented on 20 April 1763 to

the institution founded by Captain Thomas Coram for the relief of destitute children by an anonymous donor, who was in fact Dr George Garnier, Apothecary-General to the Army. The pair to it was owned at one time by the Earl of Chesterfield, and these two magnificent pieces are now reunited in the Victoria and Albert Museum.[22] They are of elaborate rococo design, having ovoid bodies with flared trumpet necks and domed covers, the knops of which are formed of gilt and white scrolls. The handles also are elaborately scrolled and picked out in gilding. The vases have a mazarine blue ground of superb quality, and in a shaped and gilt-bordered reserve on one side the 'Foundling' vase is decorated with a pastoral scene, 'Le Berger Récompensé', from an engraving by R. Gaillard after Boucher. The Chesterfield vase shows another scene from the same source, 'Le Panier Mystérieux'. On both vases the opposite side

Fig. 11.26 & 27 One of the pair of vases and covers known as the 'Cleopatra' vases, showing on one side (left) the *Death of Cleopatra*, after a painting by Gaspar Netscher (1639–84) engraved by J.G. Wilie (1715–1808), and on the other (right) exotic birds. Height 50 cm (19¾ in). 1762. The British Museum

Fig. 11.28 right Clock-case, one of a pair, decorated with a crimson ground colour, other enamels and gilding. The enamel clock face carries the name 'STRIGEL LONDON'. Height 43.8 cm (17¼ in). Mark: a Gold Anchor. *c.* 1760–65. Her Majesty Queen Elizabeth II

Fig. 11.29 below Table clock, the case in the form of a bunch of realistically coloured flowers, with the clock face set in a central sunflower. The enamel dial bears the clockmaker's name 'Fladgate'. Height 28 cm (11 in). Mark: a Gold Anchor. *c.* 1761. Museum of Fine Arts, Boston

is finely painted with exotic birds of brilliantly coloured plumage in a lobed and moulded reserve, richly gilt. The vases are each 59.7 cm (23½ inches) high, and marked with a Brown Anchor. Another pair of large vases with a mazarine-blue ground, elaborate gilding and panels decorated with scenes of the *Death of Cleopatra* and the *Death of Harmonia* and with exotic birds, which are in The British Museum [figs 11.26–7], were recorded as 'made in the year 1762 under the direction of Mr Sprimont'. They were presented to the Museum by an unknown donor on 15 April 1763.

Among other elaborate moulded and decorated items made in the Gold Anchor period are candlesticks, nests of toilet boxes [see fig. 12.4], plant pots of oblong *bombé* form; clock-cases [see fig. 11.28], some of fantastic shape, ornamented with porcelain figures; two surviving elaborate toilet mirror stands, and bouquets of porcelain flowers. A table clock-case, of which two examples are known, combines two of these items of production, since it is in the form of a bouquet of mixed flowers, with the clock face forming the centre of a sunflower. The example in the Paine Collection at the Museum of Fine Arts, Boston [fig. 11.29], was exhibited in London in 1984.[23]

Although a few figures made in the early Gold Anchor period were issued on simple mound bases, and others on plain oval or rectangular ones painted to imitate marble, the ornate type of base incorporating much gilt-decorated scrollwork which was sometimes elongated into supports soon became the most usual form. Although the underside of bases was glazed, an area round the under-edge often had to be ground free in order to get a level stance; here the naked bone-ash porcelain on many examples feels greasy to the touch. Ventilation holes are small and circular.

The Gold Anchor mark was usually placed on the base or at the back of a model, though it is occasionally hidden in the fold of drapery. On some miniature figures, toys or 'Cupids in Disguise', two conjoined anchors in red, brown or gold are used. In this case one of the 'Siamese' anchors may be in gold, the other in enamel. There was some reissue of Red Anchor models, especially among classical and allegorical subjects, but on elaborately scrolled bases and with complex floral bocages behind, for use as candle stands. Both Leda and the Swan and Venus with a Flaming Heart were treated in this way, as were the Red Anchor models of the Five Senses. The Four Quarters of the Globe, on the other hand, were produced in a new form

Fig. 11.30 A pair of Street Vendors, he with bottles, she with fruit and/or vegetables. Height of man 14.9 cm (5⅘ in), height of woman 14.6 cm (5¼ in). No marks. *c.* 1760. The British Museum

c. 1759. Here children with attendant animals, and wearing a classical form of dress, each represent one of the continents. The set must have been popular because it was copied at Derby, and continued in production there for many years.

The Monkey Band was reissued, but decorated with the brighter colouring and lavish gilding prevalent in the 1760s, and in the same vein a smaller 'Dog Orchestra' was produced, consisting of conductor, female singer, and musicians playing Pan pipes, French horn and the violin.

The 'Cupids in Disguise' appeared in a larger size than before, varying from 12.1–12.7 cm (4¾ to 5 inches) in height. Like the Monkey Band they have brighter colouring, and while some of the old models were reissued, a number of new ones appeared. 'Cupid as a Nurse maid, with a baby in a crib' and 'Cupid as a Water Carrier' with a bottle and glass and a tank on his back, are possibly among the more unusual.

Perhaps the most celebrated Gold Anchor figures are the series of so-called 'Ranelagh Masqueraders'. Their comparatively small and restrained rococo bases and lack of heavy bocage suggest that they were made quite early in the period, although some individual pieces with heavy colouring may be later in date. They are traditionally associated with the splendid masked ball held in Ranelagh Gardens on 24 May 1759, in celebration of the birthday of George Frederick, Prince of Wales. There are some fourteen different figures in the series; examples of eleven of them are in the collection at Colonial Williamsburg [see figs 11.32–3], two further models among the six once at Luton Hoo, and another illustrated by Frank Stoner.[24] One source which may have been used for these figures is a print of the Royal Birthday Ball at Ranelagh by Bowles after Maurer, although none of the porcelain figures corresponds at all exactly with those in Bowles' print. It is also a moot point whether they were really intended to represent the well-to-do in fancy dress rather than mountebanks or mummers. A figure somewhat similar to the porcelain flageolet player appears in a drawing of 1755 by Paul Sandby, where he is seen performing outside a tavern.[25]

The nine figures from this series which were exhibited informally, arranged as a crowd in real life, at the Rococo Exhibition at the Victoria and Albert Museum in 1984, were one of the highlights of that magnificent show. The whimsical clothes and vital attitudes allied to the individual characterization and brilliant colouring of each figure joined to give an impression of bursting, riotous life; one could sense the noise and music in the background. If these figures appeared for display 'at a desart', it must have been a virtuoso performance. They are all, both men and women, in the region of 20.4 cm (8 inches) in height.

Choice is almost impossible to make, but perhaps one should mention especially among the 'Ranelagh Masqueraders' the only two which form a natural pair, Jack-in-the-Green and his mate [fig. 11.32]. In the examples at Colonial Williamsburg he

Fig. 11.31 Figure of a Hunter/Musician blowing a horn, seated on a flowered stump. Height 12.6 cm(5 in). Mark: a Gold Anchor. *c.* 1760. The British Museum

half-leans against a flowering tree stump wearing no mask, but a jerkin of moulded overlapping feathers or leaves which are individually edged with turquoise. The collar and hem are trimmed with larger green leaves, and he wears a pointed feather or leaf hat. His knee breeches are rose-pink and his shoes yellow, with green leaf trim. His mate's bodice is feathered like Jack's jerkin, but nipped in at the waist and edged at the hips with a layer of pink and then a layer of yellow leaves. Her skirt seems to be of tawny satin, with an applied apron-garland of leaves and berries, and similar edging round the hem, while leaves and berries crown her head. With her left hand she holds a black mask over her face, her other arm behind her back, and she turns as she dances, laughing. If it were not an anachronism, one could see them as Papageno and Papagena in *The Magic Flute.*

The hopping or dancing stance is repeated in several of the figures, including those playing musical instruments. One of the most arresting of all is perhaps the lady who wears a drum at her waist and a trimmed tricorn hat at the back of her head over a headscarf [fig. 11.33]. She looks to her right with hands crossed over her breast, pulling round her a shawl loosely tossed over her jacket. A sword hangs from her belt on her left side. The example of this figure formerly at Luton Hoo has a puce coat, that at Williamsburg a yellow one. The former is perhaps more in keeping with her semi-military flavour.

The set of Apollo and the Nine Muses, a complete group of which are in the Bearsted Collection at Upton House, Warwickshire, are generally considered to be Joseph Willems' most notable achievement, and among the most impressive of Chelsea models, though their statuesque appearance is not perhaps so attractive as the lively, fantastic attitudes of the 'Ranelagh Masqueraders' [fig.11.34]. They stand nearly 40.7 cm (16 inches) high on detachable stands with *bombé* front and sides, which are decorated with flowers and butterflies, and rest on integral scrolled feet. The name of each figure is written in gold upon its respective stand. Two complete sets of these figures are recorded; and there is a single example of Clio in the Victoria and Albert Museum. An insertion in the *Daily Advertiser*, 13 April 1761, discovered by Mrs Valpy, gave notice that 'NORRIS and SHEPHERD, Jewellers, Goldsmiths, and Toymen, at the Crown and Pearl in Pope's Head Alley, Cornhill' were offering 'a most magnificent Set of the Muses on ornamented Pedestals of the Chelsea Porcelain, ... All of which will be sold for the most moderate Profits ...'[26] Notwithstanding, all writers on the subject agree with regret that the florid patterning of drapery and heavy use of gilding in this series go far to reduce the impact of the magnificent modelling.

The same can be said, unfortunately, of the large group of the Roman Charity (54.6 cm, 21½ inches high), one example of which is in The British Museum [fig. 11.35] and another in the Untermyer Collection. It is a dramatic representation of a dramatic story, and one of the most important of Joseph Willems' models. 'Un

Fig. 11.32 Figures of two Ranelagh masqueraders as Jack-in-the-Green and his mate. Height of male 20 cm (7⅞ in). Height of female 19.7 cm (7¾ in). Mark: an incised M beneath the plinth. *c.* 1759–63. Colonial Williamsburg Foundation, Virginia

Fig. 11.33 below Ranelagh masquerader as a *vivandière*. Height 21 cm (8¼ in). Mark: a single barb anchor painted in gold on the side of the plinth. *c.* 1759–63. Colonial Williamsburg Foundation, Virginia

Fig. 11.34 right Apollo and two muses from the complete set of Apollo and the Nine Muses. Height with base approx. 40.7 cm (16 in). *c.* 1759–60. National Trust, Upton House, Warwickshire

grouppe représentant la charité romaine' in terracotta was among the effects left after his death at Tournai in 1766. It was modelled from an engraving by William Panneels of a painting by Rubens, now in the Prado, Madrid. The subject is the saving by his daughter Pero of the aged Cimon, condemned to die through starvation in prison. On her visits she gave him her own breast milk. In 1770 the Roman Charity was offered 'either on a pea-green or mazarine blue detachable plinth, sumptuously gilded'. The largest of all Chelsea Gold Anchor figures is that of 'Una and the Lion', 66.1 cm (26 inches) in height. An example of this figure is also to be found in the Bearsted Collection. Both these models seem to be original in conception and owe nothing to Meissen.

Two uncommon models likewise in the Bearsted Collection at Upton House illustrate one of the twelve labours of Hercules: the slaying of the Hydra, with the assistance of Iolaus, who prevented the regeneration of its many heads by sealing the stumps with a red hot brand as Hercules cut them off; and Hercules in thrall to Omphale. Both groups are mounted on scrolled bases and have bocages; the one behind Hercules and the Hydra represents the Hesperides' tree with the golden apples on it. The Hydra itself was perhaps taken from a woodcut in Richard Topsell's *Historie of Four Footed Beasts and Serpents* which was published in 1608.[27]

A group of Perseus and Andromeda is more detailed than the version of the subject produced in the Red Anchor period. The ancient classical gods and goddesses represented in Gold Anchor porcelain include Jupiter in his chariot, Juno with her peacock, Diana, Minerva, Venus, Mars, and a river god rather unusually holding an oar or paddle.[28] This last figure is quite small, only 14 cm (5½ inches) high, and is on a modest circular base with only slight rococo scrolling, which suggests that it may be an early Gold Anchor, or even a transitional Red Anchor piece. An example is at Colonial Williamsburg.

The figure of Mars standing at ease by his shield with his helmet on his head is derived from Meissen, and is not unlike a similar figure in the early 'dry-edge' Derby production which also had the same original. At Chelsea, Mars is paired either with Venus and Cupid or with Minerva, and these paired figures are sometimes combined with candlesticks.

Figures representing the Four Elements were taken from Meissen models by Eberlein, which were perhaps originally inspired by garden statuary. They stand 21.6 cm (8½ inches) high, and the same models were also issued at Bow. Earth stands with a cornucopia full of fruit, and has a recumbent lion behind her. Fire (or Vulcan) is a youth standing by a flaming urn on a flower-bedecked plinth with a rising phoenix alongside. Air has wind-blown hair and drapery, and an eagle at her feet, looking up at her, while Water (or Neptune) pours a flood from a jar under his left arm. A giant dolphin behind him meanwhile spews water by his feet.

The Four Seasons appear in several different versions, one of which is a group of four putti beneath a tree on a mound base. The seasons are also represented by four pairs of putti, each pair with appropriate details and mounted beside a rococo candlestick. There are also two sets of adult seasons, both grouped in pairs. One set, the Allegorical Seasons, has Winter as a man in stocking cap and fur-lined boots skating beside Spring, a girl with a posy in her hand and an apron full of flowers. The pair to these are Summer as a girl with corn, her right hand on the shoulder of Autumn, represented as a gardener with fruit in his apron. These are large and splendid groups, about 31.8 cm (12½ inches) high, and date from *c.* 1765. Examples of both groups are in the Victoria and Albert Museum, and of Winter and Spring at Upton House.

Many other pastoral or semi-pastoral figures and groups are recorded, including harvesters, 'Sportsman and Lady', and elegant figures as 'Vendors', standing with open baskets beside them, intended to be filled with sweetmeats. But shepherds and shepherdesses in a wide variety are the most numerous of this class, their clothes decorated with elaborate patterns in brilliant enamels, and with an obligatory dog or sheep beside them. The grandest are the Imperial Shepherds on rococo scroll bases elaborately decorated with applied flowers and with a low, hip-high bocage. These figures stand 26 cm (10¼ inches) high, he supporting the stem of a crook with his left hand, she a basket of flowers beneath her right arm. In clothing smothered in patterns of dazzling colour and gold they are the epitome of the late, purely decorative phase of the Chelsea manufacture.

Fig. 11.35 Figure group, the Roman Charity. Height 53.3 cm (21 in). Mark: a Gold Anchor. *c.* 1763. The British Museum

Fig. 11.36 below Figure of John Coan, the 'English dwarf', dressed as a Yeoman of the Guard. Height 26.7 cm (10 ½ in). Mark: a Gold Anchor. *c.* 1761. National Trust, Upton House, Warwickshire

Fig. 11.37 opposite Figure group, the Dancing Lesson. Height 40.7 cm (16 in). Mark: a Gold Anchor. *c.* 1762–9. Museum of London

Two interesting and unusual figures of the Gold Anchor period are those of John Coan and David Gabarisco, the English and Prussian dwarves. These two figures were each listed three times in the 1761 sale catalogue. Coan is represented in the uniform of a Yeoman of the Guard, with the monogram of George III on his tunic. Beside him a large performing dog is about to lay the last letter of Coan's name upon the ground. John Coan, the Norfolk dwarf (1728–64), never grew taller than 96 cm. He was many times presented to royalty and was exhibited at Bartholomew Fair with Edward Bamford, the giant of Shire Lane. He had some dramatic talent, and acted and recited regularly at Tunbridge Wells Spa. During the last two years of his life, in which he suffered from premature senility, he must have been well known in Chelsea, since he was employed at the Dwarf Tavern at Five Fields to entertain customers. He died, aged thirty-six, on 28 March 1764.

David Gabarisco is represented in Cossack uniform, brandishing a sword, and with a severed head between his feet. His name is inscribed on the moulding of the base. Examples of the figure of John Coan are to be found in the Bearsted Collection at Upton House [fig. 11.36], and in the Royal Collection. An example of that of David Gabarisco is in the Untermyer Collection, Catalogue Fig. 56 (pl. 35).

Finally should be mentioned the two huge decorative groups of seated pastoral figures, the Music Lesson and the Dancing Lesson, though they were not intended as a pair. Both have a large and complex bocage in the form of a flowering tree. The Music Lesson is adapted from a Sèvres biscuit group by Etienne Maurice Falconet, which was based on the painting by Boucher of 1748. The subject of the boy with his arm round the girl's neck so that he can finger the stops of the pipe down which she is blowing was an exceedingly popular one and was reproduced on enamels, in fan painting and on Chinese painted mirrors, as well as in porcelain. The Chelsea Music Lesson stands some 38.1 cm (15 inches) high on an exceedingly elaborate terrace base which supports a dog and two or three sheep as well as the human figures. Two examples of the group are listed in the Chelsea sale catalogue of 1769, and again in 1770. One of them that year fetched £8 15s. A group of the Music Lesson is now in the Schreiber Collection at the Victoria and Albert Museum, another in the Untermyer Collection at the Metropolitan Museum of Art, New York, while a third is at Upton House.

One of only two recorded examples of the Dancing Lesson, again inspired by Boucher, whose original painting was engraved by Carle van Loo, is now in the Museum of London.[29] Here another elegant youth sits playing a hurdy-gurdy, while his companion helps a small dog dressed in jacket and trousers to stand upright and dance on the top of a marble plinth. The scrolling, applied flowers and incredible decoration are if anything more profuse than those on the former model. These two groups are perhaps the most elaborate ever produced at Chelsea, and were made *c.* 1765 [fig. 11.37].

One or two other large groups were made a little earlier, for instance 'a Fine groupe of a gypsy telling a lady's fortune under a tree, upon a rich gilt ornament foot' appeared in the sale catalogue of 1761. A rare undecorated group of George III, Queen Charlotte and a page, which is now in the Untermyer Collection may have been inspired by James MacArdell's engraving after portraits by Johann Zoffany, and was perhaps commemorative of the royal wedding in 1761. However, its attribution to Chelsea is now uncertain, since recent spectrographic analysis shows that the body contains no bone-ash, and the thick glaze shows unexplained traces of copper.

But of all the elaborate and colourful Gold Anchor porcelain, the most consistently successful groups are generally thought to be those incorporating figures from *Aesop's Fables*, or various animal subjects, mounted on gilt-scrolled bases, embellished with bocages, and issued as chamber-candlesticks.

Fig. 11.38 Fable candlestick 'The Selfish Ass'. Height 30.9 cm (12⅛ in). *c.*1765–70. Tullie House Museum & Art Gallery, Carlisle

Fig. 11.39 Fable candlestick 'The Dog in the Manger'. Height 32.2 cm (12⅝ in). *c.*1765–70. Tullie House Museum & Art Gallery, Carlisle

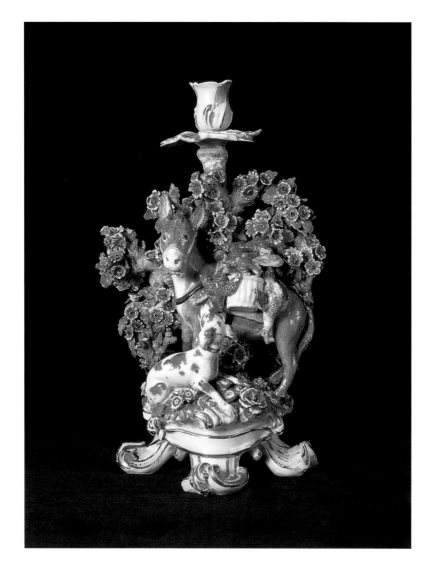

The Fable subjects seem to have been based variously on the 1666 and 1687 editions of *Aesop's Fables* which were illustrated with engravings by Francis Barlow. Among them are 'The Goat in the Well' (Fable LX), and 'The Fox in the Well' (Fable VIII). 'The Dog in the Manger' (Fable XXI) and 'The Ass Laden with Provender and the Starving Dog' (Fable VI) were apparently issued as a pair [figs 11.38–9]. In the Barlow edition of 1687 the Fables themselves were given in the rhyming version of Mrs Aphra Benn. These two are as follows:

An Envious Dog in a full manger lay,
Nor eats himself, nor to the Ox gives way,
Who griev'd reply'd – ah grudge me not that meat,
Which (cruel) thou thy selfe disdains to eate.

A sordid Ass, while on his back he bore,
Of chosen delicates, a plenteous store;
His courser Appetite with Thistles treats,
And starves beneath his load of nobler meats.

In fact, Mrs Benn rather missed the point of the second of these two Fables, which was, in contrast, that the Dog could not get at the provisions which the Ass was carrying on his back.

Other Chelsea chamberstick Fable models are 'The Foxes and Sour Grapes' (Fable XCIII), 'The Fox and Crow', 'The Tiger and Fox', 'The Leopard and Fox', 'The Maid Killing the Cock', 'The Dog with Stolen Meat', 'The Fox attacked by a Hound, while the Cat runs up a tree', 'The Fox attacked by a Dog and watched by a Hen', 'The Vain Jackdaw' and 'The Cock with a Jewel'. The two last mentioned have been attributed to the Chelsea-Derby period, but may be noticed here.[30]

The simple animal candlestick groups are also very pleasing, and include creatures such as pairs of rabbits, partridges, finches (all with bocages), and thrushes with fledglings in a cherry tree. Rather more dramatic are the 'Leopard attacked by two Dogs' paired with 'A Wild Boar attacked by Hounds'; fox and dog 'with game'; a 'Cat with a Dog' and a 'Leopard attacked by three Hounds' together with a stag, similarly assailed.

CHAPTER 12

Sprimont's Last Phase

From 1750 to 1759 Sprimont's dwelling was the house which formed the west wing of Monmouth House and was referred to in the Rate Books as 'formerly Mr Reid's'.[1] This can be deduced from an 'Indorsement' dated 18 January 1759 to a policy issued in January 1756 for Sprimont's household goods.[2]

Early in 1759, at about the same time that his pictures had nearly been sold to finance the undertaking, Sprimont left 'Mr Reid's' house and moved into the opposite part of Monmouth House, the factory warehouse. From then until the warehouse closure in 1765 he kept a lodging there, though at Lady-day 1762 to all intents and purposes he moved to Richmond, where his house 'on the Terrace' near the bridge overlooked the river.[3]

A note of uncertainty is detectable in Sprimont's newspaper advertisements in the early 1760s. In April 1761 there was a six-day sale of 'The last Year's Produce of the valuable *Chelsea Porcelaine Manufactory* ...' which, after listing a number of magnificent articles, concluded:

> ... The Proprietor N. Sprimont, after many years intense Application, has brought this Manufactory to its present Perfection; but as his Indisposition will not permit him to carry it on much longer, he takes the Liberty to assure the Nobility, Gentry and others, that next Year will be the last Sale he will offer to the Public.

The second Chelsea factory policy with the Sun Company was issued three months later on 4 July. It included Sprimont's own household goods at £400, and the warehouse stock at £2000.[4]

No sale was held in 1762. Mrs Valpy discovered a notice in the 'London' column of the *Daily Advertiser* of 24 February.[5]

N. Sprimont, Proprietor of the Chelsea Porcelaine Manufactory, having received large Orders in the Mazarine Blue and Crimson and Gold, it will

Fig. 12.1 'Warren Hastings' plate. Width 23.4 cm (9¼ in). Mark: a Gold Anchor. *c.* 1760. The British Museum

not be in his Power to complete his annual Sale till next Year, as he intended. [Amended 27 Feb. to '… as he intended, till next Year.'] He takes this Opportunity to assure the Nobility, Gentry, Merchants, etc. that it will be the last he will ever offer to the Publick, being obliged on account of the Continuance of his bad State of Health, to decline carrying on his Manufactory.

Nothing was heard for the rest of the year. This may have been the period when Sprimont was 'travelling about England' looking for some relief from his affliction; if this was the case, the factory itself evidently was not closed down.

On 7 January 1763 another notice was issued in the press, to say that Sprimont proposed 'to have a Sale sometime in March next, at Mr Burnsall's, in Charles-Street, Berkeley Square, of all the two last Year's Produce of his Porcelaine Manufactory … it will positively be his last Sale, being unfortunately obliged on account of his lameness, to decline carrying on the same …' The factory itself, both buildings and equipment, was also advertised to be sold 'and as he will retire farther into the Country, all his Household Furniture will be sold at the same Time.'

An insurance policy was issued by the Sun Company on 9 March for the Chelsea porcelain deposited 'in the Dwelling House of Mr Burnsall Auctioneer …'

Figs 12.2 & 3 Pair of cabinet beakers painted all over with flowers in natural colours against a gilt background. Height 9.4 cm (3¾ in). Mark: one on right has a Gold Anchor mark. *c.* 1760–65. The British Museum

which was valued at £4000,[6] a sum which confirms that two years' production was concerned, by comparison with the £2000 insured in the factory warehouse in July 1761. The eleven days which the sale lasted, 17–29 March, are also confirmation of this, as the sales of a single year's produce in 1760 and again in 1761 lasted only six days each.

On 25 October *Faulkner's Dublin Journal* noted that 'Mr Sprimont is not making any more [Chelsea China] on account of ill health.' The factory and Sprimont's furniture were, however, not sold in 1763 after all, and a new preliminary notice of their forthcoming sale next March was issued by David Burnsall in January 1764. A firm denial that 'his Royal Highness the Duke of Cumberland' was interested in purchasing the 'Porcelain Secret' was issued at the same time.

However, six weeks later, at the end of February, Mr Burnsall gave notice in several newspapers that 'on account of the present illness of MR SPRIMONT, the Sale of every Thing in general belonging to his Chelsea Porcelain Manufactory, as advertised to be sold in March next, must be postponed till he can be able to direct the same …' Whether this was true, or whether Sprimont simply could not bear to relinquish all connection with the factory, it is not now possible to decide.

Sprimont's ground landlord, Henry Porter, renewed the insurance policy on the little house at the corner of Justice Walk and Lawrence Street, however, on 16 May 1764.[7]

In 1764, 1765, 1766 and 1767 there were no annual sales, but small quantities of Chelsea porcelain continued to find their way to the public through general and dealers' sales, and the porcelain was often offered alongside other makes of china. In other words, a trickle was still leaving the factory.

A sensation occurred in April 1765 when M. Grosley in *A Tour to London* announced that the Chelsea factory had just fallen. This in fact referred to the closure of the old factory warehouse in Monmouth House, an event confirmed by the Rate Books.[8]

In 1765, the factory was not yet 'overthrown'. On 28 June a third factory insurance policy was issued to Sprimont by the Sun Company, in detail similar to that of 1761 with household goods, wearing apparel and the stock of china still housed on the factory premises, though now presumably in 'Mr Reid's House' instead of the Monmouth House warehouse.[9] After the closure of the double warehouse in Monmouth House, the opposite (western) wing (Mr Reid's house and the home of Nicholas Sprimont 1750–59) had become the warehouse, and was used as such until the middle of 1767. Its rating at only £19 throughout 1768 implied that the factory was indeed closed during the last year of Sprimont's ownership.[10]

The first rate for 1769 showed 'Mr Cox', jeweller and exporter of musical boxes, clocks and automata, as ratepayer for the little Corner Property, at the low rate of £10. By the middle of 1769 (second rate for the year recorded on 15 March 1770), the Corner Property was included with the 'Outbuildings', i.e., the factory, and rated at £36. Plainly production had started under James Cox's ownership. Mr Vere, the china dealer, the Indian King of Fleet Street, was at this time mysteriously paying the rate on 'Mr Reid's House'. He was apparently the last person known to have had charge of 'a book of entries bound in green vellum' which William Duesbury of Derby (to whom Cox passed on the factory lease in February 1770) particularly wanted to secure, along with the drawings, designs, models and accounts, but which had disappeared.[11]

Insurance policies offer evidence that Nicholas Sprimont invested some of his money in property. A Hand-in-Hand policy of 17 March 1766 covered five tenements belonging to him in St Andrew's parish, Holborn, for £300,[12] and in November 1770 he took over a policy issued by the Sun Company to Jonathan Jee, 'a Carpenter'.[13] This was for two houses in Gwyn's (or Gouyn's?) Buildings at the Angel end of the Goswell Road in Islington.

Early in April 1769 a preliminary notice of the sale of the Chelsea Porcelain factory, including equipment, remaining stock, and (the lease of) the buildings appeared in the *Gazeteer* and the 'London' column of the *New Daily Advertiser*.[14] The sale took place in the week beginning 15 May.

> Mr Burnsall offered to sell by auction … 'by order of Mr Sprimont … he having entirely left off making the same, All the curious and truly matchless Pieces of that valuable Manufactory; consisting of beautiful Vases, antique Urns, Perfume Pots, Table and Desert Services, Tea and Coffee Equipages, Compotiers, Leaves etc., beautiful Candlesticks of different Shapes; Variety of Figures, particularly two groups of the Roman Charity; Toilet boxes of various Forms and sizes and many other Articles, most highly finish'd in the Mazarine blue, Crimson, Pea-green and gold, finely painted in Figures, Birds, Fruits and Flowers, enriched with gold and curiously chased … N.B. Likewise will be sold all the fine Models, Mills, Kilns, Presses, Buildings, and all other Articles belonging to this most distinguished Manufactory …'

Evidently this notice caught the eye of the great potter Josiah Wedgwood, who wrote to his partner Thomas Bentley: 'The Chelsea moulds, models etc. are to be sold … There's an immense amount of fine things.' In July 1769 he wrote again: 'Pray enquire of Mr Thomas whether they are determined not to sell less than the whole of the models etc. If so, I do not think it would suit me to purchase. I should be glad if you would send me further particulars of the things at Chelsea.'

It has been doubted whether the sale of porcelain in May 1769 took place, as another advertised in almost identical terms was carried through in February 1770 by Mr Christie of Pall Mall. The priced auctioneer's catalogue for Christie's sale still exists, and the total raised was £1063 4s.

The articles in Christie's sale may have been those which Robert Boyer (who continued to work under Duesbury at Lawrence Street) said that Sprimont had removed from the factory to a room in the Cross Keys public house in mid-1769. If this is so, they could not have been the stock mentioned by David Burnsall in 1776. He stated that the cause of the sale of the whole stock and buildings in 1769 was ' … partly from the public being in great measure stocked with the kinds of wares, and partly from the fashion, or public humour, for making use of such kind of wares having abated.'

However, Mrs Chetwood (formerly Ann Sprimont) said that Nicholas Sprimont ' … did agree in the month of April 1769 to sell all the finished porcelain unto Thomas Morgan, then of Piccadilly, china dealer, for the sum of £525, and in the month of August following he sold to James Cox of London all his workshops, warehouses, fixtures, materials and utensils for carrying on the manufactory, for the sum of £600.'[15]

The sale of the remaining stock was corroborated by Susanna (Protin) Deschamps, Sprimont's sister-in-law, who gave evidence in the Exchequer suit *Chetwood v. Burnsall* in 1779.[16] She said 'that she had often been present when Nicholas Sprimont called in his chariot at the door of Thomas Morgan's in Piccadilly touching the purchase of the Chelsea porcelain in question; that he sold his remaining stock for £525; and that when he heard, afterwards, that Morgan had made a good bargain and sold it again for £900, he said he was glad of it.'

In the Exchequer document of 1776 in the case of *Chetwood v. Burnsall*, Ann (Sprimont) Chetwood described her former husband as 'a man of the most unsuspecting and benevolent disposition'. It seems in keeping with this that though he made money and died quite a rich man, money as an object in itself does not seem to have worried Sprimont unduly. Again, in the Chancery proceedings of 1772, David Burnsall said that Nicholas Sprimont once sold to Messrs Turner and Clewer 'nearly a roomful of porcelain for £500, without knowing the quality or particulars of the articles therein.' This may have been in 1760, when Thomas Turner succeeded Jerom Johnson as tenant of the former Chelsea China Warehouse in Piccadilly. Turner advertised his shop as the Old Chelsea China Warehouse; Sprimont firmly dissociated himself from Turner in an advertisement in the *Public Advertiser* in 1760.

That Sprimont was extremely proud of and very jealous of the reputation of his achievements in porcelain making is quite plain from the many advertisements which he issued during the lifetime of his factory. He and his wife Ann apparently had no children of their own, but there must have been at least some altruism as well as commercial sense in his foundation of 'a nursery of lads from the parishes and charity schools to learn the arts of designing and modelling'. Robert Boyer may have been one of the children thus educated. He said that he had been about eleven years old when he first knew Nicholas Sprimont, and was actually with Sprimont when he died.

It appears that, after all, Sprimont's collection of Old Masters was not disposed of in 1759, though the sale of the pictures had been much advertised. But twelve years later, and three months earlier, Nicholas Sprimont had at last consigned his picture collection for sale at Christie's, in a two-day sale held in Pall Mall, on Tuesday and Wednesday, 26 and 27 March 1771. A catalogue survives, marked up with the names of the buyers and the prices fetched. There were 173 lots and the total for the sale was £1,239; as Hugh Tait commented, this was 'more than double the figure that James Cox paid for the lease of the Chelsea factory in 1769.'[17]

Sprimont had sold his factory and ground lease to James Cox on 15 August 1769, and a fortnight later, on 31 August, he made his will. It seems as if in at last parting from his factory he accepted the inevitable. The will is quoted in full by F.S. Mackenna.[18] After five modest bequests to relations, the largest of which was £100 to his brother 'Jean Piers Sprimont of Liège, Jeweller', he left his wife's sister Susanna £1500. Ann Sprimont was residuary legatee. No explanation has ever been offered for the enormous legacy that Sprimont left Susanna. It could have been in grateful recognition of her assistance in setting up and running the factory, and perhaps in acting as 'house-mother' to the apprentice lads that the bequest was made. There is at least some evidence that she may have helped in this way. Alongside that of Henry Porter her signature appears as a witness on the apprenticeship indenture of Richard Dyer dated 7 February 1750/51, when Sprimont undertook to teach him the art of painting in enamel.[19] She was also one of the two witnesses who signed the lease to James Cox in 1769. We know from her own deposition in the Exchequer suit *Chetwood v. Burnsall* of 1779 that she had often accompanied Sprimont when he called at Thomas Morgan's china shop in Piccadilly; and in June 1771, about a fortnight before Sprimont's death, she gave evidence as one of his nurses that he was too ill to go to court in the case *Duesbury and Heath v. David Burnsall*. She ' … upon her Oath saith that she is Sister in Law to Nichs. Sprimont of Knightsbridge … Esquire and lives and now resides with him and had so done for several Years …' After Sprimont's death she married his friend Francis Deschamps, an upholsterer of Soho, who had a house at Petersham. It was in a tomb belonging to the Deschamps at Petersham that Nicholas Sprimont was buried.

Ann Sprimont married for a second time in April 1773. Her husband was 'John Chetwood Esq. Councillor at Law in Chancery Lane'. She may have met him in connection with the complex lawsuit over the disposal of the remaining stock of Chelsea porcelain at the time of the factory sale in 1769.

Francis Thomas, whom Sprimont employed as manager of the factory from 1752, and who, apart from Ann Sprimont's rather nominal co-operation, was in

Fig. 12.4 Nest of toilet boxes. Width of large box 14.5 cm (5¹¹⁄₁₆ in). *c.*1765. Private collection

control during the last years of its existence, seems to have been dishonest in his charge. In April 1769 Thomas apparently was instrumental in persuading Sprimont to sell the remaining finished porcelain to Thomas Morgan of Piccadilly for £525. As the Exchequer document of 1776 put it.[20]

> … your oratrix charges that the stock of finished porcelain was not bona fide sold to the said Thomas Morgan but was bought by him for the use of Francis Thomas and that the name of Thomas Morgan was only made use of to screen an atrocious fraud and imposition by Francis Thomas on the said Nicholas Sprimont. This stock was worth upwards of £2000.
>
> Your oratrix also shews that the said Francis Thomas died in the year 1770 and under his Will, David Burnsall, who was an executor, possessed himself of all the real and personal estate to the amount of £7000 and upwards …

It is known that Francis Thomas was in poor circumstances when he was first employed by Sprimont, having just failed in a small business. He had a wife and large family to support, yet without any other means of enriching himself, when he died he was worth more than £7000.

After Francis Thomas's death, his wife became 'disordered in her senses' and the suit was withdrawn in the Hilary Term 1772. Burnsall gave in, but William Duesbury had to bear the expense. Mrs Thomas later recovered and married again. From 1776 in one way and another the business dragged on for eight years or more.

CHAPTER 13

Duesbury and Company: Chelsea–Derby Wares and Figures

illiam Duesbury (1725–86), the son of a currier from Cannock, was born in Longton, Staffordshire, but by the documentary evidence of his accounts is known to have been running a decorating business for porcelain in London from 1751 to 1753. He married Sarah James of Shrewsbury, and their two elder children, William and Mary, were baptised at St James's, Piccadilly, on 5 January 1752 and 18 February 1753 respectively[1]. The Duesburys apparently returned to Longton later that year; and by 1756 William Duesbury was in partnership with the banker John Heath of Derby, for the manufacture of porcelain at Derby. China-making had already been going on in Derby for some years previously, financed by Heath and possibly conducted by the Huguenot Andrew Planché, but there is no evidence that Planché continued in the business after 1 January 1756. An agreement drawn up on that date which included his name as well as those of Heath and Duesbury was never signed: but 'W. Duesbury and Company' was the name of the firm which expanded into properties adjacent to the original Derby factory site on the Nottingham Road, east of St Mary's bridge, in April 1756. Nothing more was heard of Planché in connection with the porcelain works or Derby after July of that year.[2] Under Duesbury's regimen the Derby factory established itself firmly and began to expand. A description of a London sale of porcelains in the spring of 1757 was published in the *Public Advertiser* on 17 May, and in speaking of 'the largest Variety of the Derby, or second Dresden' sufficiently indicated Duesbury's aspirations.

The decision to purchase the lease of the failing Chelsea Porcelain factory from James Cox, whose hopes of running it had probably died with Francis Thomas, Sprimont's former manager, in January 1770, was an important one for Duesbury and Heath. Chelsea had always been their main rival, though admittedly it had also been an inspiration to them. Through its acquisition they were able to make use of the expertise and technical knowledge of Chelsea artists and workpeople, and to found a branch of the Derby business in London. The aristocratic and wealthy clientele with which Chelsea porcelain had long been associated could thus be transformed into patronage for the Derby factory, a process encouraged by Duesbury's opening of

Fig. 13.1 Two groups of putti as Elements (Fire and Water). Height of Fire 21.6 cm (8⅛ in). Height of Water 22.5 cm (8¹³⁄₁₆ in). *c.* 1773–5. Tullie House, Museum & Art Gallery, Carlisle

a London showroom in 1774. This was (like the first Bow warehouse in Cornhill), in a converted tavern. Duesbury took over the old Castle Tavern in Bedford Street, Covent Garden, which was very soon visited by King George III, and then on 23 July 1776 by Queen Charlotte. William Wood, Duesbury's agent in charge of the showroom, wrote to him at Derby about the Queen's visit.

> On Friday last her Majesty accompanied with the Duchess of Ancaster was pleased to honor with her presence Mr Duesbury's Ware Rooms in Bedford Street, Covent Garden. Condescended to express great approbation at these Beautiful articles of Derby and Chelsea Porcelain and Paintings and Encouraged the same by making some purchases.

The little documentation to do with the Chelsea Porcelain factory which has survived is concerned with these later years, and is, perhaps not surprisingly, preserved in the Duesbury Collection at the Local Studies Library in Derby. It consists largely of records of weekly payments made to the Chelsea workpeople from early in 1770 to 1773 inclusive; together with a number of bills for various items, ranging from hay and straw, bags of (bone) ashes, and saltpetre, to a 24-gallon cask of ale. The latter was ordered in February 1770, presumably so that William Duesbury's acquisition of the factory might be appropriately celebrated, though the bill for it was not settled until July 1771!

The records seem to show that, until the middle of October 1770 only five people were employed at the works and hardly more than a dozen at any time. Richard Barton was in charge, and he and Robert Boyer were then the senior workmen, capable of undertaking the various tasks of modelling, assembling (or 'repairing') and painting. Three men, named Roberts, Piggot and Inglefield, undertook the heavier manual work, which included loading and firing the kiln, working in the kiln house and mill, and attending to the horse. The horse presumably provided the power for turning the mill, which was used to break up clay for saggar-making,[3] and perhaps also to pulverize other materials.

Objects produced on the Chelsea premises mentioned in the accounts include a large number of seals of various designs, as well as vases, some figures of animals, and several types of perfume pot. It is noticeable that one variety of perfume pot (or pot-pourri jar) formed as a pigeon house was still in production in 1770, though the form was first recorded in the Chelsea catalogue of 1755. Perfume pots with a figure of Meleager or Atlanta likewise continued to be made.

From 13 October 1770 the workforce was increased by three important decorators, Mr Woollams or Wollams (the brother of Joseph Willems, the former Chelsea modeller, who had died at Tournai in 1766); Mr Jenks or Jinks, recorded at this date working on 'laying grounds';[4] and Mr Boreman, who had previously worked for

Sprimont and whose first job, in these accounts, was 'Painting a pair of Jarrs'. By February 1772 the name 'Gauron' had been added. This presumably refers to Nicholas-François Gauron, born in Paris in 1736, who became a modeller and worked first at Vincennes, then at Mennecy, and afterwards, at the age of twenty-one, became chief modeller at Tournai, 1758–64.[5]

It has never proved possible satisfactorily to attribute the porcelains produced during the Chelsea–Derby years, 1770–84. When he acquired the Chelsea works, where Chelsea porcelain had almost always been given a factory mark in one form or another, Duesbury had himself no tradition of marking his Derby porcelain. Receipt of royal patronage probably suggested the introduction of a mark in the form of a crown over a script D, usually painted in blue, though sometimes in puce. At the same time the well-known gilt monogram of a script D crossed with an anchor was probably already in use, and it is a moot point whether the D in either case stood for 'Duesbury' or for 'Derby'. John Twitchett, whose monograph *Derby Porcelain* (1980) is an authoritative work on that factory, gives it as his considered opinion that pieces from 1770 on marked with the anchor and D monogram in gold, or with a gold anchor, were decorated at Chelsea, while those marked with a crown over D were both potted and decorated at Derby. But he also feels that it is not easy to attribute Chelsea–Derby figures either to one factory or to the other. Some of those marked with a gold anchor may have been decorated at Chelsea, but if so, the decoration very closely follows the Derby tradition.

Fig. 13.2 Perfume vase and cover painted with a scene of the Trojan women carrying away the body of Polyxena, copied from a print by J. Leveau published in 1771. Height 43 cm (16⅞ in). *c.* 1771–3. Fitzwilliam Museum, Cambridge

Knowledge of the use of bone-ash as a necessary ingredient of a porcelain body soon spread from Chelsea to Derby, and typical Chelsea–Derby paste contains some 45 per cent of bone-ash. Although such a limited range of items seems to have been produced at Chelsea between 1770 and 1773, it seems certain that the manufacture of wares must have increased at Chelsea between 1773 and the end of the decade. That Duesbury continued Chelsea manufacture in the rococo manner of Sprimont for a while at least, is proved by the existence of an ornamental vase noted by J.V.G. Mallet which is marked with the Gold Anchor.[6] With its crimson ground, gilt-ornamented foot and elaborate handles, it accords entirely with the Chelsea fashion of the 1760s, but the classical scene of Vertumnus and Pomona painted in a reserve on one side is copied from an engraving not published until 1771.[7] Another rococo vase, decorated on one side with a scene of the Trojan women carrying away the body of Polyxena, was likewise probably made at Chelsea. It is now in the Fitzwilliam Museum, Cambridge [fig. 13.2].[8]

Whether made at Chelsea or at Derby, the services and vases of the Chelsea–Derby years at first followed the styles and techniques of Gold Anchor Chelsea quite closely [see, for instance, fig. 13.3]; though the plainer, simpler shapes of neo-classicism were introduced before long.[9] The tablewares of the 1770s include some of the most charming ever made, elegant in form and decorated in restrained

Fig. 13.3 Cherub or 'Fountain' vase after an engraving by Jacques Saly. Height 33.6 cm (13 3/16 in). Mark: patch marks and '19' incised. *c.* 1774. Tullie House Museum & Art Gallery, Carlisle

taste with looped floral swags, sometimes enamelled entirely in green, classical medallions *en grisaille*, and scattered coloured flowers. Length-wise brocade-like designs of wavy ribbons alternating with a line of leaves or flowers on pieces finished with simple gilt dentil edging are also characteristic, as are husk border patterns executed in black or grey, or green and gold. The use of coloured grounds almost entirely disappeared, and instead borders of a rich blue overglaze enamel, 'Smith's blue' (so named after Constantine Smith, head colourman at Derby in the 1770s, who developed it), in imitation of the Sèvres *bleu-de-roi*, were decorated with repeating designs in gold which were meticulously executed.

Classical urns of various forms provided one of the most popular and decorative motifs on Chelsea–Derby porcelain, and often appear, sometimes garlanded with roses or other flowers, in the centre of plates and dishes. The enamel colours used in all forms of decoration are much softer and sweeter than hitherto; a turquoise formerly in use at Derby was an improvement on the similar but more drab colour which Chelsea had earlier employed, and a turquoise ground, or one of gilt stripes, was frequently used on Chelsea–Derby vases. Meanwhile a Chelsea Indian red was introduced into the Derby palette. Moulded decoration of straight parallel fluting is sometimes found on Chelsea–Derby wares, and sometimes spiral fluting with the addition of fern-like fronds, which reach half-way up cups or bowls. Apart from these variations the surfaces of the wares are generally plain.

The Imari-type patterns, primarily executed in underglaze blue and overglaze red, green and gold, which later became so well known and successful as 'Derby Japans', first began to appear in the Chelsea–Derby years. Cherubs on clouds continued to decorate Chelsea–Derby wares as they once had Chelsea Gold Anchor pieces.[10]

Most of the figures made in the Chelsea–Derby period were probably produced by the Derby factory; a few that are marked with the gilt D intersected by an anchor may have been made in London, though some so marked are the products of Derby moulds. It seems safer to assume, as mentioned earlier, that the monogram D and anchor signify that the decoration in particular rather than the actual piece was executed at Chelsea.

Duesbury's first public sale 'of the last Year's Produce … of the CHELSEA and DERBY Porcelain Manufactories' took place on Wednesday, 17 April 1771 and the three following days, in Mr Christie's Great Room in Pall Mall. In the catalogue biscuit figures are listed for the first time. Porcelain figures made to be sold in the 'biscuit' or unglazed state, need to be finished to the highest standards, since there is nothing covering the surface to mask any imperfections. Nicholas-François Gauron, who had previously worked at Tournai, may have been the man who introduced the concept of figures in the biscuit to William Duesbury. Such figures were already being made at Tournai, and several of the Chelsea–Derby biscuit models – for instance, the four groups of putti representing the Elements [fig. 13.1] – were already known in Tournai biscuit porcelain. These particular groups were also made in enamelled form in the Chelsea–Derby era. The earliest version of 'The French Seasons' was made at Tournai by Gauron.

It was perhaps from Tournai that the characteristic Chelsea–Derby base, modelled to represent a pile of naturalistic rocks, was first derived. The plan of these bases is roughly circular, and they can be as much as 7.7 cm (3 inches) tall, but as the figures appear actually to clamber over them or to be informally seated on the rocky outcrops, the sense of a distinct supporting base is lost. All becomes part of the whole composition. Scroll bases were also used in the later part of the period, sometimes pierced so that they appear to stand on feet.

Nicholas-François Gauron left Tournai in 1764, and on 29 July 1765 received from the Government of the area (then ceded to the Hapsburgs and known as the Austrian Netherlands) an exclusive permit for thirty years to manufacture porcelain, faience, etc., but with the stipulation that only materials from the principality of Liège were to be used. He was associated with François Lefébrve, a wealthy Frenchman from Epernay in Champagne, in a factory established at Caronmeuse, Liège, and the undertaking is said to have made a very great quantity of wares. Nevertheless, Lefébrve, the principal proprietor, lost a great deal of money, and the factory went into receivership. Lefébrve blamed Gauron, who had apparently left, taking tools and some equipment with him. Gauron already had considerable renown as a modeller, and his most celebrated work at Tournai had been a magnificent biscuit and parcel-gilt group of eleven figures representing the Apotheosis of Charles d'Oultremont, Prince-Bishop of Liège. It is now housed at the Oultremont's château at Warfusée, in Belgium. Being the only documented piece of modelling by Gauron at Tournai, it offers a reliable basis for attributions of his work.[11]

In 1770 Thomas Morgan, the London china dealer, wrote to William Duesbury in Derby to say that he had been informed by 'Mr. De Viveur of Tournay ... of one Garon who he says is a very ingenious Modeller, who he says has infinite (other) merits than Sc(ulpting) gave me his direction at Bruxeles and when there I sent for him and find that if you can find him Employ he is willing to come to England ...'[12]

Although no reference to Gauron at Chelsea has survived earlier than 19–26 June 1773 among the Chelsea wage invoices now preserved in Derby Public Library, the item of that date shows that Gauron was then receiving a wage twice, and sometimes three times, as much as any other similar worker at Chelsea. Timothy Clifford suggests that as Christie's were in 1771 already selling models of figures in Chelsea porcelain comparable to those Gauron had made at Tournai, Gauron had indeed come to England in 1770, and had begun to work at Chelsea then. How long he continued to work for Duesbury has not been established, but no new models of Gauron type appear to have been produced by Duesbury after *c.* 1774.

Other grouped figures for which Gauron is thought to have been responsible,

Fig. 13.4 Figure of Charles Pratt, Baron (later Earl) Camden, as Lord Chancellor, after a model attributed to J. Bacon. Height 31.2 cm (12¼ in). Mark: a Gold Anchor. *c.* 1770–75. National Trust, Upton House, Warwickshire

though at one time it was suggested that Pierre Stephan was their modeller,[13] are those of putti representing 'Minerva crowning Constancy' and 'Hercules Slaying the Hydra'. Again the protagonists are represented as chubby naked children, and again the biscuit prototypes are found at Tournai.

Duesbury's figure models seem to have been marked with incised numbers beneath, to correspond with the numbering of a price list from about the time of the

Fig. 13.5 'Pensent-ils au Raisin?', group after Boucher of a shepherdess feeding a grape to a shepherd. Height approx. 22.9 cm (9 in). *c.* 1775. Museum of London

opening of the Bedford Street showrooms in London in 1774. Such a list, though unfortunately without a given source and undated, was published by John Haslem in 1876.[14] This list (and another published some twenty years later by William Bemrose)[15] does not include several models known to have been made between 1770 and 1773, among them the 'Minerva' group mentioned above, and the figure of Baron Camden [fig. 13.4]. From this omission it might be argued that these pieces could have been made at Chelsea, but many known to have been made at Derby were not included. Chelsea manufacture, however, might be suggested for the pair of early Chelsea-Derby chamber candlesticks in the Bearsted Collection at Upton House, representing the fables of 'The Cock and Jewel' and 'The Vain Jackdaw'. Each has two candle nozzles supported on flowering may-trees. The paste and the use of the bright overglaze 'Smith's blue' enamel on some of the plumage are pointers to Chelsea–Derby, rather than Gold Anchor, as the correct period of attribution.

The weekly Chelsea wage lists give positive proof that Nicholas-François Gauron was working at Chelsea in the early 1770s; but the other important modeller of the early Chelsea–Derby years, Pierre Stephan, the Frenchman who was chief resident modeller for the combined factories, worked only at Derby. Yet it is Pierre Stephan whose figure models have perhaps the truest flavour of the early Chelsea-Derby years. The use of a bone-ash paste deriving from Chelsea gave much more freedom for the production of large and elaborate figures and groups to modellers used to the more difficult body formerly employed at Derby; and this new paste in the hands of men trained on the Continent was worked into figures which were quite plainly inspired by the allegorical or pastoral productions of Sèvres. They are also redolent of the more superficial and sentimental ethos of the time [see fig. 13.5].

Typical of such pastoral fantasies is the group attributed to Stephan of a shepherd piping to a shepherdess beside a plinth on which a candle nozzle masquerades as a neo-classical urn. The whole is decorated in the palette of delicate, sweet colours associated with Chelsea–Derby production. An example is in the Derby Museum, another in the Bearsted Collection at Upton House [fig. 13.6].

Most common, however, and perhaps not surprisingly at a time of revived interest in classical art, were figures of the ancient Greek and Roman gods and goddesses, Juno, Jupiter, Minerva, Calliope, and, particularly, Eros in the guise of cupids and putti produced by the thousand. To Stephan are now credited a set of the Elements, and possibly the Derby version of the 'French Seasons' introduced *c.* 1770, at the time Stephan began to work there. The large group of 'Time clipping the Wings of Love' which derives from a painting by Rubens is also assigned to him. Stephan is likewise thought responsible for groups representing Prudence and Discretion, and Cephalus and Procris, as well as those of 'Two Virgins awakening Cupid', and 'Bacchantes adorning Pan'. All these models, also a gardener and companion, are mentioned in Duesbury's sale catalogue of 1771.

Fig. 13.6 Group of a shepherd and sleeping shepherdess near a fountain and an urn. Height 29.2 cm (11½ in). *c.* 1775. National Trust, Upton House, Warwickshire

Stephan was at one time thought to be the author of a series of figures of national heroes made at Derby, but this is now disproved. In later years he modelled small busts of Admiral Duncan and Earl St Vincent in feldspathic stoneware for the Herculaneum Pottery, Liverpool, two of which busts he signed. Figures of John Wilkes and General Henry Seymour Conway made at Derby were in fact reissues of earlier models of the 1760s, and so cannot be unequivocally attributed to Stephan.

Josiah Wedgwood, pre-eminent among the Staffordshire potters of the eighteenth century, and William Duesbury, the proprietor of the Derby porcelain factory, were extremely fortunate in that they could both call upon John Bacon (1740–1799), one of the foremost sculptors of his time, to provide them with designs and models for their respective manufactures.

As Timothy Clifford has shown,[16] Bacon had early come into contact with ceramic modelling when he was apprenticed at the age of fifteen to Nicholas Crisp, the jeweller and porcelain maker with premises in Bow Churchyard, Cheapside. From 1752–9 Crisp was a partner with John Sanders making porcelain at Nine Elms near Vauxhall. He was also a friend of William Shipley who founded the Society of Arts, and was one of the Society's earliest members. Such a beginning must have influenced Bacon, and through Crisp he could have met a number of influential people in the art and manufacturing worlds of the time.

In the mid-1760s Bacon set up as a stone carver and modeller on his own in Spitalfields, but in 1769 Mrs Eleanor Coade opened her Artificial Stone Manufactory in Lambeth. Bacon began to model for her, before long becoming her co-proprietor in the business. He is in fact credited with saving it from failure. A large variety of items were made there, not only architectural pieces such as ornamental keystones, plaques and balustrades, etc., but 'an immense variety of items from candelabra to wine coolers, from altar tables to clock cases'.

Some objects were available in plaster at a cheaper price, and provided first-class original models at little expense for other manufacturers. Wedgwood, by 5 June 1777, had bought models of Bacchus, Apollo, Andromache and Companion, and the Four Seasons, all supplied by Bacon 'from plaisters we bought near Westminster Bridge', i.e. at Mrs Coade's Manufactory.

When William Duesbury of Derby bought the Chelsea porcelain factory in 1770, it must have been partly in order to capitalise on Chelsea's great reputation. Timothy Clifford lists three categories of style for Chelsea–Derby productions, whether figures, groups or ornamental wares. They were either reissued from the old Chelsea rococo moulds, or modelled in the 'French Taste' by Pierre Stephan and Nicholas Gauron, or else produced in the new, neo-classical style by a very distinguished unnamed modeller. Vases, ewers, lamps, pedestals and a few figures appear to have been in production for the opening of the Chelsea–Derby showroom in London. The unnamed modeller may have been Bacon.

There are a few surviving papers to show that he was supplying the factory with models between July 1769 and February 1771, but unfortunately individual pieces are not described. The judgement of Bacon's style as compared with some of the Coade productions is all that can be relied on. A class of rare Derby figures including Baron Camden and an Admiral, who may be Keppel, or Duncan, are, however, very similar to some of Bacon's monumental sculptures. Timothy Clifford particularly mentions the statue of Henry VI (1786) in the Ante Chapel of Eton College, and that of Judge Blackstone (1784) at All Souls, Oxford. He concludes that it is apparent from a letter of 23 April 1787 preserved in Derby Public Library, and written by the London agent of the Derby factory, Joseph Lygo to William Duesbury the younger, that Bacon had provided models for the factory, but by then no longer did so. However, Bacon's influence continued at both Wedgwood's and at Derby through the employment of various younger modellers who had been trained by him.

Almost all Chelsea–Derby figure models were probably made at Derby, and any other contemporary modellers who can be named are known to have been working at Derby and not at Chelsea. During the Chelsea–Derby years, like water sinking into sand, the tradition and style of Chelsea gradually faded and died away so that ultimately all was overlaid by the Derby influence. The Chelsea factory as an individual note in the harmony of English porcelain-making was effectively silenced on the day that Nicholas Sprimont relinquished his proprietorship, 15 August 1769, though its echoes could be heard for almost another fifteen years.

William Duesbury's ground lease on the Chelsea factory ran out in 1780; but was renewed for one year, and then again for three years.[17] Between 1771 and May 1784 he had held eight London auction sales of the 'Produce of the Derby and Chelsea Porcelaine Manufactories', and three, in 1778, 1779 and 1783, at which only porcelain actually made at Chelsea was apparently sold. Besides porcelain, the catalogue for the sale of December 1783 included all the factory buildings and fixtures, as well as a quantity of artificial stone figures, various moulds, old plaster and five or six tons of 'chalk-stones'. On 17 May 1784 and the following six days was held the final sale including both Chelsea and Derby porcelain. Before this, however, on 18 February 1784, Robert Boyer had already written to William Duesbury the famous letter which records the final destruction of the Lawrence Street factory:

Lawrence Strt., Chelsea, Feb[y] 18th 1784.

Sir, – I Wright to Inform you how we are pretty forward in the pulling Down of the buildings at Chelsea. I think a little better than a fortnight they will all be down to the ground and Cleared of the primeses, wich I shall be glad to my hart; for I am tired of it ...[18]

CHAPTER 14

Fakes, Forgeries and Collecting

Fig. 14.1 Figure of a crouching leveret after the model illustrated opposite. Twentieth century, probably made at Torquay, Devon. Sotheby's

Fig. 14.2 Figure of a leveret. Length 10.2 cm (4 in), height 7.7 cm (3 in). Chelsea Raised Anchor period, 1750–52. Private collection

In a paper on 'Reproductions and Fakes of English Eighteenth Century Ceramics' which was published in 1939,[1] Wallace Elliot, one of the founder members of the English Ceramic Circle, gave detailed definitions of what he understood by the terms 'reproduction' and 'fake', as applied to English eighteenth-century ceramics.

A reproduction, he said, was 'a copy of an original 18th century piece of porcelain, earthenware or stoneware made with the intention of deceiving, or likely to deceive, an intending purchaser'; while he defined a fake as any piece of eighteenth-century ceramic which has in some way been added to or altered, with the intention, fraudulent or no, of increasing its value as an object for sale. He qualified these terms by adding that they referred only to pieces made or altered after the date of c. 1862, about which time eighteenth-century English wares began seriously to be collected. This of course enabled objects decorated in the eighteenth century outside their factories of origin by independent workshops to be excluded: the chief consideration is whether pieces were made or changed more recently in order to extract greater sums of money from collectors.

Reproductions, Wallace Elliot considered, were either made complete, or in some cases had a later, added, mark. Fakes, however, needed a more complicated definition, and he listed six variants. Of these the first three are concerned with genuine eighteenth-century pieces either originally plain white, or with simple decoration (e.g. underglaze blue) or with more decoration; all of which have had extra overglaze decoration and sometimes marks as well, spuriously added. His fourth group comprises nineteenth-century pieces with false decoration and again sometimes false marks, added in eighteenth-century style.

The fifth group consists of continental-made pieces of any period which were complete when produced, to which spurious

English eighteenth-century marks have been added. In some cases, the original mark was removed either by acid or by means of a file.

Wallace Elliot's last group is the one which, sixty years and more after he defined it, is the most likely to be disputed today – genuine English eighteenth-century pieces which have been damaged and restored. Since he wrote, the number of collectors has grown so much and good and interesting antique ceramics have become so scarce and therefore so expensive, that there can now be very few private collections of eighteenth-century wares which do not include restored pieces. Methods of restoration have greatly improved, and nowadays sale room catalogues mention the fact if objects they offer have been restored. Prices adjust themselves accordingly, and as a collector one would feel indignant indeed to be told that one's cabinets held nothing but a collection of fakes.

So far as Chelsea porcelains are concerned, reproductions have certainly been made which match Wallace Elliot's first definition, i.e. reproductions which are complete in themselves. Some of these copies may also be included in the fifth class of fakes, by removal of the maker's mark and the addition instead of a spurious Red or Gold Anchor. Perhaps the best known of all Chelsea reproductions are the imitations of Gold Anchor figures and candlesticks made in the nineteenth and earlier part of the twentieth century by Messrs Samson of Paris, who copied items from several English factories and even made spurious models of their own in similar styles. I have in my possession a charming figure of a lady, copied in fact from Watteau's *Embarkation for the Island of Cythera*, with the Derby Crown and crossed batons mark in red. But she is not composed of any kind of soft-paste English porcelain, or even of bone china; she is formed of a good class continental hard paste. The qualities of these imitative figures are now more appreciated, and Samson productions are collected in their own right, but a glance at the originals will immediately make plain the gulf between Chelsea and Samson.

The firm of Edmé Samson was founded in 1848, and originally merely enamelled porcelain which had been bought in the white from other contemporary factories. Emile Samson, the founder's son, expanded the business, and between 1870 and 1913, when he died, reproductions were produced not only of eighteenth-century English porcelain figures, but of faience and oriental and European useful wares as well.

The moulds for Samson's figure reproductions were taken directly from the originals, so that his copies are always slightly smaller. The hard-paste body and the glaze used are of

Fig. 14.3 Rabbit tureen and cover. Length 36.9 cm (14½ in). Red Anchor period, *c.*1755. Chelsea Porcelain. Fitzwilliam Museum, Cambridge

course quite different from the eighteenth-century English soft-paste porcelains and lead glazes. Enamels sink into an eighteenth-century glaze; on the Samson copies they stand out, glossy, on the surface. The firm claimed to have put its own marks on all its productions, but this is certainly not the case. The spurious Gold Anchor is sometimes used, but frequently there is no mark at all.

It was the showy Gold Anchor figures, so much appreciated in Edwardian drawing-rooms, on which the firm concentrated particularly, for example, copies of a shepherd and shepherdess of *c.* 1765, with elaborate rococo scrolled bases, half-bocages and heavily coloured and gilt clothing. One of the most elaborate Gold Anchor Chelsea productions, the Dancing Lesson, was in the Samson repertoire, as were simpler and meaner copies of some of the Fable candlestick groups such as the 'Cock with a Jewel'. In candlesticks the bocages of the originals are often reduced to a mere wreath of leaves, and the bases are much simpler and flatter than the Chelsea ones, though more exact and therefore expensive copies were also made.

Samson et Cie also reproduced figures made at Bow and at Derby, some of the latter being marked with a spurious Gold Anchor, since early in the twentieth century their originals were still mistakenly thought to be Chelsea.

The Gold Anchor is also used on figures made in a pseudo-eighteenth-century style which bear no relation to any known genuine models; these were made at Sitzendorf in Thuringia. Recently small hard-paste porcelain Staffordshire-type animal models of sheep or cats on rectangular bases, also marked with a Gold Anchor, have appeared on the market, but they could hardly be expected to deceive anybody. Such pieces probably also come from German factories. Copies in hard-paste porcelain of 'Girl-in-a-Swing' and Gold Anchor scent-bottles which seem to be slightly *larger* than the originals must be among the more recent continental reproductions (or fakes).

On all the pieces so far mentioned the garish enamels and brassy gilding are far removed from the quality of genuine Chelsea. However Chelsea manufactures were copied in England as well as on the Continent [see fig 14.1], and among the best known of these reproductions are those of the Goat-and-Bee jugs made at Coalport in the early part of the twentieth century. To anyone familiar with the Chelsea Triangle paste they should pose no problem, since they are made of a bone china which has a colourless translucency and does not show the lighter 'pinholes' to be seen in true Triangle porcelain. Their surface appears very white, without the warm glow of early Chelsea, and the glaze often extends over the base, which on originals shows the bare porcelain. On genuine Goat-and-Bee jugs any Triangle mark or inscription was

Fig. 14.4 Rabbit tureen and cover in imitation of the one opposite. Twentieth century. Sotheby's

incised by hand while the paste was soft, and the burred edges can be plainly seen. Triangle marks on faked pieces were impressed, and sometimes even appear to have been scratched on after the piece was fired, so do not show the rough-edged grooving of a genuine piece.

On decorated Coalport Goat-and-Bee jugs the colours are more garish than on the originals, and the bee, which is usually over-large, is sometimes given the black and yellow stripes of a wasp. Details of the goats also help to distinguish the genuine from the spurious. Chelsea goats have short horns and upturned tails, and the flowers in the moulding have convex-formed petals. The opposites pertain to Coalport. The Coalport factory also reproduced some of the Gold Anchor vases. Once again the body employed should be a pointer to origin.

Spurious Red Anchor plates, made by no one knows whom, are identified by the uncharacteristic paste of which they are made, as well as by bad or unsuitable decorative painting, and sometimes by a Gold Anchor on a supposed Red Anchor piece.

About 1911 a rare, possibly unique, Raised Anchor figure of a young Dr Baloardo, from the Italian Comedy, was repaired by a restorer in London. It was bought by Mr and Mrs Sigmund Katz, and is now with the pieces from their collection in the Museum of Fine Arts, Boston. After they had purchased it, not long before the beginning of the First World War, several reproductions of the figure appeared in the salerooms. The original is of the beautiful Raised Anchor period paste, and stands 28.6 cm (11¼ inches) high, but the copies are in a phosphatic soft paste and measure only 24.2 cm (9½ inches) in height. These forgeries required knowledge, skill and money to manufacture; the perpetrator obviously felt that his expenditure of all three would nevertheless bring in a worthwhile return. But because of the outlay required, such good quality even if incorrect forgeries are fortunately rare.

Another early piece reproduced by a firm which was active in Torquay, Devon over forty-five years ago is a Dancing Girl of the 'St James's' type. This figure was made of a phosphatic semi-porcelain, and decorated in a similar manner to an original issued in the white and coloured in recent times. Again this is an example of a rare model, which the perpetrator hoped would pass to an unknowledgeable collector for a very high price.

It must by now be obvious and should be emphasized that any would-be-collector of English eighteenth-century porcelain must do his best to become acquainted with the differences between hard paste, soft paste and bone china. The knowledge is essential, but it takes time to acquire, and since one must handle the pieces, it cannot be learned in museums. Viewing days at the sale room, friends, and among these particularly a kind and reputable dealer, are all of the greatest importance in the acquiring of this knowledge. A true dealer is not only someone who buys and sells porcelain. A dealer and an individual collector can become real friends over the years, and appreciate each other as such. A dealer can observe which way a collector's interests are turning and draw attention to pieces which are likely to suit an individual collection, or warn against a tendency which seems to be mistaken. In the larger sale rooms nowadays it is wise to allow such a dealer to bid on one's behalf, both to save running up the price, and to preserve anonymity.

To collect Chelsea porcelain is not cheap, but neither need it be an impossible extravagance. It is still possible to acquire examples of each of the Chelsea periods, even marked examples, and a small amount of damage, a crack or a chip, does not necessarily spoil the effect of a piece on display, though it may reduce the price to one more easily afforded. It is wise to know the aims of one's collecting at the outset; wares are less expensive and more easily obtainable, whereas figures, especially many of those of the Red Anchor period, are now not only rare, but extremely highly priced. But however few the pieces that can be afforded – even if only a single item – the collector nevertheless has the thrill of possessing something which comes from the earliest days of English porcelain manufacture, made at the most prestigious factory of eighteenth-century England, and can feel directly in touch with the excitement, worries and perseverance of the man who was instrumental in founding it, Nicholas Sprimont.

Appendices

I Names associated with the Chelsea Porcelain Factory

Modellers
Flanchet
Gauron, Nicholas (Snr.)
Gauron, Nicolas (Jnr.)
Harrop, Joseph?*
Harrop, William?*
Nollekens?
Willems, Joseph

Painters
Abbot, Thomas (possibly the same as J. Abbot)
Askew, Richard
Banfield, James?
Banford, James
Billingsley, William, Sen.ʳ
Boreman, Zachariah
Brown, William
Duvivier, Fidele?
Duvivier, Joseph
Duvivier, William
Dyer, Richard
Ferg, Paul, Jnr.
Jinks, or Jenks, –
Lefebre, J.
Lenthall, Rose
O'Neale, J.H.
Snowden, –
Welch, James*
Willems, –
Withers, Edward

Potters
Barton, Richard
Boyer, Robert
Martin (turner)
Parr, Samuel*
Phenix, Robert*
Simpson, Aaron

Workmen
Inglefield, –
Mason, Alfred*
Pavett, Henry*
Piggott, –
Roberts, –

Others
(Early period c. 1744–53)
Briand, Thomas (chemist)?
d'Ostermann (chemist)
Gouyn, Charles (1st proprietor)?
Sprimont, Nicholas (proprietor in middle period with Sir Everard Fawkener)
Supply, Anthony (chemist?)

(Middle period c. 1753–69)
Abbott, J. (witness to Sprimont's will, August 1769)
(Abbott, Margaret)
Betts, Nathaniel
Brunsall, David (London auctioneer)
Duvivier (draughtsman)
Fawkener, Sir Everard (2nd proprietor with Nicholas Sprimont, who was 3rd proprietor from 1758)
Ford, Richard (London auctioneer)
Jones, Jenkyn (accounts)
Lagrave, Andrew (arcanist?)
Mead, William (arcanist?)
Porter, Henry (1st ground landlord)
Porter, Isaac (2nd ground landlord)
Protin, Susannah (later Deschamps)
Sprimont, Ann (née Protin)
Taylor, Margaret (witness to Sprimont's will, August 1769)
Thomas, Francis (factory manager)

(Late period 1769–84)
Cox, James (4th proprietor)
Duesbury, William (5th proprietor)
Ross, Charles (3rd ground landlord)

*Also worked at Bow

II Some museums in the British Isles with Chelsea Porcelain in their collections

Alton, Hants: Allen Gallery (Hampshire County Museum Service)
Barnard Castle, Co. Durham: Bowes Museum
Bath, Avon: Holburne Museum of Art
Bedford: Cecil Higgins Art Gallery
Birmingham: Birmingham Museum and Art Gallery
Bristol: City Museum and Art Gallery
Cambridge: Fitzwilliam Museum
Cardiff: National Museum of Wales
Carlisle, Cumbria: Tullie House Museum and Art Gallery
Cheltenham, Glos: Art Gallery and Museum
Derby: Museum and Art Gallery
Doncaster, S. Yorks: Museum and Art Gallery
Dublin: National Museum of Ireland
Edinburgh: National Museums of Scotland
Exeter, Devon: Royal Albert Memorial Museum
Glasgow: Glasgow Art Gallery and Museum
Hastings, E. Sussex: Hastings Museum and Art Gallery
Horsham, W. Sussex: Museum
Hove, W. Sussex: Museum and Art Gallery
Ipswich, Suffolk: Christchurch Mansion
Lincoln: Usher Gallery
Liverpool: National Museums and Galleries on Merseyside
London: The British Museum, Museum of London, Victoria and Albert Museum
Maidstone, Kent: Maidstone Museum and Art Gallery
Manchester: Manchester City Art Gallery
Newcastle upon Tyne: Laing Art Gallery
Northampton: Central Museum and Art Gallery
Norwich: Norwich Castle Museum
Nottingham: Nottingham Castle Museum and Art Gallery
Oxford: Ashmolean Museum
Plymouth, Devon: Plymouth City Museum and Art Gallery
Preston, Lancs: Harris Museum and Art Gallery
Rotherham, S. Yorkshire: Clifton Park Museum
Salisbury, Wilts: Salisbury and South Wiltshire Museum
Sheffield, S. Yorkshire: Sheffield City Museum
Stoke-on-Trent, Staffs: Potteries Museum and Art Gallery
Truro, Cornwall: Royal Cornwall Museum
Warrington, Cheshire: Warrington Museum and Art Gallery
Wolverhampton, W. Midlands: Bantock House Museum
Worthing, W. Sussex: Museum and Art Gallery

Some American Museums

Birmingham, Alabama: Museum of Art
Boston, Massachusetts: Museum of Fine Arts
Charlotte, N. Carolina: Mint Museum
Cleveland, Ohio: Museum of Art
Indianapolis, Indiana: Museum of Art
New York: Metropolitan Museum of Art
Providence, Rhode Island: Rhode Island School of Design
San Francisco, California: M.H. de Young Memorial Museum
San Marino, California: Huntington Art Gallery
Washington, D.C.: Smithsonian Institution
Williamsburg, Virginia: Colonial Williamsburg
Winterthur, Delaware: Du Pont Museum, Winterthur

Some Australian Museums

Launceston, Tasmania: Queen Victoria Museums and Art Gallery
Melbourne: National Gallery of Victoria
Sydney: Art Gallery of New South Wales
Sydney: Museum of Applied Arts and Sciences

Some Canadian Museums

Toronto: George R. Gardiner Museum of Ceramic Art
Toronto: Royal Ontario Museum

Notes

Chapter 1

1 Preface to the *Description of Strawberry Hill* (1784).
2 *Court and Private Life in the Time of Queen Charlotte: Mrs Papendiek's Journals* (London 1887), i, 181. Discovered by Geoffrey Wills, quoted by Bevis Hillier (London 1968), p. 81.
3 The French Protestants were followers of John Calvin (1509–64), but the beginning of the Wars of Religion in 1562 heralded the beginning of their persecution. In 1598 Henry of Navarre, who had himself been a Protestant but who had to abjure his faith in order to ascend the throne, signed the Edict of Nantes which guaranteed the Huguenots freedom of worship in France.
4 Young 1998, p. 37.
5 Mallet 1984, p. 237.
6 Hillier 1996, with new findings on Dr Anthony Supply and John Offley.
7 Hillier 1996, referring to *Roll of the Indian Medical Service* by Lt-Col D.G. Crawford (London 1930), p. 247.
8 Hillier 1996, quoting Consultation of 1 February 1705, Records of Fort St George, *Diary and Consultation Book of 1795* (Madras 1927), p. 15.
9 Guildhall MS 8674, vol. 66, p. 141. Policy 3320. 12 September 1744.
10 *Publications of the Huguenot Society*, vol. XXVII, p. 110.
11 The British Library, Lansdowne MSS no. 829, fol. 21.
12 Mountford 1969, pp. 88–90.
13 John Wedgwood papers. City Museum & Art Gallery, Stoke-on-Trent.

Chapter 2

1 There has been some confusion between Nicholas Sprimont and his older *cousin*, Nicolas-Joseph (brother of Jean-Joseph Sprimont) in the works of various authorities, but the matter is settled by reference to the inscription on Sprimont's tomb at Petersham, Surrey, where his age is given as fifty-five years. This corresponds with a birth date of 1716.
2 Society of Genealogists, Register of Apprentices. Discovered by E. Benton (Benton 1976), p. 56.
3 E.C.C. *Trans.*, vol. 2, no. 6 (1939), p. 27 *et seq.*
4 Christopher Garibaldi and Helen Jones, paper read to the Silver Society, June 1997.
5 Young 1999, p. 35.
6 E.A. Jones, *The Old English Plate of the Emperor of Russia* (Letchworth and London 1909), pl. 49, no. 1, p. 100.
7 J.A. Rouquet, *Present State of the Arts* (London 1755).
8 Monmouth House was possibly let to Sprimont by Sir Everard Fawkener, whose relative, James Chase, had built it *c.* 1704.
9 Mackenna 1952, p. 9.

Chapter 3

1 Guildhall MS 8674, vol. 66, p. 141. Hand-in-Hand Fire Insurance Policy 3320.
2 Middlesex Deeds Register 1753 Book 2, no. 535. Greater London Record Office.
3 Legge 1984, p. 22.
4 Austin 1977, item no. 7.
5 Glendinning and MacAlister 1935.
6 Mallet 1984, cat. 03, p. 244.
7 Glendinning and MacAlister 1935, pl. XVIIb.

8 Mackenna 1948, pl. 13, figs 31, 32.
9 Hackenbroch 1957, pl. 3, fig. 5.
10 Clarke 1959, p. 50, pl. 20b.
11 Mackenna 1948, pl. 14, fig. 33.
12 These teapots are at The British Museum. A second guinea-fowl teapot is at Colonial Williamsburg, Virginia.
13 Mackenna 1948, pl. 15, fig. 36.
14 Mallet 1984, cat. 05.
15 A less sophisticated version of this group is also known in the St James's ('Girl-in-a-Swing') class and is in the National Museum of Ireland.
16 Chaffers 1965, vol. II, p. 302, and Wills 1959, fig. iii. Two cream jugs of the strawberry leaf (or acanthus) moulding, which carry the underglaze blue crown and trident mark, are recorded. One, at Colonial Williamsburg, is undecorated; the other has flower sprays and insects enamelled in colours. This example was item no. 207 in the *E.C.C. Exhibition Catalogue* (1948), and was sold by Christie's on 20 October 1986, lot 136.
17 Gilbert Bradley has kindly drawn to my attention five inventories of ceramics belonging to the Earl of Bristol (probably kept at Ickworth) of which three are dated 1767, 1768 and 1775 respectively. Copies of the lists were sent to Mr Bradley by the late Richard Kilburn and the originals are kept in the P.R.O. ref. C103 174 Pt. 1 Earl of Bristol.
The list for 1767 includes an amount of blue and white Chelsea porcelain:
Chelsea porcelain
Blue and White Plates 35, 17 broken
A Blue and White Sugar Dish
A Cover to Ditto
Blue and White Saucers, 3.
Blue and White round Comport Plates 6
Blue and White Desert Plates 12. All broken.
18 Sold by Sotheby's, 18 April 1967, lot 112. Two Goat-and-Bee jugs with their bases streaked with blue and manganese are also known.
19 Legge 1984, pl. 16.
20 Mallet 1967 (reprinted 1971, with revisions and the addition of fig. 6A).
21 Baker 1997, pp. 223–5.
22 William Salt Library, Stafford, MS 4788.

Chapter 4

1 E.C.C. *Trans.*, vol. 7, pt 3 (1970), p. 160.
2 The Rate Book entries can also be taken to suggest that Mr Supply died in the autumn of 1750, as after December 1750 he is always referred to there as 'late Mr Supply'.
3 Hilary Young (Young 1999, ch. 6, note 35) points out that parallels between St James's modelling and the plasterwork of Bartholomew Cramillion, carried out in Dublin in 1755, were noted by Bernard Watney (Watney 1972b, p. 821). Young adds that in the light of suggestions that St James's figures were modelled by an amateur 'it is interesting...that a Mrs Anne Gouyn "At Mrs Carnsu's, Hosier, Piccadilly", had artistic aspirations and exhibited "Two pieces of flowers, cut in card" at the Free Society in 1763'.
4 Lane and Charleston 1962, p. 111.
5 Shaw 1829, p. 167. Facsimile reprint, Beatrice C. Weinstock, Great Neck, New York 1968.

Chapter 5

1 It is generally considered that he probably made not porcelain but white salt-glazed stoneware. This was first drawn to my attention by Miss M. Macfarlane, former Keeper of Ceramics for the Hampshire County Museum Service. It was published in an article, 'The Clay Industries of Oxfordshire and Oxfordshire Potters', by Nancy Stebbing, John Rhodes and Maureen Mellor, included in the Oxfordshire Museum Service's Publication No. 13, 1980.
2 Valpy 1994, p. 325.
3 B.C.V. Caen, Manuscript in-quarto, 171, vol.1, folios 127vo–130vo.
4 Actually written by Hellot in brackets.
5 Frank Britton, *London Delftware* (London 1987), records William Jackson at the Norfolk House pottery, Lambeth, 1747–62.
6 Valpy 1983, extracts from the *Daily Advertiser*, 1747–1956, p. 198.
7 Westminster Public Library, MSS D.438 and D.540.
8 Drummond's Bank customer ledgers (DR/427), The Royal Bank of Scotland Archives, Regent's House, 42 Islington High Street,

London N1 8XL. Material from the archives of Drummond's Bank is published by courtesy of the Royal Bank of Scotland.

9 Gouyn's will was proved on 12 January 1785.

10 Sun Assurance, Guildhall MS11936/138:83790, 15 July 1761.

11 Cox 1980, p. 202.

12 Valpy 1990, p. 110.

13 Lane and Charleston 1962.

14 Another 'Winter' is in the Museum of London: and an identical figure in the white seated on part of an Ionic capital and produced purely as an ornament, was shown some years ago at a meeting of the English Ceramic Circle.

15 Mallet 1977, pp. 222–5.

16 Adams 1981, p. 24.

17 Synge-Hutchinson 1968, pp. 96–8.

18 Watney 1972b, p. 821.

19 In the Kulturen Museum, Lund, Sweden.

20 Foster 1967, pp. 284, 287.

21 Mackenna 1948, p. 54.

22 Mackenna 1970, pp. 46, 47, and fig. 83.

23 Sotheby's, 18 April 1967, lot 111, and 6 May 1969, lot 117.

24 Illustrated by Dr H. Bellamy Gardner, *Antique Collector* (August 1938). Katz Collection, Museum of Fine Arts, Boston, Mass., USA.

25 Klaber 1984, p. 70.

26 Watney 1968, p. 63.

27 Watney 1972a, pp. 226, 227.

28 Godden 1985, p. 48.

Chapter 6

1 Benton 1976, pp. 54, 55.

2 Adams 1981, p. 27.

3 See Chapter 8.

4 Guildhall MS 11936/133:176294, 27 June 1760, Sun Assurance policy.

5 GL Record Office, Middlesex Deed Registers, 1750 (Book 3), nos 49 and 50; and Guildhall Library MS 8674/89, 72516, p. 25, 10 May 1751. Nicholas Sprimont was the tenant.

6 Formerly among Sir Thomas Phillipps' MSS at Thirlestone House, Cheltenham. Quoted by the Earl of Ilchester in 'A Notable Service of Meissen Porcelain', *Burlington Magazine* (October 1929), pp. 189–90.

7 10 November.

8 It is interesting in this connection also, to note the remarks made by John Campbell in the *Political Survey of Great Britain* (London 1774), vol. 2, p. 18, where he discusses the porcelain manufactures of Bow, Worcester and Chelsea. 'If we reflect on the short space of Time in which these several Attempts have been made, and how far they have already advanced, notwithstanding the capital Obstacle in their Way, by which I mean the moderate price of true China, and the Necessity imposed thereby of selling cheap in order to force a Market. If at the same Time we remember that these difficulties were encountered in the very Infancy of these several Manufactures; which however were carried on without any of those public Encouragements which were given to the Establishments in other Countries, we need not surely despair of seeing a successful issue to this important and now promising Undertaking.'

He added that 'The high Price of (Chelsea) Ware was the sole Objection to it, and yet the Sale at these Prices afforded little profit.'

9 See Charleston and Mallet 1971, pp. 113–15.

10 Mackenna 1951, p. 15.

11 Public Record Office, Kew, Prob. PCC 11 922 1–280.

12 Westminster Public Library, MS D. 520.

13 Guildhall MS 11936/106:141089, Sun Insurance policy. 'Henry Porter at the Chelsea Porcelaine Warehouse in Pall Mall Dealer in Carpetts'. Stock £200. 30 May 1754. Catherine, daughter of Henry and Ann Porter, born 4 December and baptised 8 December 1752 at St George's Church, Hanover Square.

Chapter 7

1 The lead content of the Raised Anchor paste is about 0.55 per cent, alumina about 6 per cent. Other ingredients remained much the same: silica at 65 per cent, lime at 25 per cent, soda and potash together at 4.3 per cent.

2 Legge 1984, cat. no. 23, ill. p. 32.

3 On the other hand, a set of Japanese beakers *c.* 1700 at Burghley House were provided with matching *Chelsea* saucers.

4 Described in Chapter 2.

5 Chinese blue-and-white porcelain 'bowl-shaped jugs' with a small pointed spout were sold at Christie's, Amsterdam, The Nanking Cargo, 28 April-2 May 1986, lots 4066–4130.

6 King 1922, pl. 19, fig. 1.

7 Illustrated in Mackenna 1948, pl. 28, no.62. These were probably decorated later.

8 Mackenna 1948, p. 37.

9 At the International Ceramics Fair, Dorchester Hotel, London, 1986.

10 Mackenna 1948, p. 37, and pl. 29, no. 63 (square bottles). Two small flat extremely translucent porcelain scent-bottles, moulded and faceted in imitation of glass, and with delicate Kakiemon-type decoration, are illustrated in Bryant 1925, pl. 1 nos.1 and 3, and by him attributed to the Raised Anchor period. However, they are now thought to have an affinity with the earliest Bristol/Worcester productions, although scientific analysis shows that the body is a 'glassy' soft-paste porcelain, containing neither soapstone nor bone-ash.

11 References in John Bowcock's Memorandum Book 1756 (The British Museum, Dept of Medieval and Modern Europe).

12 Frank Tilley (*Antique Collector*, March–April 1947, pp. 65–7) thinks these figures may have been inspired by Löwenfinck's work on Meissen porcelain *c.* 1730. The second jug is noted by Dr Paul Riley, E.C.C. *Trans.*, vol. 12, pt 2 (1985), p. 109.

13 Mackenna 1948, pp. 34, 35.

14 Mackenna 1948, pl. 25, fig. 55 and pl. 27, fig. 59.

15 Riley 1985, pp. 110, 111.

16 Two saucer dishes with shaped edges, each 11.5 cm (4.5 inches) in diameter and decorated respectively with the fables of the Wolf and the Crane, and the Wolf and the Lamb, said to date from the Triangle period 1744–9, were sold by Sotheby's from the Selwyn Parkinson Collection (lots 115 and 116) on 21 June 1966.

17 King 1922, p. 42 and pl. 30.

18 See Chapter 12.

19 Bradshaw 1981, p. 86.

20 Watney 1972b. Watney believes it to have been copied from the head of a full-length plaster figure of a male infant, examples of which were probably in use as sculptors' models at the time.

21 Zorka Hodgson, 'Chelsea Boy's Head after Francois Duquesnoy-Il Fiammingo', E.C.C. *Trans.*, vol. 15, pt 2 (1994), pp. 184–9.

22 Lane 1961, p. 61.

23 A Chelsea group of two goats, 16.5 cm (6.5 inches) wide, marked with a raised Red Anchor, and thought to be painted in the workshop of William Duesbury, was sold by Christie's on 20 October 1986, lot 140. Their white coats have black and brown patches, and the shaped oval rockwork base has raised coloured flowers applied and is painted with moss. (See fig. 7.36.)

24 Bradshaw 1981, appendix B, pp. 290, 291.

25 C. Vecellio, *Degli Habiti Antichi e Moderni di tutto il Mondo* (Venice, 1590), pp. 269, 270.

26 Baker 1997.

27 An example of the Rose-seller in the white is in a private collection in Melbourne, Victoria; and another with polychrome decoration is in the Museum of Fine Arts, Boston, Mass.

28 Bradshaw 1981, pl. 23, p. 95.

Chapter 8

1 F. Tilley, *Antique Collector* (March–April 1947), p. 65, fig. 1. Mackenna 1951, p. 20 and pl. 4.

2 Mackenna 1951, p. 67.

3 Quoted by J.C. Austin (Austin 1977), p. 12.

4 The 1755 catalogue is reprinted in full by W. King (King 1922) and by J.C. Austin (Austin 1977). The catalogue for 1756 was reprinted by R.W. Read, *A Reprint of The Original Catalogue of One Year's Curious Production of the Chelsea Porcelain Manufactory Sold by Auction by Mr Ford* (Salisbury 1880) and by G. Savage (Savage 1952).

5 See T.H. Clarke, 'Das Northumberland Service aus Meissner Porzellan', *Keramos* 70 (October 1975), pp. 9–92, and 'Pachyderms among the Peonies', *Country Life*, vol. CLXXVIII, no. 4601 (24 October 1985), pp. 1178–80.

6 Catalogue, *Treasure Houses of Britain* (Washington D.C. 1985), Board of Trustees, National Gallery of Art, no. 420, p. 484. Another Boar's Head tureen is in The British Museum, yet another in the Campbell Collection at

Winterthur Museum, Delaware.

7 Now in the care of the National Trust.

8 The Japanese name for this person was Shiba Onko.

9 Illustrated by Mackenna 1951, pl. 10.

10 Tilley 1957, colour pl. E.

11 Austin 1977, no. 54.

12 Austin 1977, no. 55.

13 Gerald Coke, *In Search of James Giles* (Kent 1983), pp. 4–7.

14 Part of another, later, edition exists, formerly in the Tapp collection. A photocopy is in the Victoria and Albert Museum.

15 Honey 1977, p.42.

16 Honey 1977, p. 44 and pl. 8D.

17 Mackenna 1951, pl. 53.

18 Sotheby's sale of *Rous Lench Collection*, vol. 1, lots 213 and 214, 1 July 1986.

19 *Rococo: Art and Design in Hogarth's England* (Victoria and Albert Museum, 1984), cat. D6.

20 Honey 1977, pl. 80.

21 P.S. Hutchinson, 'Sir Hans Sloane's Plants', *Connoisseur Year Book* (1958), and 'G.D. Ehret's Botanical Designs on Chelsea Porcelain', *Connoisseur* (October 1958).

22 Pl. II *Abrotanum humile*, pl. IV *Acacia*, pl. VII *Acanthus*, pl. XXXVII *Anonis*, pl. XXXVIII *Anthemis*, pl. XL *Antholyza*.

23 It may be of interest to note that Philip Miller occupied the west wing of Monmouth House, just north of the Lawrence Street factory, and formerly Sprimont's home, in 1771 and 1772.

24 Preserved among the Daniel MSS at the Spode factory, Stoke-on-Trent.

25 Hist. MSS Comm. of the Earl of Charlemont, pp. 311, 312, 313. See Watney 1981, pp. 48, 49.

26 Valpy 1984, p. 79.

27 A yellow ground part tea service, *c.* 1760, is in the Bearsted Collection, Upton House, Warwickshire. The other examples given are in the Paine Collection, Museum of Fine Arts, Boston, Mass. See Austin 1977, no. 71, p. 82, note 1.

28 Austin 1977, no. 76. These jars were formerly in the collection of Frank Hurlbutt, and then in that of F.S. Mackenna.

29 An example of this clock-case is illustrated in Blunt 1981, pl. 10, no. 119.

Chapter 9

1 Bradshaw 1981, Appendices A, B, C, D.

2 R. Blunt, *Country Life* (14 February 1925), quoted by Dr H. Bellamy Gardner (Gardner 1928), p. 18.

3 A shop famous for the sale of luxurious trifles ('Toys') such as snuff boxes, gold and silver small wares, enamel goods made in South Staffordshire, or London, china ornaments, etc. kept 'At the Sign of the Golden Door over against Suffolk Street' Charing Cross, at least from 1731 by Paul Daniel Chenevix and Mrs Chenevix. He was of Huguenot descent, she was the daughter of John and Mary Deards, who had a toyshop in Fleet Street. After Paul Chenevix's death, Mrs Chenevix gained a fine reputation as 'toy-woman à la mode'. In 1747 Horace Walpole had purchased the lease of Strawberry Hill, Twickenham, from her.

4 T.H. Clarke, 'Sir Charles Hanbury Williams and the Chelsea Factory', *E.C.C. Trans.*, vol. 13, pt. 2 (1988), pp. 110–20, and 'Pachyderms among the Peonies', *Country Life*, vol. CLXXVIII, no. 4601 (24 October 1985), pp. 1178–80.

5 Lane 1961, p. 66.

6 Savage 1952, pl. 30.

7 Mackenna 1951, pl. 62, figs 122, 123.

8 Mackenna 1951, pl. 63, figs 124, 125, and pl. 64, figs 126, 127, 128.

9 Mackenna 1951, pl. 65, fig. 129, and Bradshaw 1981, pl. 38 and Lane 1961, pl. 18a and b. The figure of Winter apparently derives from an etching of the *Blind Beggar and Companion* by Jacques Callot (1592–1634). The Blind Beggar himself was also translated into Chelsea Red Anchor porcelain: see Bradshaw 1984, pp. 26–8.

10 Two representing Geography and Astronomy are illustrated in Legge 1984, cat. no. 68.

11 Watney 1972b, no. 837, p. 821.

12 Watney 1972b, ibid.

13 Mackenna 1951, fig. 144.

14 Derby Reference Library, Duesbury Collection, Box 1, item 1043.

15 At Saltram House, Devon (no. 267. T), The National Trust.

16 Also at Saltram House. Both Fisherman figures are illustrated

in *The Treasure Houses of Britain* (National Gallery of Art, Washington, 1985), no. 415, p. 480.

17 Hackenbroch 1957, pl. 27, fig. 41.

18 Watney 1972b, p. 818. Illustrated in Legge 1984, cat. no. 65, p. 43.

19 Lane 1961, p. 68, pl. 17.

20 Nearly two years after Sprimont's death, a sale 'by order of the Executrix' was held by Mr Gerard at his house in Litchfield Street, St Anne's, Soho, for nine consecutive evenings from 19 March 1773 of 'the entire Collection of Prints, Drawings, Books of Prints and Architecture of the late Mr NICHOLAS SPRIMONT, Proprietor of the Chelsea Porcelain Manufactory'.

21 The fiddler at least is known as an individual figure; an example is in the Katz Collection, Museum of Fine Arts, Boston, Mass. The original wax model was found among the old Chelsea equipment at the Spode factory in Stoke-on-Trent, and was given to the Victoria and Albert Museum by Alexander Lewis in 1960. See Young 1999, p. 115, fig. 48.

22 Information given by J.V.G. Mallet and published in Bradshaw 1984, p. 107.

23 *Recueil des cents estampes représentant les différentes Nations du Levant.*

24 Mackenna 1951, pl. 59, fig. 118.

25 Coustou was the sculptor with whom L.F. Roubiliac, Sprimont's friend, had trained.

26 Lane 1961, appendix I, p. 136.

27 A. du Boulay, 'Religious Rococo Revived', *Country Life* (5 June 1986), p. 1636, pl. 3.

28 Examples of both figures, the nun differently decorated, in the Museum of Fine Arts, Boston, are illustrated in Lane 1961, pl. 19A and B.

29 Illustrated in Dixon 1952, pl. 22.

30 Savage 1952, pls 28B and 62C.

31 An example is in the Katz Collection, Museum of Fine Arts, Boston, Mass.

32 In the Schreiber Collection, Victoria and Albert Museum.

33 Legge 1984, p. 85.

34 Valpy 1982, p. 126.

35 Cox 1980, pp. 202, 204.

36 Guildhall MSS 11936/105:141087 and 11936/108:143155, Sun Assurance Co.

37 Hackenbroch 1957, pl. 62, fig. 92 and pl. 63, fig. 91.

38 Hackenbroch 1957, pl. 63, fig. 89.

39 Foster 1966, pls 55, 59.

40 A single bottle of this form was sold at Christie's on the 20 October 1986, lot 163.

Chapter 10

1 Guildhall MS 11936/113:148790 3 October 1755, and Indorsement Book no. 9, p. 429, 3 April 1758.

2 Valpy 1982, p. 128.

3 Westminster Public Libraries, MS D.583.

4 Chaffers 1965, p. 292.

5 GL Records Office, Middlesex Deeds Register 1759, Book 1, nos 444, 445.

6 GL Records Office, Middlesex Deeds Register 1759, Book 3, nos 9, 10.

7 Valpy 1984, p. 64.

8 Ibid.

9 Guildhall MS 11936/133:176294, 27 June 1760, Sun Assurance Co.

Chapter 11

1 See Charleston and Mallet 1971, pp. 113–15.

2 Charnwood Antiques, Spring 1988.

3 It is perhaps of interest to note that this was the first sale of Chelsea porcelain to be undertaken by David Burnsall, whose appointment as auctioneer was advertised as being 'by the Desire of several Persons of Distinction', in March and April 1759. It is noticeable that after the death of Sir Everard Fawkener in November 1758, Richard Ford of the Haymarket, who had formerly undertaken all the Chelsea auctions, was never again employed by Sprimont, though he disposed of Sir Everard's effects in two sales for Lady Fawkener in February 1759 and March 1760. The identity of the 'persons of Distinction' who recommended Burnsall is a point for speculation.

It was not until after Sprimont's death in 1771 that Richard Ford once again undertook a sale in connection with the Chelsea factory. He was advertised, apparently at short notice, as the auctioneer of the 'valuable Produce of last Year' of the 'Derby and Chelsea Porcelaine Manufactories', a six-day sale, held intermittently between 4 and 13 May 1772. James Christie of Pall Mall had at first been engaged, but for some reason could not fulfil the commission. The few later sales connected with the Derby and Chelsea factories were conducted by Messrs Christie and Ansell.

4 Tait 1998/1999, pp. 24–33.

5 Christie's six-day sale of the effects of a gentleman 'Going Abroad' after the tragic death of his fiancée, began on Monday, 16 February 1767. It included a number of interesting articles of Chelsea porcelain. One such was lot 87, of the fourth day, which by the catalogue description must have been of Gold Anchor manufacture. 'A superb table service, containing fourteen dishes, five sizes/ fifty-one table plates/ twenty-three soup ditto/two tureens, covers and dishes/nine salad dishes/four sauceboats/all richly gilt and enamell'd in flowers'. It was bought, as was so much Chelsea porcelain in the early catalogues of James Christie's sales, by Thomas Morgan, 'a Chinaman', who made a speciality of Chelsea productions, for £28 7s. I am grateful to Mrs Pat Halfpenny for drawing my attention to entries in Christie's early catalogues.

6 See Chapter 5.

7 Mallet 1999a, pp. 52–4.

8 Mallet 1999a, pp. 55, 56. Commonplace Book. Wedgwood MSS. E39-28408, vol. 1, p. 33.

9 Mallet 1999a, pp. 56–9. It has been suggested that 'engine turning' may have been produced on the Chelsea plates by pressing each over a *mould* previously engine turned. As yet it has not been discussed who was responsible for making these moulds, although the method was known in France by 1701, when *L'Art du Tourneur* was published at Lyon by M. Plumier.

10 Mallet 1999b, pp. 126–63.

11 See ch. 10, note 9.

12 Mallet 1999b, p. 158, note 2.

13 Young 1997, pp. 218, 219.

14 Young 1997, p. 281, quoting Llewellynn Jewitt, *The Ceramic Art of Great Britain*, vol. II (London 1878), p. 89.

15 Young 1997, p. 221, note 8. Major William H. Tapp, 'Zachariah Boreman' *Connoisseur*, vol. XCII (January 1934), p. 28.

16 Comment by Hilary Young.

17 J.V.G. Mallet, 'The Contribution of Chelsea, 1770–84' in J. Murdoch and J. Twitchett, *Painters and the Derby China Works*, exhibition catalogue (Victoria and Albert Museum, 1987), p. 21, quoted by Hilary Young.

18 W. Mankowitz and R.G. Haggar, *The Concise Encyclopaedia of English Pottery and Porcelain*, 2nd imp. (London 1968), p. 28.

19 Franklin A. Barrett, *Worcester Porcelain*, 2nd edn (London 1966), pp. 53, 54.

20 There is a story that Rose Lenthall, the daughter of an advocate in Stirling, who met the Duke of Cumberland when he was on campaign in Scotland in 1745, followed him to London, and that he later contracted a morganatic marriage with her. In the meantime, vouched for by Paul Sandby, who was attached to the Duke's staff as a military artist, she lived with the Sandbys in Fleet Street, and is said to have worked as a paintress at Chelsea. This information was provided by Patrick Latham to whom I am much obliged.

21 Mackenna 1952, p. 56. See also Chapter 13.

22 Victoria and Albert Museum, nos. C. 52 and 53 – 1964. See Mallet 1965a, pp. 29–37.

23 *Rococo: Art and Design in Hogarth's England* (Victoria and Albert Museum, 1984), cat. 043.

24 Stoner 1955.

25 *Rococo: Art and Design in Hogarth's England*, cat. F 43, pp. 97, 98.

26 Valpy 1984, p. 66.

27 H. Bellamy Gardner, E.C.C. *Trans.*, vol. 1, no 2 (1934), pp. 17–21, pl. VIIA and fig. 4.

28 A set of three figures of Diana, Venus and Hercules, *c.* 1765, all on high plinths, picked out in gilding, are in the Bearsted Collection at Upton House, Warwickshire. The first two figures are 19.1 cm (7½ inches) high; Hercules 18.5 cm (7¼ inches).

29 The other is at West Dean House, Chichester, West Sussex.

30 See Chapter 13 for their discussion in greater detail.

Chapter 12

1 Alexander Reid, Surgeon to the Royal Chelsea Hospital, had left the property in 1718 to move to a larger one in Cheyne Walk.

2 Guildhall MS 12160, Indorsement Book no. 8, p. 559. Guildhall MS 11936/115:150782.

3 The house occupied by Sprimont in Richmond was the second from the East (really South) end of the five which subsequently became the Morshead (later Richmond Gate) Hotel. The properties were owned by the Trustees of the Marshalsea Prison. (Information given by John Cloake, local historian of Richmond.)

4 Guildhall MS 11936/137:183484.

5 Valpy 1984, p.66.

6 Guildhall MS 11936/146:197290.

7 Hand-in-Hand policy 816. 'Henry Porter, St Martins in Fields, Gent. renewal in possession Sprimont'. 16 May 1764.

8 First rate for 1765, recorded 11 September 1765.

9 Guildhall MS 11936/164:228159.

10 A notice of 12 March 1768 in the *Gazetteer* and the 'London' column of the *New Daily Advertiser* stated that 'the Warehouse at Chelsea continues to be open every day with the usual attendance by Mr F. Thomas (the Manager) till all is sold'.

11 Public Record Office, Chancery proceedings, *Duesbury & Heath v. Burnsall*, 1772.

12 Guildhall MS, Hand-in-Hand policy 58226.

13 Guildhall MS 11936/164:228159. Sun Assurance Company.

14 Valpy 1984, p. 68.

15 P.R.O. Hilary Term 1776. Exchequer B & B, Geo. III. London and Middlesex, 2231.

16 Ibid.

17 Tait 1998/1999 p. 27.

18 Mackenna 1952, pp. 8, 9.

19 L. Whiter, *Spode* (London 1970), p. 232, note 46, drawn to my attention by Patrick Latham.

20 See note 15 above.

Chapter 13

1 This William died in infancy. William Duesbury II was not born until 1763.

2 For details of Planché's later life and connections with the theatrical world see Barkla and Barkla 1996, or the resumé of their paper for the E.C.C in E.C.C. *Trans.*, vol. 15, pt 3 (1995), p. 367.

3 28 April to (4 May) 1770: 'Piggot 1 day Working the hors in the Mill Grinding Case Clay'.

4 See Chapter 11.

5 Clifford 1969, pp. 109, 110.

6 R.J. Charleston (ed.), *English Porcelain* (London and Toronto 1965), p. 38, pl. 7B. This vase is in the Victoria and Albert Museum (Illidge Loan no. 9) and is also illustrated in Honey 1977, pl. 34, where it is dated to 1756.

7 This was engraved after Boucher by St Aubin and Leveau, and was an illustration for l'Abbé Banier's *Les Metamorphoses d'Ovide*, IV (Paris 1771).

8 The scene of the Trojan women was taken from a picture by C. Monet engraved by Leveau, also published in *Les Metamorphoses d'Ovide*, IV (Paris 1771).

9 There were signs of neo-classical influence in some vases even before Sprimont sold the factory in 1769.

10 See Chapter 11.

11 Information on the career of N.F. Gauron is contained in Clifford 1986.

12 The letter was first published by Timothy Clifford (see Clifford 1986). The original is in the Derby Public Library (MS 1024).

13 Barrett and Thorpe 1971, p. 40.

14 J. Haslem, *The Old Derby China Factory* (London 1876), pp. 170–78.

15 W. Bemrose, *Bow, Chelsea and Derby Porcelain* (London 1898).

16 Clifford 1985a. This article contains much detailed information about John Bacon.

17 The last known fire insurance policy for the Chelsea Porcelain factory was taken out with the Sun Company by 'William Duesbury and John Heath of the Town of Derby China Manufacturers' on 10 October 1771. (Guildhall MS 11936/209:303537) The total was for only £1500, including Stock and Utensils at £1300 and the buildings at £200 only. See Adams and Redstone, *Bow Porcelain* (London 1981), p. 53 or 2nd edn (1991), p. 40.

18 Derby Reference Library, Duesbury Collection.

Chapter 14

1 Elliot 1939, p. 67.

Bibliography

ABBREVIATIONS

D.P.I.S.: Derby Porcelain International Society
E.C.C. *Trans.*: *Transactions of the English Ceramic Circle*
E.P.C. *Trans.*: *Transactions of the English Porcelain Circle*

PRINTED SOURCES

Adams, Elizabeth, 'The Bow Insurances and Related Matters', E.C.C. *Trans.*, vol. 9, pt 1 (1973), pp. 67–108.
Adams, Elizabeth, 'A Suggested Chronology of Chelsea Porcelains 1743–54', *Apollo*, vol. 113, no. 227 (January 1981), pp. 24–8.
Adams, Elizabeth, 'The Sites of the Chelsea Porcelain Factory', *Ceramics* (December 1985), pp. 55–62.
Adams, Elizabeth, 'Chelsea Aer and Fire', *Ceramics* (July/August 1986), pp. 94–7.
Adams, Elizabeth, 'Nicholas Sprimont's Business Premises', E.C.C. *Trans.*, vol. 13, pt 1 (1987), pp. 1-17.
Albert Amor Ltd., London, Exhibition Catalogue *The Golden Age: Masterpieces of 18th Century English Porcelain* (1980).
Austin, John C., *Chelsea Porcelain at Williamsburg* (Williamsburg 1977).
Baker, Malcolm, 'Roubiliac and Chelsea in 1745', E.C.C. *Trans.*, vol. 16, pt 2 (1997), pp. 222–5.
Barkla and Barkla, R. and R., 'Andrew Planché – Life after Derby', D.P.I.S. *Journal* III (1996), pp. 26–43.
Barrett, F.A. and Thorpe, A.L., *Derby Porcelain* (London 1971).
Beaver, Alfred, *Memorials of Old Chelsea* (London 1892). Reprinted 1971 (Wakefield, Yorkshire).

Bemrose, William, *Bow, Chelsea and Derby Porcelain* (London 1898).
Benton, Eric, 'Payments by Sir Everard Fawkener to Nicholas Sprimont', E.C.C. *Trans.*, vol. 10, pt 1 (1976), pp. 54–8.
Blunt, Reginald (ed.), *The Cheyne Book of Chelsea China and Pottery* (London 1924). Reprinted with an extended introduction by J.V.G. Mallet (Wakefield, Yorkshire 1973, 1981).
Bradshaw, Peter, *18th Century English Porcelain Figures 1745–1795* (Woodbridge 1981).
Bradshaw, Peter, 'A Beggar, a Snuff-taker, and a Lady', E.C.C. *Trans.*, vol. 12, pt 1 (1984), pp. 26–8.
Bryant, G.E., *The Chelsea Porcelain Toys: Scent Bottles, Bonbonnières, Etuis, Seals and Statuettes, made at the Chelsea Factory, 1745–1769, and Derby Chelsea, 1770–1784* (London 1925).
Bunford, A.H.S., 'Some Remarks on Claret Colour', E.C.C. *Trans.*, vol. 1, pt 5 (1937), pp. 24–9.
Burrell, Francis E., 'Some Advertisements of Ceramic Interest', E.C.C. *Trans.*, vol. 5, pt 3 (1962), pp. 176–9.
Chaffers, William, *Marks & Monograms on European and Oriental Pottery and Porcelain*, 15th edn (London 1965).
Chapel, Jeannie and Gere, Charlotte, *The Fine and Decorative Art Collections of Britain and Ireland* (London 1985).
Charleston, R.J. and Mallet, J.V.G., 'A Problematic Group of Eighteenth Century Porcelains', E.C.C. *Trans.*, vol. 8, pt 1 (1971), pp. 80–121.
Charleston, R.J. and Towner, Donald, *English Ceramics 1580–1830: A Commemorative Catalogue of Ceramics and Enamels to Celebrate the 50th

Anniversary of the English Ceramic Circle 1927–1977* (London 1971).
Christie's London: English Porcelain (13 February 1984). Fine British Ceramics (20 October 1986).
Clarke, T.H., 'French Influences at Chelsea', E.C.C. *Trans.*, vol. 4, pt 5 (1959), pp. 45–57.
Clifford, Timothy, 'Derby Biscuit', E.C.C. *Trans.*, vol. 7, pt 2 (1969), pp. 108–17.
Clifford, Timothy (1985a), 'John Bacon and the Manufacturers', *Apollo* CXXII (October 1985), pp. 288–304.
Clifford, Timothy (1985b), 'The Chelsea–Derby Royal Family Groups', *Burlington Magazine* CXXVII (supplement, September 1985), pp. 13–15.
Clifford, Timothy, 'Nicholas Gauron: A Virtuoso Modeller at Tournai and Chelsea' in C. Hind (ed.), *The Rococo in England: A Symposium* (Victoria and Albert Museum, London 1986), pp. 161–74.
Cox and Cox, Drs A. and A., 'Chelsea, Bow and Worcester – Some Early Invoices', E.C.C. *Trans.*, vol. 10, pt 4 (1980), pp. 200-13.
Dixon, J.L., *English Porcelain of the 18th Century* (London 1952).
Dragesco, B., *English Ceramics in French Archives: The Writings of Jean Hellot, the Adventures of Jacques Louis Brolliet and the Identification of the 'Girl-in-a-Swing' Factory* (privately printed, London 1993).
Eccles, Herbert and Rackham, Bernard, *Analysed Specimens of English Porcelain* (Victoria and Albert Museum, London 1922).
Elliot, Wallace, 'Reproductions and Fakes of English Eighteenth Century Ceramics', E.C.C. *Trans.*,

vol. 2, pt 7 (1939), pp. 67–82.
Encyclopaedia Britannica, 11th edn (1911).
English Ceramic Circle, 'A Miscellany of Pieces', E.C.C. *Trans.*, vol. 7, pt 2 (1969), pp. 118–19, pls 129–30.
Foss, Arthur, *Country House Treasures* (London 1980).
Foster, Kate, *Scent Bottles* (London 1966).
Foster, Kate, 'Chelsea Scent Bottles: "Girl in a Swing" and another Group', E.C.C. *Trans.*, vol. 6, pt 3 (1967), pp. 284–91.
Gabszewicz, Anton, 'Chelsea Porcelain from the Schreiber collection', *The Antique Dealer and Collectors Guide* (August 1983), pp. 14–17.
Gardner, Dr H. Bellamy, 'A Contribution to the History of Chelsea Porcelain', *Connoisseur* LXIV (October 1922), pp. 97–102, and pt 2, LXV (March 1923), pp. 150–59.
Gardner, Dr H. Bellamy, 'The Earliest References to Chelsea Porcelains', E.P.C. *Trans.*, vol. 1, no. 1 (1928), pp. 16–22.
Gardner, Dr H. Bellamy, 'An Early Allusion to English Porcelain, Gouyn's Will, and some Chelsea Models', E.P.C. *Trans.*, vol. 1, no. 2 (1929), pp. 23–6.
Gardner, Dr H. Bellamy, 'The Chelsea Birds', E.P.C. *Trans.*, vol. 1, no. 3 (1931), pp. 55–64.
Gardner, Dr H. Bellamy, 'Sir Hans Sloane's Plants on Chelsea Porcelain', E.P.C. *Trans.*, vol. 4 (1932), pp. 22–5.
Gardner, Dr H. Bellamy, 'Sir Hans Sloane's Chelsea Porcelain Heirlooms in the possession of Major R.C.H. Sloane-Stanley' and "Silvershape" in English

Porcelain', E.C.C. *Trans.*, vol. 2, pt 6 (1939), pp. 26–30.

Gardner, Dr H. Bellamy, 'Further History of the Chelsea Porcelain Manufactory', E.C.C. *Trans.*, vol. 2, pt 8 (1942), pp. 136–41.

Glendenning, Oliver and MacAlister, Mrs Donald, 'Chelsea, the Triangle Period', E.C.C. *Trans.*, vol. 2, pt 3 (1935), pp. 20–35.

Godden, Geoffrey, 'Chelsea Porcelain Discovery', *The Antique Collector* (May 1983), pp. 96–9.

Godden, Geoffrey, *Eighteenth-Century English Porcelain* (St Albans 1985).

Hackenbroch, Yvonne, *Chelsea and Other English Porcelain, Pottery, and Enamel in the Irwin Untermyer Collection* (Cambridge, Mass. 1957).

Haggar, Reginald, 'Three Frenchmen in search of a Patron', E.C.C. *Trans.*, vol. 10, pt 5 (1980), pp. 248–59.

Hillier, Bevis, *Pottery and Porcelain 1700–1914* (London 1968).

Hillier, Bevis, 'Nicholas Crisp and the Elizabeth Canning Scandal', E.C.C. *Trans.*, vol. 16, pt 1 (1996), pp. 20–25.

Honey, William Bowyer, *Old English Porcelain* (London 1928). Rev. edn (London 1977).

Ilchester, the Earl of, 'A Notable Service of Meissen Porcelain', *Burlington Magazine* LV (October 1929), pp. 188–90.

Jewitt, Llewellynn, *The Ceramic Art of Great Britain* (London 1878).

Jottrand, Mlle M., 'Tournai Porcelain and English Ceramics', E.C.C. *Trans.*, vol. 10, pt 2 (1977), pp. 130–35, pls 58–63.

King, William, *Chelsea Porcelain* (London 1922).

Klaber, Pamela, 'The Enid Goldblatt Collection of Continental Porcelain', vol. 55, no. 7, pt 1, *The Antique Collector* (July 1984), pp. 69–73.

Lane, Arthur, *English Porcelain Figures of the Eighteenth Century* (London 1961).

Lane, Arthur and Charleston, R.J., 'Girl-in-a-Swing porcelain and Chelsea', E.C.C. *Trans.*, vol. 5, pt 3 (1962), pp. 111–44, pls 126–40.

Legge, M., *Flowers & Fables* (National Gallery of Victoria, Melbourne 1984)

MacAlister, Mrs Donald (ed.), *William Duesbury's London Account Book,*

1751–53 (London 1931).

Mackenna, F.S., *Chelsea Porcelain: The Triangle and Raised Anchor Wares* (Leigh-on-Sea 1948).

Mackenna, F.S., *Chelsea Porcelain: The Red Anchor Wares* (Leigh-on-Sea 1951).

Mackenna, F.S., *Chelsea Porcelain: The Gold Anchor Wares* (Leigh-on-Sea 1952).

Mackenna, F.S., *18th Century English Porcelain* (Leigh-on-Sea 1970).

Mackenna, F.S., *The F.S. Mackenna Collection of English Porcelain Pt 1: Chelsea 1743–1758* (Leigh-on-Sea 1972).

Mallet, J.V.G., 'Upton House, The Bearsted Collection: Porcelain' (National Trust, 1964).

Mallet, J.V.G. (1965a), 'Two Documented Chelsea Gold-Anchor Vases', Victoria and Albert Museum *Bulletin* (January 1965), vol. 1, no. 1, pp. 29–37.

Mallet, J.V.G. (1965b), 'Chelsea', in R.J. Charleston (ed.), *English Porcelain 1745–1850* (London and Toronto 1965), pp. 28–41.

Mallet, J.V.G., 'A Chelsea Talk', E.C.C. *Trans.*, vol. 6, pt 1 (1965), pp. 15–29.

Mallet, J.V.G., 'Rococo in English Porcelain, a Study in Style', *Apollo* XC (August 1969), pp. 100–13.

Mallet, J.V.G., *Hogarth's Pug in Porcelain* (Victoria and Albert Museum, London 1971). Reprinted with revisions from Victoria and Albert Museum *Bulletin* (April 1967), vol. 3, no. 2, pp. 45–54.

Mallet, J.V.G., 'The Site of the Chelsea Porcelain Factory', E.C.C. *Trans.*, vol. 9, pt 1 (1973), pp. 115–31.

Mallet, J.V.G., 'A Chelsea Greyhound and Retrieving Setter. Some Early Chelsea Figure Models, perhaps by Sprimont', *Connoisseur* 196 (November 1977), pp. 222–5.

Mallet, J.V.G., 'Chelsea Porcelain – Botany and Time', *Burlington House Fair Catalogue* (September 1980), pp. 12–15.

Mallet, J.V.G., 'Rococo in English Ceramics', and notes in Porcelain section, in Michael Snodin (ed.), *Rococo: Art and Design in Hogarth's England* (Victoria and Albert Museum, London 1984), pp. 236–42.

Mallet, J.V.G., 'A painting of Nicholas Sprimont, his family and his Chelsea vases', *Les Cahiers de*

Mariemont 24/25 (1993/1994), pp. 77–95.

Mallet, J.V.G. (1999a), 'Engine-turning on ceramics before Wedgwood' in Tamara Préaud (ed.), *Mélanges en souvenir d'Elisalex d'Albis 1939–1998*, privately printed 1999, pp. 51–9.

Mallet, J.V.G. (1999b), 'Gold Anchor Vases – Part 1 The Forms' E.C.C. *Trans.*, vol. 17, pt 1 (1999), pp. 126–61.

Mankowitz, W., and Haggar, R.G., *Concise Encyclopaedia of English Pottery and Porcelain*, 2nd imp. (London 1968).

Mountford, A., 'Thomas Briand – A Stranger', E.C.C. *Trans.*, vol. 7, pt. 2 (1969), pp. 87–99.

Nightingale, J.E., *Contributions towards the History of Early Porcelain, from Contemporary Sources* (Salisbury 1881; reprinted East Ardsley 1973).

Palmer, J., 'Lord Fisher's Collection of English Porcelain in the Fitzwilliam Museum', E.C.C. *Trans.*, vol. 5, pt 2 (1964), pp. 252–7.

Perry, Norma, *Sir Everard Fawkener* (Voltaire Foundation, Banbury, Oxon. 1975); vol. 133 in the series, *Studies in Voltaire and the Eighteenth Century*, ed. Theodore Besterman.

Poole, Julia, Exhibition catalogue, *Plagiarism Personified?* (Fitzwilliam Museum, Cambridge 1986).

The Quiet Conquest, The Huguenots, 1685 to 1985 Exhibition catalogue (Museum of London, London 1985).

Riley, Paul, 'Two Chelsea Cream Jugs' and 'Sir Hans Sloane's Butterflies and Moths on Chelsea Porcelain', both E.C.C. *Trans.*, vol. 12, pt 2 (1985), pp. 109–11.

Savage, George, *Eighteenth Century English Porcelain* (London 1952).

Savage, George, *English Pottery and Porcelain* (New York 1961).

Shaw, Simeon, *History of the Staffordshire Potteries and the Rise and Progress of the Manufacture of Pottery and Porcelain* (Hanley 1829).

Skinner, Miranda, 'The Meissen Influence on Chelsea Raised Anchor Figures', E.C.C. *Trans.*, vol. 12, pt 1 (1984), p. 6.

Sotheby's catalogues: Very fine English and Welsh Porcelain (16 May, 1961). Fine English and

Continental Porcelain (26 November 1963). Important English Porcelain (18 April 1967). Very Fine English Porcelain (7 May 1968). Important Collection of English Porcelain (Lady Corah), (20 July 1971). Highly Important English Porcelain (Mr & Mrs J. McG. Stewart, Halifax, Nova Scotia), (13 November 1973). Important English Pottery and Porcelain (28 October 1980). Rous Lench Collection, English Pottery and Porcelain (1 July 1986).

Sotheby Parke Bernet Inc, New York: Important European Porcelain, Pottery and Objects of Vertu, A Collection formed by Nelson A. Rockefeller … (11 April 1980).

Stoner, F., *Chelsea, Bow and Derby Porcelain Figures* (Newport, Mon. 1955).

Synge-Hutchinson, Patrick, 'Some Chelsea Porcelain in the Collection of Her Majesty Queen Elizabeth the Queen Mother', *Connoisseur* CXXXIV (September 1954).

Synge-Hutchinson, Patrick, 'G.D. Ehret's Botanical Designs on Chelsea Porcelain', *Connoisseur* (October 1958), pp. 88–94.

Synge-Hutchinson, Patrick, 'The Masterpiece of an unknown craftsman', *Connoisseur* (June 1968), pp. 96–8.

Tait, Hugh, 'Outstanding Pieces in the English Ceramic Collection of the British Museum', E.C.C. *Trans.*, vol. 4, pt 3 (1957), pp. 45–54.

Tait, Hugh, 'Nicholas Sprimont at Chelsea, His Apprentice William Brown, and The Anchor and Dagger Mark', *Ars Ceramica*, vol. 15, 1998/1999, pp. 24–33.

Tapp, William H., 'The Chelsea Fable Painter', E.C.C. *Trans.*, vol. 1, pt 4 (1937), pp. 71–4.

Tapp, William H., 'Chelsea China Factory Catalogues and the Fable Painter', pt 1, *Apollo*, vol. XXXIII (June 1941), pp. 140–43, and pt 2, *Apollo*, vol. XXXIV (July 1941), pp. 15–19.

Tilley, Frank, *Teapots and Tea* (Newport, Mon. 1957).

Toppin, Aubrey J., 'Recent Discoveries: II: A Note on Excavations at Chelsea in 1843', E.P.C. *Trans.*, vol. 1, no. 3 (1931), pp. 68, 69.

The Treasure Houses of Britain Exhibition catalogue (National

Gallery of Art, Washington D.C. 1985).

Twitchett, John, *Derby Porcelain* (London 1980).

Valpy, Nancy, 'Extracts from Eighteenth Century London Newspapers', E.C.C. *Trans.*, vol. 11, pt 2 (1982), pp. 122–30.

Valpy, Nancy, 'Extracts from Eighteenth Century London Newspapers and Petworth House Archives', E.C.C. *Trans.*, vol. 11, pt 3 (1983), pp. 187–211.

Valpy, Nancy, 'Extracts from Eighteenth Century London Newspapers', E.C.C. *Trans.*, vol. 12 pt 1 (1984), pp. 58–89.

Valpy, Nancy, 'Extracts from the *Daily Advertiser* and Additional Manuscripts', E.C.C. *Trans.*, vol. 14, pt. 1 (1990), pp. 106–17.

Valpy, Nancy, 'Charles Gouyn and the "Girl-in-a-swing" Factory', E.C.C. *Trans.*, vol. 15, pt. 2 (1994), pp. 317–20.

Watney, Bernard, 'The King, the Nun and other Figures', E.C.C. *Trans.*, vol. 7, pt 1 (1968), pp. 48–58.

Watney, Bernard (1972a), 'A Hare, A Ram, Two Putti and Associated Figures', E.C.C. *Trans.*, vol. 8, pt 2 (1972), pp. 223–7.

Watney, Bernard (1972b), 'Origins of Designs for English Ceramics of the 18th Century', *Burlington Magazine* CXIV (December 1972), pp. 818–28.

Watney, Bernard, *English Blue and White Porcelain of the 18th Century*, rev. edn (London 1973).

Watney, Bernard, 'A China Painter Writes to an Earl', E.C.C. *Trans.*, vol. 11, pt. 1 (1981), pp. 48–9.

Young, Hilary, 'A Problematic Print by Zachariah Boreman and an Unpublished Drawing by J.H. O'Neale', E.C.C. *Trans.*, vol. 16, pt. 2 (1997), pp. 217–21.

Young, Hilary, 'Anti-gallicanism at Chelsea: Protestantism, Protectionism and Porcelain', *Apollo* CXLVII (June 1998), pp. 35–41.

Young, Hilary, *English Porcelain 1745–95* (Victoria and Albert Museum, London 1999).

Young, Hilary, 'Pierre Stephan: The Career of a Derby Modeller Reviewed', D.P.I.S. *Journal*, vol. 4 (2000), pp. 83–93.

MANUSCRIPTS AND 18TH CENTURY CATALOGUES

Local Records
Chelsea Rate Books
    Chelsea Reference Library, Old Town Hall, King's Road, SW3.
Middlesex Deeds Registers
    Greater London Records Office, 40 Northampton Road, EC1.
St Luke, Chelsea, Parish Registers (Originals) GL Record Office, 40 Northampton Road, EC1.
Westminster Rate Books
    Westminster Reference Library, Buckingham Palace Road, SW1.

Insurance Records
Sun Assurance Company Policy Registers
    Guildhall Library, EC2.
Sun Assurance Company, Indorsement Books
    Guildhall Library, EC2.

Other
Duesbury Papers
    Derby Local Studies Library
William Duesbury's London Account Book 1751–53

English Ceramic Circle Monograph ed. Mrs D. MacAlister (1933).

Chelsea Catalogues – Reprints
1755 – discovered by Mrs Radford (1915), reprinted by W. King (1922) and J.C. Austin (1977).
1756 – discovered by Raphael W. Read (1880) and reprinted by G. Savage (1952).
1761 – reprinted by F.S. Mackenna (1952) and in *Apollo* 34 (1941), pp. 15–19.
1770 – and catalogues of Chelsea–Derby period – reprinted by J.E. Nightingale (1881).

Christie's Eighteenth-century Catalogues
5 December 1766 and 4 following days Household Furniture etc. of a Noble Personage, deceased.
16 February 1767 and 5 following days Effects of a Gentleman 'Going Abroad' after the tragic death of his fiancée.
30 January 1775 and 2 following days Household Furniture etc. of Joseph Tullie Esq. deceased.
10 and 11 February 1775 Pictures, Oriental and European China, Late the Property of the Hon. Charles Dillon.

Illustration Acknowledgements

The author and publishers are most grateful to all the galleries, museums, photographic libraries, institutions and individuals who have kindly either given permission for their objects to be reproduced as illustrations in this book and/or supplied photographs. Special thanks are due to photographers Saul Peckham (Photography and Imaging, The British Museum) and Henry Wilson.

half-title page: The British Museum (MLA 1913, 12–20, 150)
frontispiece: Private collection (photo: courtesy of Errol Manners)
title page: The British Museum (MLA PC II 36)
1.1: The British Museum (MLA 1940, 11–1, 67)
1.2: Guildhall Library, Corporation of London
2.1: V&A Picture Library
2.2: V&A Picture Library
2.3: Courtesy of Museum of Fine Arts, Boston: Jessie and Sigmund Katz Collection
2.4: By courtesy of the National Portrait Gallery, London
2.5: London Metropolitan Archives
2.6: Crown copyright reserved
2.9: London Metropolitan Archives
3.1: The British Museum (MLA PC II 97)
3.2: The British Museum (MLA 1938, 3–14, 57 and MLA PC II 18)
3.3: Private collection (photo: The British Museum Press)
3.4: Private collection (photo: The British Museum Press)
3.5: The British Museum (MLA PC II 13)
3.6: The British Museum (MLA PC II 14)
3.7: Private collection (photo: The British Museum Press)
3.8: The British Museum (MLA 1905, 2–18, 6)

3.9: The British Museum (MLA 1905, 2–18, 6)
3.10: Colonial Williamsburg Foundation (acc#1963–55)
3.11: Private collection; ex Schreiber collection (photo: The British Museum Press)
3.12: The British Museum (MLA PC II 12)
3.13: The British Museum (MLA 1938, 3–14, 72)
3.14: The British Museum (MLA 1938, 3–14, 96)
3.15: Private collection (photo: The British Museum Press)
3.16: The British Museum (MLA PC II 6a)
3.17: Trustees of the Cecil Higgins Art Gallery, Bedford, England
3.18: Private collection (photo: The British Museum Press)
3.19: Private collection (photo: The British Museum Press)
3.20: The British Museum (MLA PC II 7)
3.21: Private collection (photo: Sotheby's)
3.22: Private collection (photo: The British Museum Press
3.23: The British Museum (MLA PC II 90)
3.24: Private collection (photo: The British Museum Press)
3.25: Private collection (photo: © Christie's Images Ltd 2001)
4.1: Private collection (photo: The British Museum Press)
5.1: The British Museum (MLA 1938, 3–14, 89 & 90)
5.2: Private collection (photo: The British Museum Press)
5.3: Guildhall Library, Corporation of London
5.4: Private collection (photo: The British Museum Press)
5.5: Private collection (photo:

The British Museum Press)
5.6: V&A Picture Library
5.7: The British Museum (MLA 1988, 12–2, 1)
5.8: Courtesy of The Potteries Museum & Art Gallery, Stoke-on-Trent
5.9: Courtesy of Museum of London
5.10: V&A Picture Library
5.11: National Museum of Ireland
5.12: Reproduction by permission of the Syndics of the Fitzwilliam Museum, Cambridge (accession no. C.22–1941)
5.13: Tullie House Museum & Art Gallery, Carlisle: Williamson Bequest
5.14: Reproduction by permission of the Syndics of the Fitzwilliam Museum, Cambridge (accession no. C.3–1975)
5.15: V&A Picture Library (C.587–1922)
5.16: The British Museum (MLA 1936, 3–17, 1)
5.17: Courtesy of Museum of Fine Arts, Boston
5.18: The British Museum (MLA PC II 2)
5.19: V&A Picture Library
5.20: Private collection; ex Blohm collection (photo: Robyn Robb)
5.21: © Christie's Images Ltd 2001
5.22: V&A Picture Library (C.49 & a – 1969)
5.23: Courtesy of The Potteries Museum & Art Gallery, Stoke-on-Trent (with permission from Geoffrey Godden)
6.1: Ashmolean Museum, Oxford (with private collector's permission)
6.2: Private collection (photo: The British Museum Press)
6.3: V&A Picture Library
6.4: Colonial Williamsburg Foundation (acc#1960–899)
6.5: Private collection (photo: The British Museum Press)
6.6: Courtesy of The Potteries Museum & Art Gallery, Stoke-on-Trent
6.7: The British Museum (MLA PC II 1)
6.8: By courtesy of the National Portrait Gallery, London
6.9: London Metropolitan Archives
7.1: Private collection; ex Mackenna collection (photo: The British Museum Press)
7.2: The British Museum (MLA 1938, 3–14, 65)
7.3: Courtesy of Museum of Fine Arts, Boston
7.4: The British Museum (MLA 1970, 1–4, 116)
7.5: The British Museum (MLA PC II 21)
7.6: © Salisbury & South Wiltshire Museum
7.7: Private collection (photo: Elizabeth Adams)
7.8: Colonial Williamsburg Foundation
7.9: Private collection (photo: Sotheby's)
7.10: © Salisbury & South Wiltshire

Museum
7.11: © Salisbury & South Wiltshire Museum
7.12: Private collection; ex Dr and Mrs Paul Riley collection (photo: The British Museum Press)
7.13: Private collection; ex Geoffrey Phillips collection (photo: The British Museum Press)
7.14: Private collection; ex Raison collection, Dr and Mrs Paul Riley collection (photo: Robyn Robb)
7.15: Private collection (photo: The British Museum Press)
7.16: Private collection (photo: The British Museum Press)
7.17: Private collection; ex Dr and Mrs Paul Riley collection (photo: Phillips)
7.18: Private collection; ex F. Severne Mackenna collection, Dr and Mrs Paul Riley collection (photo: Phillips)
7.19: The British Museum (MLA PC II, 20, 1 & 2)
7.20: Private collection (photo: The British Museum Press)
7.21: Private collection (photo: The British Museum Press)
7.22: The British Museum (MLA 1981, 1–1, 231)
7.23: Private collection (The British Museum Press)
7.24: Private collection; ex Wallace Elliott collection, Frank Hurlbutt collection, F. Severne Mackenna collection, Dr and Mrs Paul Riley collection (photo: Robyn Robb).
7.25: Courtesy of Museum of London
7.26: The British Museum (MLA PC II 76)
7.27: The British Museum (MLA PC II 244)
7.28: Colonial Williamsburg Foundation
7.29: Ashmolean Museum, Oxford
7.30: V&A Picture Library
7.31: Private collection (photo: Albert Amor)
7.32: Reproduced by permission of the Syndics of The Fitzwilliam Museum, Cambridge (acc. no. C.20–1973)
7.33: The British Museum (MLA 1938, 3–14, 103)
7.34: The British Museum (MLA PC I 3)
7.35: Ashmolean Museum, Oxford
7.36: Private collection (photo: © Christie's Images Ltd 2001)
7.37: V&A Picture Library
7.38: Private collection (photo: The British Museum Press)
7.39: Colonial Williamsburg Foundation (acc#1962–57)
7.40: Courtesy Museum of Fine Arts, Boston

8.1: Private collection; ex Raby Castle (photo: The British Museum Press)

8.2: Colonial Williamsburg Foundation

8.3: Reproduced by permission of the Syndics of The Fitzwilliam Museum, Cambridge (acc. no.C.24A&B–1941)

8.4: Private collection (photo: The British Museum Press)

8.5: Private collection (photo: The British Museum Press)

8.6: The British Museum (MLA 1959, 11–2, 147)

8.7: Private collection (photo: The British Museum Press)

8.8: Private collection

8.9: Private collection (photo: The British Museum Press)

8.10: Reproduced by permission of the Syndics of The Fitzwilliam Museum, Cambridge (acc. no.C.3–1958)

8.11: Courtesy, Winterthur Museum, gift of John Dorrance, Jr. Campbell Collection of Soup Tureens at Winterthur (reg. no. 96.4.1a–c)

8.12: National Museum of Wales, Cardiff (private loan, reproduced with the owner's permission)

8.13: Ashmolean Museum, Oxford (J216)

8.14: Trustees of the Cecil Higgins Art Gallery, Bedford, England (C.296)

8.15: Courtesy Museum of Fine Arts, Boston: Jessie and Sigmund Katz Collection

8.16: Colonial Williamsburg Foundation (acc#1962–87)

8.17 & 18: Private collection; ex Dr and Mrs Paul Riley collection (photo: The British Museum Press)

8.19: Private collection (photo: The British Museum Press)

8.20: Private collection (photo: Simon Spero)

8.21: Private collection (photo: The British Museum Press)

8.22: Courtesy of Museum of London

8.23: Private collection (photo: Robyn Robb)

8.24: The British Museum (MLA 1940, 11–1, 67)

8.25: The British Museum (MLA 1959, 11–2, 137)

8.26: Birmingham City Museum & Art Gallery

8.27 & 28: Private collection (photo: The British Museum Press)

8.29: Courtesy of Museum of London

8.30: Tullie House Museum & Art Gallery, Carlisle: Williamson Bequest

8.31: The British Museum (MLA PC II 32)

9.1: The British Museum (MLA PC II 35)

9.2: Private collection (photo: Robyn Robb)

9.3: The British Museum (MLA PC II 36)

9.4 & 5: Private collection (photo: The British Museum Press)

9.6: Courtesy of the Museum of London

9.7: V&A Picture Library (414: 173–1885 [Sch.1–135])

9.8: V&A Picture Library (Sch.1–171)

9.9: Trustees of the Cecil Higgins Art Gallery, Bedford, England

9.10: Private collection (photo: The British Museum Press)

9.11: The British Museum (MLA 1948, 12–3, 55 & 56)

9.12: The British Museum (MLA 1930, 4–19, 1 & PC II 27)

9.13: Reproduced by permission of the Syndics of The Fitzwilliam Museum. From the collection of Lord & Lady Fisher (Fisher Loan 76)

9.14: Reproduced by permission of the Syndics of The Fitzwilliam Museum. From the collection of Lord & Lady Fisher (Fisher Loan 109)

9.15: Private collection

9.16: © National Trust Photographic Library/Angelo Hornak

9.17: Reproduced by permission of the Syndics of The Fitzwilliam Museum. From the collection of Lord & Lady Fisher (Fisher Loan 67)

9.18: Reproduced by permission of the Syndics of The Fitzwilliam Museum. From the collection of Lord & Lady Fisher (Fisher Loan 68)

9.19: Trustees of the Cecil Higgins Art Gallery, Bedford, England

9.20: Tullie House Museum & Art Gallery, Carlisle: Williamson Bequest

9.21: Reproduced by permission of the Syndics of The Fitzwilliam Museum. From the collection of Lord & Lady Fisher (Fisher Loan 99)

9.22: The British Museum (MLA 1940, 10–1, 1)

9.23: © National Trust Photographic Library

9.24: © National Trust Photographic Library

9.25: Private collection (photo: The British Museum Press)

9.26: Private collection (photo: The British Museum Press)

10.1: Private collection; ex Raby Castle (photo: The British Museum Press)

10.2: Private collection (photo: The British Museum Press)

10.3: Private collection (photo: The British Museum Press)

10.4: Private collection (photo: The British Museum Press)

10.5: Private collection (photo: The British Museum Press)

11.1: Private collection (photo: The British Museum Press)

11.2: The British Museum (MLA 1956, 11–6, 1 & 2)

11.3: The British Museum (MLA 1957, 12–1, 34)

11.4: The British Museum (MLA PC II 94)

11.5: The British Museum (MLA 1913, 12–20, 147)

11.6: The British Museum (MLA PC II 93)

11.7: The British Museum (MLA PC 11 8, Franks Bequest)

11.8: The British Museum (MLA 1923, 12–18, 4)

11.9: Private collection (photo: The British Museum Press)

11.10: The British Museum (MLA 1923, 12–18, 6)

11.11: The British Museum (MLA 1923, 12–18, 9)

11.12: The British Museum (MLA 1948, 12–3, 60))

11.13: V&A Picture Library

11.14: Private collection (photo: The British Museum Press)

11.15: Private collection (Photo: The British Museum Press)

11.16: The British Museum (MLA 1940, 11–1, 73)

11.17: Tullie House Museum & Art Gallery, Carlisle: Williamson Bequest

11.18: Private collection (photo: The British Museum Press)

11.19: The British Museum (MLA 1940, 11–1, 74)

11.20: The British Museum (MLA PC II 30)

11.21: The British Museum (MLA 1913, 12–20, 154)

11.22: The British Museum (MLA 1940, 4–1, 10)

11.23: The British Museum (MLA PC II 29)

11.24: The British Museum (MLA 1913, 12–20, 153)

11.25: V&A Picture Library (C.52–1964)

11.26 & 27: The British Museum (MLA PC II 28)

11.28: The Royal Collection © 2001, Her Majesty Queen Elizabeth II (RCIN 2915; Jagger p.96, ill. 134/135)

11.29: Courtesy of Museum of Fine Arts, Boston: Gift of Richard C. Paine

11.30: The British Museum (MLA 1945, 12–1, 3 & 2)

11.31: The British Museum (MLA 1940, 11–1, 20)

11.32: Colonial Williamsburg Foundation (Acc. no. # 1952–606, 1–2)

11.33: Colonial Williamsburg Foundation (Acc. no. # 1952–611)

11.34: © National Trust Photographic Library/Upton House (Bearsted Collection no. 48)/John Bethell

11.35: The British Museum (MLA 1927, 4–11, 1)

11.36: National Trust

11.37: Courtesy of Museum of London

11.38: Tullie House Museum & Art Gallery, Carlisle: Williamson Bequest

11.39: Tullie House Museum & Art Gallery, Carlisle: Williamson Bequest

12.1: The British Museum (MLA 1981, 1–1, 227)

12.2 & 3: The British Museum (MLA 1923, 12–18, 8)

12.4: Private collection

13.1: Tullie House Museum & Art Gallery, Carlisle: Williamson Bequest

13.2: Reproduced by permission of the Syndics of The Fitzwilliam Museum, Cambridge (acc. no. C.31–1938)

13.3: Tullie House Museum & Art Gallery, Carlisle: Williamson Bequest

13.4: © National Trust Photographic Library/Upton House (Bearsted Collection no. 54)

13.5: Courtesy of Museum of London

13.6: © National Trust Photographic Library/Upton House (Bearsted Collection no. 68)

14.1: Sotheby's

14.2: Private collection (photo: The British Museum Press)

14.3: Reproduced by permission of the Syndics of The Fitzwilliam Museum, Cambridge (acc. no. C.11.1945)

14.4: Sotheby's

Index

Page numbers in *italics* refer to illustrations.